# SOUTH KOREA

# SOUTH KOREA

## THE ENIGMATIC PENINSULA

MARK DAKE

DUNDURN
TORONTO

Editor: Allison Hirst
Design: Laura Boyle
Cover Design: Sarah Beaudin
Cover photos by the author
Printer: Webcom

**Library and Archives Canada Cataloguing in Publication**

Dake, Mark A., author
South Korea : the enigmatic peninsula / Mark A. Dake.

Issued in print and electronic formats.
ISBN 978-1-4597-3145-5 (paperback).--ISBN 978-1-4597-3146-2 (pdf).--
ISBN 978-1-4597-3147-9 (epub)

1. Dake, Mark A.--Travel--Korea (South). 2. Canadians--Travel--Korea (South). 3. English teachers--Travel--Korea (South). 4. Korea (South)--Description and travel. I. Title.

DS902.4.D34 2015 915.19504'5 C2015-906014-1
C2015-906015-X

1 2 3 4 5 20 19 18 17 16

Canada Council
for the Arts

We acknowledge the support of the **Canada Council for the Arts** and the **Ontario Arts Council** for our publishing program. We also acknowledge the financial support of the **Government of Canada** through the **Canada Book Fund** and **Livres Canada Books**, and the **Government of Ontario** through the **Ontario Book Publishing Tax Credit** and the **Ontario Media Development Corporation**.



Printed and bound in Canada.

**VISIT US AT**

Dundurn.com | @dundurnpress | Facebook.com/dundurnpress | Pinterest.com/dundurnpress

Dundurn
3 Church Street, Suite 500
Toronto, Ontario, Canada
M5E 1M2

In memory of my father, who passed away in 2013, and who would leave the sports section of the *Globe and Mail* on the breakfast table in the winter for me when I was a kid so I could read about my beloved Toronto Maple Leafs.

To my mother, who loved reading epic novels late into the night, thank you for introducing me to literature.

# CONTENTS

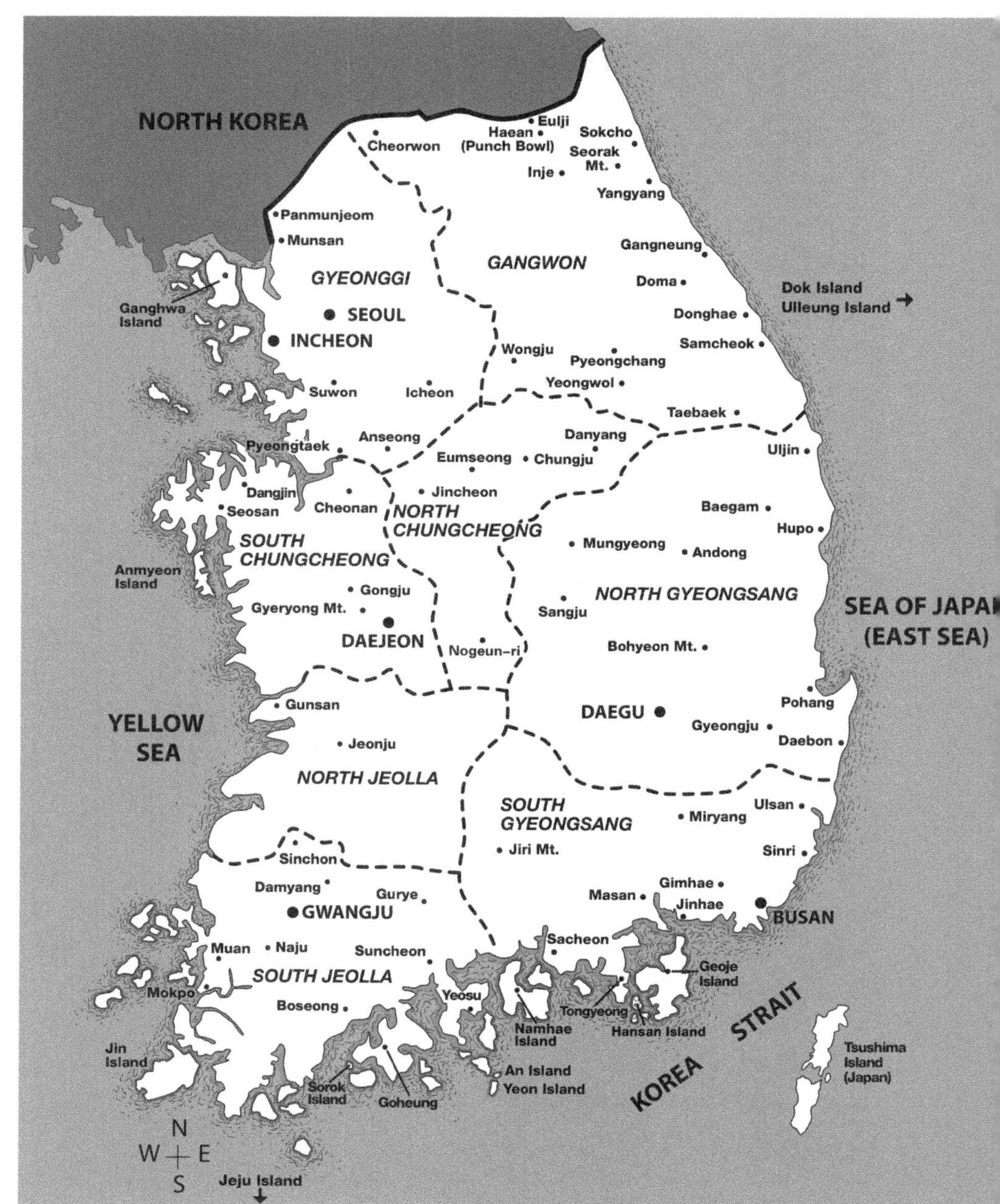


*Map by Jing (Vera) Chen and Jing Yun (Joyce) Tao.*

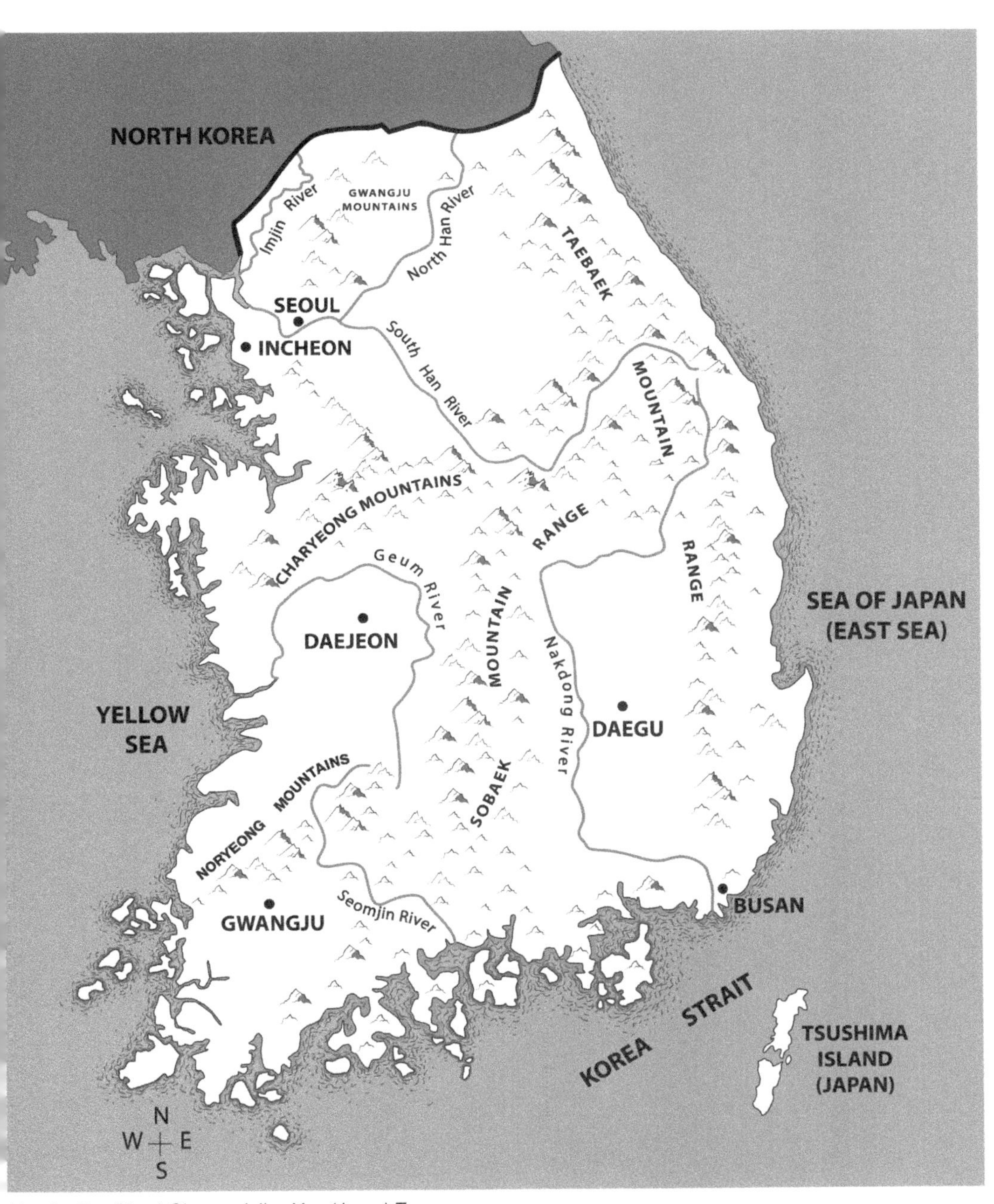


*Map by Jing (Vera) Chen and Jing Yun (Joyce) Tao.*

# CHAPTER 1

A young U.S. soldier — our "security escort" into Panmunjeom — stepped on the tour bus and walked slowly up the aisle, handing out identification tags to me and each of the forty or so other Westerner tourists aboard. His name tag read Sergeant Naumenkof. He was wholesome-faced and sleepy-looking, and spoke with a slow Midwestern American drawl. I envisioned him working on a farm in Kansas rather than aiming a rifle toward North Korea.

"These ID tags must be prominently displayed on your jackets at all times," he announced. "There will be no flash photography. Turn off your cellphones."

We were parked in front of Camp Bonifas. Two and a half kilometres north were Panmunjeom and the Joint Security Area, which formed the border between North and South Korea. The *Washington Post* described Camp Bonifas as a "small collection of buildings surrounded by triple coils of razor wire just 440 yards south of the DMZ [demilitarized zone]," which, minus minefields and soldiers, "resembled a big Boy Scout camp."

It was true; the camp's entrance was utilitarian, like one of those cut-rate summer camps your parents sent you and your sister to when you were ten years old. But looks can be deceiving. Camp Bonifas is the base for the United Nations Command Security Battalion, comprised of a crack contingent of approximately six hundred men, 60 percent of whom are Republic of Korea (ROK) soldiers, the rest American; though to get a confirmation of precise numbers in this high-risk security area can be a challenge. The battalion provides protection in the JSA for visiting military officers, government officials, other guests, and most important today, for me! These soldiers are in a constant state of readiness; one never knows when the belligerent and unpredictable North Korean border soldiers might act up.

* * *

Four hours earlier, our bus had departed Seoul from Yongsan Garrison, headquarters for the United States Forces Korea (USFK), which is responsible for organizing, training, and supplying approximately twenty-eight thousand American troops on the Korean peninsula. The mid-April morning was cold and miserable, a shroud of mist clinging to the ground and a hard, slanting rain falling. Our bus proceeded northwest out of the city toward Panmunjeom, sixty kilometres away. En route, we passed the satellite city of Ilsan, where a staggering number of white high-rise apartment blocks dominate the skyline. We then travelled into the fertile Paju lowlands, formed by the Imjin River basin. The land here is sectioned into small rectangular plots where predominantly rice is grown between the pockets of low, wooded hills. These hills are part of the Gwangju mountain range, an outlier of the grand Taebaek range that rises in the east. The mountains surround Seoul to the north, east, and west, and the ridges, peaks, and steep hills are a picturesque feature of the city.

The bus travelled north onto the Freedom Expressway, which parallels the eastern shore of the indomitable Han River. The windows were so fogged up that we needed to constantly wipe them to be able to see out. The expressway was wide, modern, and for the most part devoid of vehicles due to its proximity to the North Korean border — if you're not a soldier based in the area, a local farmer, or a tourist visiting Panmunjeom, there really isn't any reason for you to be there.

Our route followed the general path of the river, which flows northwest out of the capital and is joined forty-five kilometres downriver by the Imjin, which flows southwest from North Korea. In the pelting rain, the Imjin that day was swollen, yellow, and wide. Just a few kilometres north, on the other shore, is North Korea. No vessels are permitted to ply the river here due to security concerns.

We soon approached the area of Imjingak and the Unification Bridge that spans the Imjin River. Just south of here is Munsan village. Munsan Station is the last rail stop on the regular Gyeonggi Rail Line, which runs north from Seoul. A special DMZ train that is designated for sightseeing begins in Seoul, continues the short distance from Munsan to Imjingak Station, then crosses Freedom Bridge — just south of Unification Bridge — and culminates about a kilometre and a half north at Mount Dora Observatory, where passengers can look out over the DMZ. No civilian vehicles are permitted north of the Imjin River.

After crossing Unification Bridge, we entered the Civilian Control Zone (CCZ), a restricted area that runs south of and along the entire length of the 250-kilometre-long DMZ. Within this coast-to-coast corridor are security checkpoints and military personnel and hardware, including tanks, attack helicopters, and rocket launchers. East of us are two long south–north passes that move through the Gwangju Mountains, one reaching north from Seoul through the cities of Uijeongbu, Dongducheon, and Yeoncheon to the border. Along this route there are several military camps, temporary home for an ever-changing number of ROK and U.S. soldiers. When North Korea launched its assault against South Korea on June 25, 1950, triggering the Korean War, many of its troops marched south into Seoul through this corridor.

It may seem like overkill that myriad troops and military hardware inhabit such remote, lonely and largely mountainous terrain. But since Korea split into North and South in 1948, the North has demonstrated a continued history of trying to infiltrate, sending spies and commandos across the DMZ into the South. Not to mention occasionally launching missile strikes, as well as kidnapping South citizens and hauling them back to the North. There's good reason the DMZ's four-thousand-metre-wide buffer zone was established in 1953; it keeps both sides' militaries a respectable distance apart. The DMZ's notorious claim to fame is that it's the most heavily militarized border in the world. My main concern was that we would soon be in the JSA, where there is no buffer zone, and we'd be standing almost face to face with angry North border soldiers, men who eat iron for breakfast and ore for dinner.

Along a lonely narrow road leading to nearby Panmunjeom, the bus stopped just south of the DMZ, at a parking lot populated with scores of tour buses, and next to the entrance to Tunnel No. 3, the third of four tunnels covertly dug by the North under the DMZ. It was discovered by the South in 1978 and is now a popular tourist destination.

We hopped off the bus and made our way to the entrance, a tunnel dynamited and drilled by the South in 2003 to connect with the tunnel hollowed by the North much farther underground. Inside it was clammy and humid, and myriad tour groups were congregated, including Chinese and Japanese visitors, their languages clearly audible in the echoey underground chamber. We donned yellow hard hats, so we wouldn't crack our skulls on the low granite ceiling.

We descended to about sixty metres below the surface to the North-built tunnel, which took five years to construct, and though it is just two metres tall and wide, would have provided enough space to allow tens of thousands of North Korean troops to hustle into the South if there was war. The South was alerted to the location of the tunnel by a North Korean defector.

After the tour, we returned to the bus, which took us to a nearby cafeteria crowded with several hundred tourists. After lunch, we were shuttled toward Camp Bonifas.

"This is the most dangerous area in the world ... are you ready?" joked our Korean tour guide over the bus loudspeaker, as we approached the DMZ.

Well, more hazardous locales did exist: Iraq, Syria, and Somalia, came to mind. But there have been thousands of incidents along the DMZ since the war ended in 1953. Granted, many of the incidents were minor — North guards spitting on the shoes of American and ROK guards, name-calling, guns going off. But border clashes have claimed a reported 1,375 lives since 1953; more than ninety Americans, five hundred South Koreans, and at least nine hundred North Koreans. A tragedy occurred in 2008, when a group of South Korean tourists were on one of the government-sanctioned excursions to the Geumgang Mountain Resort, located just north of the border along the east coast. A housewife, Park Wang-ja, decided to take a solo early-morning stroll from the hotel, and mistakenly wandered into an off-limits area. A North Korean soldier in a guard tower reportedly ordered her to halt, but the poor woman likely panicked and ran. One of the guards shot her dead.

I don't mean to be an alarmist, but according to the English-language *JoongAng Daily,* the North had 1.19 million soldiers, 3,900 tanks, 420 battleships, 840 fighter jets, and 8,500 pieces of field artillery as of a few years ago. South Korea possessed less of everything: 655,000 troops, 2,300 tanks, 120 battleships, 490 fighter jets, and 5,200 artillery weapons. Excuse me, but by my calculation, North Korea has way more military hardware! It also has Rodong and Scud missiles aimed south — possibly equipped with chemical, biological, or even nuclear weapons — according to an international military journal. I was obviously on the wrong side of the border!

But the ROK does enjoy a significant military advantage due to the high-tech naval and air power and artillery, thanks in part to the Americans. A U.S. tank commander in Seoul told me that his weapons system could hone in on a North tank across the border simply by detecting heat generated when the vehicle's engine roared to life. At U.S Osan Air Base south of Seoul are A-10 Thunderbolt 11 fighter jets nicknamed "Tank Killers" for its missiles that can penetrate tank armour. Most of the North's weapons are aged. The regime has quantity, not quality, firepower. And it takes big money to keep those tanks and planes fuelled — money the regime doesn't have. Still, the enemy is formidable and war would be a spectre.

Naumenkof walked up the aisle of the bus handing each of us a sheet of paper. "This is a visitor's declaration page that you all have to sign," he informed us. I glanced over it and saw that one paragraph read: "The visit to the Joint Security Area at Panmunjeom will entail entry into a hostile area, and possibility of injury or death as a direct result of enemy action."

About 150,000 foreigners take government-sanctioned tours into the JSA each year (native South Koreans take separate tours). Though I had yet to read about anyone on these sojourns being kidnapped and hauled into the North, I thought, *there's always a first time*. On December 14, 1969, a North agent abducted fifty people aboard Korean Air flight YS-11 flying from the east coast city of Gangneung to Seoul, and ordered the pilots to fly the plane to Pyongyang. Two months later, thirty-nine passengers were returned through Panmunjeom. But, to this day, the plane, four crew members, and seven passengers have not been returned. If a commando was capable of stealing a plane, one would certainly be able to nab little ol' me in the JSA. I'd probably be whisked away to a remote mountain gulag, where I'd spend the remainder of my sad existence hoeing desiccated fields and unearthing shrivelled potatoes with a small trowel. I did not like the prospect of this, not at all.

I signed the form, releasing the South Korean government of any liability if a North soldier decided to use me as a punching bag or for target practice.

Once we had all inked our signatures, Naumenkof escorted us off the bus and into a small auditorium, Ballinger Hall, named in honour of Robert M. Ballinger, a U.S. Navy Commander who died on November 20, 1974, along with an ROK soldier when there was an explosion in Tunnel No. 1, about twenty-five kilometres northeast of Panmunjeom, and the first North tunnel discovered. Naumenkof took the stage.

"Did you guys read the waiver you signed?" he asked. "What does it say?"

I guess discussing the rules we must adhere to in the JSA was necessary — it would only take one nutcase among us to do something really foolish, provoking what could be an embarrassing international incident. "If something happens to you it's not our fault," he deadpanned.

We all laughed.

One fellow in our group called out that no photos were allowed. Naumenkof confirmed this. Another announced there was no fraternization with North guards.

"No fraternization," echoed Naumenkof.

If anyone was daft enough to approach a North soldier, drape an arm around him, and attempt to take a selfie, I thought he deserved to wind up on a permanent North Korean vacation.

"No gestures, no pointing," offered another tour member.

"No pointing," reiterated Naumenkof.

"Stay in your group," someone called.

"Stay in your group."

"Follow instructions."

"Absolutely," agreed Naumenkof.

"Don't defect to North Korea!" I blurted out.

The audience guffawed. The young sergeant stared at me with a gaze that I deciphered as being half restrained humour and half wanting to deliver a taekwondo kick my way. Thank goodness witnesses were on hand to deter such unwarranted action. "Do not defect to North Korea," he repeated dryly, after a long pause. "That's the number one rule around here. The biggest thing is, this area we're going to go up to, it's a dangerous area. As recently as three weeks ago we had incidents up there. So it's important you follow instructions. Your safety does depend on it. And if you don't, then you just signed a waiver saying we're not responsible for anything that happens to you. But most important, do not point, do not wave, and do not gesture to the North Koreans. These are violations of the Armistice Agreement."

He then surrendered the stage to a young American UNC soldier who began to recite a speech about the DMZ. UNC soldiers presiding over tour groups in Panmunjeom memorize a thirteen-page history of the Korean War. This soldier obviously had taken the task of learning it to heart, because he morphed into autopilot, and sounded like he was trying to win a Guinness World Record for the quickest-delivered speech. Without a single pause, it took him just nine minutes and forty-seven seconds (I timed him).

"Your-tour-group-will-be-escorted-into-Panmunjeom-by-soldiers-of-the-UN-Security-Force-who-are-above-the-average-aptitude-of-normal-soldiers," he concluded speedily.

What a relief knowing we would be accompanied by Ivy-Leaguers.

In front of Ballinger Hall, we transferred to a military bus that would convey us the final two kilometres to the JSA. En route, we passed a hamlet called Daeseong-dong, population about 250, and through a retinue of trees I could make out tightly grouped village homes and farm units. The village is the only settlement permitted to exist in the DMZ by South authorities, and is only four hundred metres south of the DMZ's midpoint. The reason for its existence seems to be for propaganda; it's as if the South government thumbs its nose at the enemy, and refuses to be cowed. Only those who grew up in the village or have direct descendents in it, are permitted to reside there. They receive government perks for doing so: they pay no taxes, the men are exempt from mandatory two-year military conscription, and farm sizes average twenty-two acres, far greater than the average two to three acres in the rest of the country. The downside is that there is twenty-four-hour military protection, and the village shuts down at nightfall, the residents required to remain in their homes with all their windows and doors locked until morning.

North Korea used to blare out propaganda slogans over speakers in Panmunjeom clearly audible in Daeseong-dong. "This is paradise. Come over so you can have a good meal of rice," was a common adage. What was conveniently excluded, though, was the warning, "Savour the few grains that you'll be lucky we feed you, because you'll shrink to a gaunt bag of bones after working seventeen-hour days in the fields at Hotel Gulag."

Our bus was stopped briefly at UNC Checkpoint 2, at the entrance to the JSA, my first opportunity since arriving in Seoul in 1995 to stand on the doorstep of North Korea. Fortunately, by the time we debarked in the JSA, the torrent of rain that had been falling was relegated to a light mist. Our protectors accompanying us into the JSA were two strong and intimidating-looking Korean UNC guards — taller and larger than the average ROK soldier — who possessed first-degree black belts in martial arts and basic fluency in English. Good to know that as I was being hauled kicking and screaming by North soldiers toward the dark recesses of their secretive nation, my two bodyguards would helpfully holler, "Don't worry, we'll write!' in grammatically and phonetically perfect English.

The JSA seemed very desolate and peaceful — a square of utilitarian grey concrete about eight hundred metres in diameter. Of course, we weren't seeing the real DMZ, the lonely 250 kilometres that reached west and east and was guarded by a ten-foot-tall chain link barrier and a roll of coiled barbed-wire above, watchtowers every few hundred metres, floodlights shining into the no-man's-land, so that if any North commandos attempted a sortie, they would be shot.

In the centre of the square, along the Military Demarcation Line (MDL) that divides the two countries, is a row of seven low barrack-style buildings referred to as Conference Row. Several of the units belong to the North, and several to the UNC. Three are a sky-blue colour. Across in the North, directly behind Conference Row, is the formal white concrete, three-storey "Panmungak," or Panmun Building. Behind us in the South was the large steel and glass "Freedom House." There are a total of twenty-four buildings located within the JSA.

What I didn't know until later was that this sense of tranquility was deceiving. Apparently, hidden in one or more of the surrounding units on both sides of the border are contingents of soldiers with heavy weapons, poised to rush into action if needed. Naumenkof informed us that the highly-trained UNC soldiers could be outfitted in full combat gear within ninety seconds, "which is really fast," he added.

Such soldiers were forced to scramble into action on November 23, 1984. On that day, a group of Russian students who were attending Kim Il-sung University in Pyongyang, North Korea, had been bused to the JSA for a tour. One student, Andrei Lankov — now a professor at Kookmin University in Seoul — told me later that his classmate, Vasily Matauzik, was standing by Conference Row snapping photos.

Matauzik, twenty-two, suddenly sprinted across the demarcation line into the South, Lankov explained in his Russian-accented English. (This was the Cold War era, and communist-bloc citizens attempting to defect to other countries was not unusual). Immediately, a KPA guard raced after Matauzik. Then all hell broke loose, said Lankov, estimating that a dozen or more KPA guards equipped with Kalashnikov automatic rifles raced out of Panmungak.

Major Wayne A. Kirkbride, who had been assigned to a U.S. infantry battalion near Panmunjeom in 1975 and is the author of *DMZ: A Story of the Panmunjom Axe Murder* and *Panmunjom: Facts about the Korean DMZ*, wrote that "twenty to thirty KPA guards opened fire and ran across the MDL in an effort to prevent the defection." In response, UNC soldiers bolted out from their unit carrying heavy weapons to confront the North soldiers. Ironically, the July 27, 1953 Armistice Agreement stipulated that soldiers in the DMZ should use minimum force and be armed only with non-automatic weapons. Both sides ignore that rule.

"For twenty minutes bullets were flying everywhere," recalled Lankov, who had dashed into Panmungak to escape the hail of gunfire.

The battle resulted in one ROK and three KPA soldiers dead and five others injured. Matauzik made it safely across the line, though Lankov referred to him as a "spoiled brat" who was responsible for four deaths.

* * *

Our tour group members stood next to the Military Armistice Commission (MAC) building on Conference Row. Between 1953 and 1976 more than four hundred meetings took place between the North and South in this building. During these powwows, greetings and handshakes were rarely exchanged. In fact, North brass would sometimes go all out to unnerve their counterparts, including making wild accusations and showing deaf indifference to logic. They would distort the truth and insist on outrageous demands, sometimes repeating the words "U.S. Imperial aggressor" up to three hundred times in a single encounter, wrote Kirkbride.

Facing us across the demarcation line just fourteen metres away was a KPA guard with a short, slight frame inside his brown-green uniform and sporting a Soviet-style wide-brimmed hat. It seemed as if a stiff gust of wind would have blown him away. The Korean UNC guard on our side stood ramrod straight, his feet apart, arms out by his side, as if he were about to draw his gun in an American Wild West shootout. He wore a helmet and a pistol holder on his waist, his muscular chest and biceps evident through his tight-fitting short-sleeve shirt.

While the physical stature of the American and ROK soldiers in the JSA can intimidate the smaller North guards, the latter have been known to compensate by massing against a lone soldier, or psyching themselves up into an unnerving mental and emotional fervour. UNC soldiers are trained to not react to these minor provocations. This show of physique by the UNC was just that — a show. It was our boys who were intimidated by the "war faces" of the KPA guards and their unrelenting, unflinching, and unnerving glares that locked in like lasers to the eyes of the UN guards. These were cold, hard, barely suppressed stares of hatred. Our boys wore reflector sunglasses. The sunglasses gave them some refuge from those baleful glares.

Located in Sinchon County, North Korea, southwest of Pyongyang, is the Sinchon Museum of American War Atrocities, which remembers the deaths of about 35,000 North civilians, who the North accused the U.S military of torturing and executing during the latter's occupation of the country from October to December 1950 (the U.S. vehemently denies any involvement). And the North hasn't forgotten that U.S. planes dropped 635,000 tons of bombs — including 32,557 tons of napalm — on it during the war.

That KPA soldier across from me had no way of knowing, of course, that I was not an American, his arch enemy. He would not know I was Canadian — a good guy, neutral, who wouldn't hurt a flea.

The MAC building is long and spartan, with windows running the length of the room. In the centre along the side were long wooden tables and a few chairs. One half of one table was in the South, the other half in the North. Once we were inside, one of our ROK guards positioned himself against the wall, the other by the far door, which opened into North Korea. Stand in the near south side of the room, you are in South Korea; cross over the centre to the far side, you're in the North. Visit two countries for the price of one. Neat!

"Do not interfere or touch the ROK soldiers," warned Naumenkof. "They will physically stop you if you cross in front or behind them. Do not go near the door to the North. Two KPA guards are standing outside. There have been incidents where tourists and ROK soldiers have been pulled through the door and brutalized."

Naumenkof told us that in 2002, U.S. president George W. Bush stood in this room with then South Korean president Kim Dae-jung. Two KPA guards walked in, and one took down the American flag and began polishing his shoes with it, while the other removed the ROK flag and blew his nose on it. Not wanting a future repeat, the South had the silk flags replaced with plastic ones.

Naumenkof took questions from us, and told us we could "take photos with the ROK soldiers, but don't get too close to them. I don't want any accidents or you guys to get hurt." I decided to pass on the photo-op. He then led us outside onto the nearby steps of Freedom House. "Do you see the North Korean guard standing on the steps of Panmungak?" he asked us.

We gazed across into the North, the guard distinguishable a hundred metres away by his uniform and tall hat. "Yes," we answered.

"He's staring back at us with binoculars," said Naumenkof. I straightened my shoulders and nodded to the enemy. We were not permitted to wave.

A short time later, we boarded a military shuttle bus, which transported us a kilometre from the JSA along a lonely road through the woods to the remote UNC Checkpoint 3, located just south of the midpoint of the DMZ. We were greeted by a young, enthusiastic Korean soldier named Han. He announced that the North was monitoring our tour group at this moment from KPA Checkpoint 5, located in close proximity. "Their radio tower is jamming our hand phone signals," he told us, adding rather gleefully that if we tried to use them now they would be inoperable.

Our view north out over the DMZ was limited by a soupy veil of white mist hugging the ground and reducing visibility to less than a kilometre. Photos in Major Kirkbride's book on Panmunjeom show the area north of the DMZ as sparsely populated, a terrain of rugged foothills and brush. In the distance was a ridge of low, steep hills.

Because the DMZ's long swath has remained untouched by humans and development since 1953, its nearly one thousand square kilometres of flora and fauna has grown unchecked for seven decades. Each winter, for example, several hundred rare red-crowned cranes — delineated by a small red patch on their head, and by snowy-white plumage and black necks and tails — arrive from their home in northeast China and Siberia to feed in the Cheorwon area in the DMZ about sixty kilometres east of Panmunjeom. Occasionally, a deer or small animal detonates one of the estimated one million landmines both sides have planted since the end of the war. In 2013, a South farmer was killed when he stepped on a landmine. In 2015, two soldiers on an ROK patrol in Paju, near Panmunjeom, had their lower appendages blown off after stepping on mines.

One has to wonder what happened for Korea to create this obtrusive border in 1948. Korean history books state that Korea as a society came into existence during the Gojoseon period (*go* means ancient), which began in about 2300 BC. Since that time, although the country's kingdoms having had their share of royal murders and court intrigue, dynastic upheavals, peasant revolts, coup d'états, and foreign invasions, it has remained a singular nation. Prior to the 1948 divide, one could travel from Busan on the south coast all the way north to the shared border with China and Russia, a distance of about 1,400 kilometres. Today, though, the distance from Busan to the DMZ is only about five hundred kilometres.

We need to go back to August 15, 1945, when Japan's thirty-five-year period of colonization suddenly ended upon its surrender ending the Second World War. About seven hundred thousand Japanese citizens living in Korea at the time fled back to their country. The Soviets, who had declared war on Japan on August 8, arrived in the northern part of Korea to ostensibly oversee the Japanese departure. The U.S. Army arrived in Seoul from Japan to provide a semblance of law and order in the chaos and confusion. Because the U.S. feared the Soviets might try to sweep south and impose a communist regime on the entire peninsula, the United States stipulated that the 38th parallel, just north of Seoul, would be the arbitrary line the Soviets could not proceed past. It turned out that the U.S. fears were well-founded.

The Soviets respected the 38th, but began to promulgate their form of rule, confiscating private land, farms, and livestock from the wealthy. They transferred 90 percent of private industry, banks, railways, and communications to the nascent state. They propped up a charismatic Korean, Kim Il-sung, as ruler. The Americans requested meetings with the Soviets in an attempt to eradicate the 38th line, but both sides held fast that their forms of government — a nascent rough-and-tumble form of democracy in the south, Communism in the north — would prevail.

When Japan surrendered, Koreans were ecstatic, looking forward to living under democratic rule. Those who had fled the country during colonization flooded back from Manchuria, China, and Japan, and many from north of the 38th headed south, many to Seoul. Between 1945 and 1947, the population in the southern half of the peninsula skyrocketed from 16 to 21 million. In 1947, Kim Il-sung made it more difficult for Koreans in the north to flee south.

The United Nations then mandated that elections should take place in Korea. The Soviets refused. With UN backing, the south held its own elections on May 10, 1948, and a U.S.-educated Korean, Rhee Sung-man, also known as Syngman Rhee, was elected president.

Believing there was no hope for uniting the country, Rhee established the Republic of Korea on August 15 of that year. Three weeks later, on September 7, the Democratic People's Republic of Korea (DPRK) was formed in the North.

About ten million families — brothers, sisters, mothers, fathers, cousins, uncles, and aunts — who lived on different sides of the 38th, were now permanently separated. If you resided in Seoul, and your parents and relatives lived in Pyongyang, you would never see them again. As the regime in the North intensified its stranglehold, Kim Il-sung, using intimidation and assassinations to rid himself of political opponents, and backed by the Soviet Union, launched an attack on the South on June 15, 1950, in an attempt to unify the two counties under his dictatorship. His troops waltzed into Seoul. The Korean War had begun.

The conflict was brutal, and didn't end until the summer of 1953. China contributed about 1.3 million soldiers to fight alongside the North. More than three hundred thousand U.S. soldiers, and considerably smaller numbers from sixteen other UN nations, fought for the South. The war left more than two million dead. In the aftermath there were half a million South Korean war widows and about one hundred thousand orphans. The South's economy, land, and infrastructure were left in tatters; its per capita income about $89 annually.

In fact, the Korean War has never really ended. The July 27, 1953 Armistice Agreement was not a peace treaty; rather, it was an armed truce, now the longest ongoing armed truce in history. It would be nearly twenty years after the war ended, not until 1974, that the South and North, via Red Cross meetings, could bring themselves to have official contact.

In June 2000, an historic Summit Meeting took place between presidents Kim Dae-jung and Kim Jong-il in Pyongyang. Between then and 2015, there have been twenty rounds of family reunions, each usually involving several hundred North and South family members. I have watched televised news coverage of reunions, and long-lost brothers and sisters, mothers and sons, clung to each other, refusing to let go. Adult sons bowed deeply to mothers. Tears flowed unabashedly; the anguish, angst, and loneliness of six decades apart rushed out. It was even enough to get me emotional. The harder part for families comes a day or two later, when they are forced to split up again and return to their respective country. Only 66,000 war-divided family members remain in the South; half of them are more than eighty years old.

* * *

Our guide, Mr. Han, pointed to the DMZ and asked if we could see the A-frame building. In the thick mist, I could not spot it. He said it was the North Korean Peace Museum. "It holds the two axes the North soldiers used in the 1976 murders in the JSA."

The museum, and the JSA, are located in the ancient farming village of Panmunjeom. In 1951, Panmunjeom was chosen as the site where the main participants in the Korean War would meet and iron out an end to the conflict. For two years, South, North, Chinese, and American officers sat at that MAC building table for countless meetings. The Korean Armistice Agreement that put an end to the fighting was signed in Panmunjeom in July 1953. But the resulting DMZ swallowed up the village, and all that remains of it today is the building in which the agreement was signed, now home to the so-called North Korean Peace Museum.

The axe murders Han was referring to claimed the lives of two U.S. officers, and brought the peninsula to the brink of conflict. About a hundred metres from where we stood was the Bridge of No Return, where, on August 18, 1976, Captain Arthur G. Bonifas and First Lieutenant Mark T. Barrett met their fates. The Bridge of No Return was so-named because when POWs from the Korean War were exchanged between April and September 1953, the predominantly American, Chinese, North, and South Korean POWs' decision to cross from or into North and South Korea was irrevocable. Until 1976, the bridge and the road over it was the only land route connecting the two countries. Just fifteen kilometres northwest, over the bridge along the road into the North, was Gaesong, the capital of Korea's Goryeo Kingdom, the latter in existence from 918 to 1392.

Han informed us that a poplar tree by the bridge had been the trigger for the murders. He permitted us to stroll down to the bridge — a long, single-lane slab of now darkened, worn concrete — which moved over a small stream overgrown with bushes. In 1976, on this side of the bridge, was the modest UNC Checkpoint 3; across from it was KPA Checkpoint 4 (both posts are now gone). Two lush, broad and leafy poplar trees once grew close to the UN checkpoint. One of the trees partially blocked the view of UNC guards stationed at our current location (where Han met us). The UNC would occasionally trim the poplar to ensure the view was unobstructed between the two posts.

At ten thirty in the morning on Wednesday, August 18, 1976, Bonifas and Barrett, and a modest security team and work crew, conveyed out in a work truck to trim the tree. Three men carried axes up the ladders. Within two minutes, nine KPA guards and a senior lieutenant by the name of Pak Chul dashed across the bridge to the poplar.

Lieutenant Pak's rank was equivalent to that of an American staff sergeant, wrote Kirkbride, adding UNC brass considered Pak a tough officer, with a reputation for discipline, demanding law and order from his soldiers in the JSA. The UNC had nicknamed him "Bulldog," for his penchant for provoking incidents. In 1974, for example, when a high-ranking U.S. officer was touring the JSA, UNC guards prevented the KPA from snapping the officer's photo. Pak, in response, "kicked an American officer in the groin."

As the UNC work crew began trimming the tree, Pak confronted Bonifas and ordered him to instruct his men to cease work. It was 10:50 a.m. Bonifas told his crew to continue. Pak became incensed and threatened to kill him. He called for reinforcements. By eleven a.m. there were about thirty KPA soldiers gathered under the tree.

Pak then slipped off his wristwatch, wrapped it in a white handkerchief, put it in his trousers pocket, and shouted, *"Mi gun a chu I cha!"* ("Kill the U.S. aggressors!").

"He pounced upon Captain Bonifas, striking him in the back and knocking him to the ground," wrote Kirkbride. "Bonifas was [then] beaten to death by at least five other KPA guards."

The melee lasted about four minutes and was only stopped when Bonifas's truck driver positioned his vehicle over his commander's mutilated body. Four U.S. enlisted men and four ROK soldiers were injured. Meanwhile, Barrett was separated from the other men and systematically bludgeoned with an axe.

The incident was captured on film by a UN guard stationed at one of the posts who had a movie camera with a telephoto lens. Clips from the footage were shown on American television news programs the following night. In *DMZ: A Story of the Panmunjom Axe Murder*, Kirkbride included sixteen still frames from that assault, twelve depicting KPA soldiers massing around the officers, swinging axes. The two Americans were subsequently taken to hospital, but it was too late. Both had succumbed to their injuries. Bonifas, a West Point graduate, had volunteered to be sent to Korea, and was scheduled to return home to Newburgh, New York, to his wife and three young children, in just two weeks.

In Washington, the National Military Command Centre and Joint Chiefs of Staff at the Pentagon were notified within two hours of the deaths. Washington taxed Eighth Army Commanding General Richard G. Stilwell in Seoul with devising a response plan. Stillwell and his officers hatched Operation Paul Bunyan. It called for sixteen ROK engineers to be sent to the tree to cut it down, protected by infantry, attack helicopters and tanks. Sixty-four members of the elite 1st ROK Special Forces Brigade would surround the tree. In the air above would be twenty American UH-1 Huey helicopters carrying U.S. troops to be placed on the ground if KPA forces responded. Eight American Cobra attack helicopters would be circling, another eight idling on the ground, and seven on standby. An American platoon of twenty Sheridan tanks would be moved to the JSA, ready to level it with shells, to allow forces to evacuate if the KPA attacked.

And there was more, much more. Within twenty hours of the killings, the Pentagon ordered U.S. air and naval reinforcements to Korea, and a squadron of F-111 fighter jets stationed in Idaho flew nonstop to Suwon Air Base, just south of Seoul. A number of F-4 Phantom fighters stationed in Okinawa and two B-52 bombers from Guam were also sent to Korea. The U.S. Fifth Air Force in Yogota, Japan, was placed on increased readiness. Parts of the U.S. Seventh Fleet and the aircraft carrier USS *Midway* were directed to the peninsula. In the South, the 38th Air Defense Artillery Brigade — which would control an air war — went into full readiness. The ROK's 600,000 and the U.S.'s 37,000 troops in the South were put on alert for a mission they knew little about. This was big.

Two days later, on August 19, Operation Paul Bunyan was approved by official channels in Washington. Later that day, President Ford gave final approval. By late evening, General Stilwell, in Seoul, still had not received official word when the mission would go. He needed to know by midnight if he was to carry out the plan the next day. With fifteen minutes to spare, he got his reply: commence operations at seven a.m. He briefed ROK and U.S. battalion commanders, who briefed their soldiers.

"Pray we can get through the next day without war," Stilwell told his wife, the military weight of the ROK and U.S. Army, Air Force, and Navy, directed at Panmunjeom.

Just after seven the next morning, three days after the murders, a U.S. officer entered the JSA and announced to a North officer that the operation was commencing. Minutes later, the operation's first element crossed into the DMZ. Major Kirkbride, who spoke some Korean, had a first-hand view as interpreter for the ROK troops. The sixty-four ROK Special Forces, clutching long wooden clubs, formed a human ring around the engineers at the tree. Nearby, ROK Reconnaissance troops were concealed at the line of trees and U.S. helicopters buzzed low overhead.

To cut through the poplar's three massive limbs required thirteen chainsaws — each kept getting gummed up with sap. Four burned out. By seven forty-five, the tree was finally down. All forces, except ROK Reconnaissance, began to depart. By eight o'clock, the operation was complete. A U.S officer in an overhead helicopter said he sighted upwards of five hundred KPA soldiers in the JSA, dashing about in all directions, many in groups of two, three, or more, apparently confused about the show of force. From a tunnel in the JSA previously unknown to UNC, KPA soldiers had emerged wearing helmets and carrying rifles.

By four thirty in the afternoon, all U.S. and ROK forces, except aviators, had returned to their home bases to wait out the night on alert. No one knew how North Korea would react. General Stilwell, who had managed to get only an hour of sleep in the previous seventy-two hours, took the opportunity to get some shuteye. In the following weeks, numerous meetings between the two sides were held at the MAC building in the JSA. The UNC demanded an apology for the murders. Kim Il-sung offered a half-hearted response. After a month, all UNC units returned to normal duties.

Changes came in the JSA because of the incident. Personnel from both countries, once free to wander the entire compound, were now relegated to their own side. A concrete sidewalk — today visible along Conference Row — was poured to delineate the demarcation line. As well, The Bridge of No Return was permanently shuttered. As for Lieutenant Pak, he continued to patrol the JSA. But after the 1984 firefight involving the Russian, Matauzik, Kirkbride claims that Pak was not seen again, and speculated he may have been one of the three KPA guards killed during that gun battle.

* * *

The military bus returned us to Camp Bonifas. It was late afternoon. We transferred back onto our tour bus and prepared to leave for the trip back to Seoul. Fortunately, I had not been manhandled, bullied, or ridiculed by North guards, or by Naumenkof or any fellow tour members. As we motored toward Seoul, at the front of the bus, our loquacious Korean guide was talking a mile a minute over the loudspeaker — just as he had that morning on our way north. He spoke a language I was not familiar with, though snippets reminded me of English. His pronunciation was so garbled and indecipherable, it sounded like his mouth was full of marbles. So that's what I called him.

"Do you understand what Marbles is saying, Gail?" I asked my fellow Canadian seatmate, a woman from Kamloops, British Columbia, who was in Seoul visiting her daughter, who was also teaching English.

"No," Gail said, grinning.

"Neither do I."

We crossed back over the Imjin River and an hour later were back among Seoul's mass of concrete and steel. Our trip ended where it had begun that morning: at Yongsan Garrison at the USO compound in Camp Kim. Yongsan was built by the Japanese in 1910, and was later the base for the U.S.'s Korean headquarters. It's located in south central Seoul, just north of the Han River and near Itaewon, a crowded and bustling area of old and new shops, and bars and restaurants commonly patronized by foreigners. Just north is the singular, broad, and wooded Nam Mountain. Yongsan base may be the world's only military camp located in a major city.

Inside the USO compound were a few civilians and a smattering of young soldiers wearing military fatigues. As a well-deserved reward for having successfully survived my trip to the JSA unscathed, I treated myself to a chocolate bar and a Coke at the snack bar, then relaxed on a big comfortable sofa in front of a big-screen TV. It was tuned to FOX, and the blonde host was pontificating about something or other, so I soon left and took the subway back to my small flat in Myeongil-dong in southeast Seoul.

I've noticed that South Koreans seem almost blasé about the border tension. In decades past, though, when there was a serious military flare-up along the border, citizens reportedly would dash to the grocery stores to stock up on supplies, including boxes of fried noodles. These days, while border confrontations and skirmishes may create world headlines, people here have, I suppose, heard it all before; so they just get on with their lives. Mothers fret about their children's educations. Schoolgirls are enraptured with the latest boy bands. Boys roughhouse with friends on the way home from school. Fathers work late. Citizens scurry about to earn a living. Yet, their grandfathers and grandmothers, parents, sisters and brothers in the North live largely in poverty, and have been held hostage in a closed and internationally isolated country for nearly seventy years by a despotic Kim lineage of ruthless dictators. Being separated must be heartbreaking for the older generation in both nations. Yet, for many young South Koreans, North Korea is so distant, so intangible, it might as well be Mars.

# CHAPTER 2

I had been living in Seoul for more than a decade when my Aunt Irene in Toronto sent me a book written by American Bill Bryson. I had never heard of Bryson, but I read the book, *In a Sunburned Country*, which is a comic narrative of his fascinating trip through Australia. I was smitten, cognizant of why millions of readers were hooked on this bestselling author. I had not thought a simple travel book — the genre, in my mind, reminiscent of wanderers writing dull prose about what should have been fascinating adventures — could be so breezy, humorous, and illuminating.

I read Bryson's other gems: *Notes from a Small Island*, about his trek through Britain, and *A Walk in the Woods*, which recounted his long, exhausting hike along the Appalachian Trail. I had a walloping grand time tagging along with Bryson on these excursions, too. I got to thinking that he was most definitely needed in South Korea to trundle through the country, to put it on the map by writing another bestseller. Goodness knows the peninsula could use his help. Except for its immediate neighbours, China and Japan, very few others seem to visit the country for leisure or for pleasure. (In 2014, about 5.5 million Chinese and 2.5

million Japanese tourists visited Korea, representing about 80 percent of all incoming foreign tourists. Many arrive for shopping or gambling junkets.) Most of the rest of the world seemed to know little, if anything, about South Korea. It is dominated in the media attention department by its mad-hatter neighbour, North Korea — run currently by Kim Jung-un, one of our planet's most notorious dictators. Compared to the North, South Korea is like that standup comedian who has to follow Jerry Seinfeld on stage; he is always going to be second fiddle. Not that the South Korean government seems to do much to promote the country for tourism. When was the last time you saw an advertisement on television or in print inviting you to visit one of its sandy beaches or its ancient Buddhist temples, or hike its craggy granite mountain ridges?

It astonishes me how little Westerners seem to know about the country. When I'm back in Canada and I speak with people about my time in Korea, they sometimes ask "North or South?" Koreans living in Canada have told me with a sigh that they have been asked if they're from the North or the South. Well, more than two million South Koreans have emigrated to North America; while the number of North Koreans is miniscule. Chances are slim that a Korean you run into at a shop or on the street will be from North Korea.

One day, in the small town of Brockville, Ontario, I was at the local post office inquiring about sending a parcel to a friend in Korea. The clerk behind the counter checked a country list and announced with a hint of bewilderment that there were two Koreas. *Well, no shit, Sherlock.*

"Which Korea is the parcel going to?" she asked me.

"It can only go to one place; mail doesn't go to the other," I replied politely, hoping by simple deduction she would conclude the correct country. She didn't.

"So ...which one?" she asked.

"South Korea," I answered. "You can't get in or out of the North. There's no international mail delivery there."

She looked surprised. "Oh, I didn't know that."

Even people who read newspapers and watch the news, like my mother, were pretty much clueless about South Korea. She was a school librarian in Toronto for many years, and I would have thought that in her downtime she may have wandered to the East Asia section and perhaps taken a peak at a book on, say, South Korea, considering her son was living there.

Just prior to my parents' visit to Seoul in the early fall of 2000, my mother phoned me to ask, concerned, "Do we need to get inoculated for disease before we arrive?"

*Of course, Mom — we all suffer from dengue fever and typhoid in Korea.*

She next wondered innocently, "Should we bring purification tablets to put in our drinking water?"

I sighed, shook my head, and said, "Mom, South Korea is not a third-world country." When my parents arrived in Seoul, my mother looked at all the high-rise apartments and modern buildings, and remarked with surprise, "I didn't think there would be so many buildings," as if she had been expecting mud huts with straw roofs.

Poor South Korea; seemingly ignored and passed over. The country has always suffered from a lack of drawing power as a travel destination. Heck, it was 1882 before Korea opened her borders for the first time to international visitors and trade. In the previous five hundred years, the conservative, Confucian-based government kept the nation cloistered and sequestered, zealously guarding against any encroachment by foreigners. This was a country where, in 1653, the government would not permit the thirty-six survivors of the Dutch ship *Sparrow Hawk*, wrecked off Jeju Island, to depart. Had eight of *Sparrow Hawk*'s crew not taken a boat and escaped to Nagasaki thirteen years later, then to The Netherlands — the endeavour described by crew member Hendrik Hamel in *Hamel's Journals and a Description of the Kingdom of Korea, 1653–1666* — they may have never escaped the peninsula.

Lillias Stirling Horton, an American missionary doctor who arrived in Incheon in 1888, and became the personal physician to Empress Myeongseong (known as Queen Min), wrote in her 1904 book, *Fifteen Years Among the Topknots, or Life in Korea*, that "people back home [have] never even heard of Corea."

It has really only been in the past twenty years or so that the words *Korea* and *vacation* could be reasonably uttered in the same breath. The country was a colony of Japan from 1910 to 1945. Then came the Korean War. This was followed, until 1988, by a period of rule by a series of authoritarian military-backed presidents. In May 1980, for instance, President Chun Doo-hwan sent the army in to Gwangju to brutally put down a civilian uprising, killing more than six hundred — hardly an environment conducive to a family vacation.

Even today, it is not an easy place for an individual backpacker or a family to travel through. Language is but one issue. Korea has also been slow to introduce amenities and accommodation that would fit North American and European tastes, unlike Korea's southerly neighbours — the Philippines, Thailand, Indonesia, and Vietnam. It seems Koreans and Westerners even view vacationing differently. We tend to go for quiet, and where nature and aesthetics loom large, maybe at a nice country cottage or place by the sea with activities provided. These are rare finds in Korea. Koreans love crowds and action and noise. The simple pleasure of being alone has not yet seemed to have made much of a dent in the Korean national psyche.

During my first summer in Seoul, my academy owner, Mr. So, invited me to join his family and friends on a camping trip for four days. He told me they would be pitching their tents by a stream in Seorak Mountain National Park in Gangwon Province along the east coast. I accepted. But once we arrived at the shallow pebbly river that wound its way through picturesque farmland, hills, and woods, we sat for excruciatingly long breakfasts, lunches, and dinners, served atop large mats laid out on the grass. The meals were prepared and served by the patient ladies in the group. Between meals we sat around some more.

On the third day, we were hustled into the van and driven to a nearby mountain, where there was a hiking trail. *Wonderful,* I thought, *finally some activity*. I was looking forward to jettisoning the bloated feeling you get after eating seemingly non-stop for three days. I hoped my blood — which had congealed into petroleum jelly — would begin to flow again on the challenging hike. We parked, walked along a clear narrow stream that flowed over granite rock, and two minutes later, entered a wooden chalet, a restaurant, it turned out, where we all sat down for a two-hour lunch. After our meal, we were driven back to the campsite to sit some more. I don't think I've eaten as much and used fewer calories over four days in my entire life.

* * *

I arrived in South Korea on June 1, 1995. I had departed Los Angeles International Airport in the early afternoon, and what always seems surreal to me, the almost ten-thousand-kilometre, twelve-hour flight touched down at Gimpo International Airport in northwestern Seoul that same afternoon. We flew in low over Seoul. The day was clear and sunny. I peered out the window at the beauty below: a smattering of craggy, rugged granite ridges covered in the full bloom of trees, in stark contrast to the innumerable clusters of white, high-rise apartment buildings. The juxtaposition: nature versus concrete, of two dominant vivid colours: dark green and white — was visually stunning. I immediately liked Seoul.

For the first few months, I lived in Cheonho-dong, in the eastern reaches Seoul, along the shore of the Han River, which divides the city into approximate north and south halves. When I looked across the kilometre-wide Han from Cheonho-dong, my view was of the long, low ridge of Acha Mountain that followed the river. The academy where I taught was in nearby Myeongil-dong.

I soon discovered that within a ten-minute walk of my front door, I could find almost anything I could possibly desire. There were dry-cleaners; supermarkets; hardware, grocery, convenience, drug, and clothing stores; chicken, pizza, and Chinese food delivery restaurants; barbers and hairdressers; academies; saunas and fitness clubs; and outdoor markets supplying fresh fish, vegetables, and fruit at good prices. Nearby, there were also wooded trails, red earth tennis courts, and a multiplex movie house. Olympic Park, site of the 1988 Olympics, was within a twenty-minute walk. Running alongside the Han River was a forty-kilometre walking and cycling path. In my free time, I'd rollerblade along the path or play tennis on the courts.

But the day I arrived, this was all unknown to me. The sun was setting, darkness enveloping the city as I was dropped off on the main street by the Cheonho subway station, and headed toward my little room in a *yeogwan* (old traditional inn) located along a back lane near a bustling outdoor market.

Cheonho-dong at night is abuzz with lights and colours, of rapid movement and palpable energy. I had never seen such packed sidewalks. Many in the crowd were young women decked out in the latest fashions — often miniskirts and high heels. There were schoolchildren in smart uniforms coming and going from the various academies, and women out shopping or socializing in ubiquitous coffee shops. The streets were crammed with old city buses, cars, and taxis, horns honking. A constant stream of buses screeched to a loud, squeaky halt at the bus stops. The sound of traffic, of bus and car engines, was a constant, and at night the haze from the diesel hung in the yellow illumination from street lamps like a cloak of London fog.

I was not used to all this energy and mass of humanity. Not at all. I loved the urgency and visual delights. The multi-storied commercial buildings that lined the streets were plastered with neon signs in greens, oranges, reds, and yellows, advertising coffee shops or restaurants or other businesses. Red neon crosses rose high above small churches across the city.

In residential suburbs across the West you don't see people out on neighbourhood streets. After arriving home by car from work, a North American won't be seen again until the following morning. They camp out for the night in their carpeted basement rec rooms on their recliners and surf 150 channels on their big-screen televisions while eating TV dinners. Maybe the room has a bar and a billiards table. During winters — November to March — such citizens hibernate and perhaps do all sorts of unnatural acts. You rarely see them outside, though occasionally they'll poke their heads out the door to see if spring has arrived.

To me, it is the opposite in Korea. People view their apartment/homes as a place to simply lay their heads for the night. When I visit apartments there, often the only furniture in the living room is a sofa, chair, and a big flat-screen TV on the wall, not much else. I think Koreans prefer to be with friends, to talk and have fun out and about at coffee shops, cafés, restaurants, saunas, bars, and shops. That's perhaps why the streets, cafés, and restaurants are busy well into the night.

About 10.5 million people live in Seoul, and about 26 million — half the country's population — in the Seoul Capital Area, which includes satellite cities built with armies of high-rise apartment buildings. Consider that Australia, seventy-seven times larger in area than South Korea, has just 24 million people.

Korean cities employ a concept that I find appealing: residential and commercial areas intertwine, so that from my flat in Myeongil-dong, I could walk to the hardware, convenience, or grocery store, tailor, barber, bike shop, restaurant, or outdoor market along adjacent lanes in a jiffy. Having people out and about is how a residential place is supposed to be. I enjoy the interaction, hearing kids squealing in delight, school students gabbing loudly, housewives chatting, grandfathers debating. If North America decided to upgrade their moribund and tomb-like suburbs from their current catatonic status, to one in which people out for a walk don't feel like the last human on Earth, they ought to check out the Korean system.

There are lots of positives about living in Korea. It's generally a safe place. There are stringent laws here to ensure that owning a gun is a near impossibility. A good thing, too, I say, because with Koreans' quick temperament and penchant for drinking, there may not be many people left in the country if purchasing a firearm was as easy as applying for a library card, the way it is in America.

For reasons I can't explain, the homicide rate seems to be a closely guarded secret. I had asked my good Korean friend, Heju, to try to acquire the statistics, and she visited several local police stations. Officers informed her that they weren't at liberty to divulge the information. To obtain it, they insisted, she'd need to fill out a form and send it to the "Shady and Secretive Department of Homicides." She didn't bother. But judging from newspapers, homicides are certainly not an everyday occurrence, and those that are committed seem often to be a crime of passion.

Young kids freely play outside and have little fear of approaching, for example, a stranger like me, to have a go at practising a few words of English. On subways and buses, strangers who sit down beside mothers holding babies or with young kids will sometimes touch or hold the little ones.

Korea has historically been a peace-loving nation. Unlike countries such as Italy, Portugal, Spain, France, Germany, the Netherlands, Belgium, Britain, Japan, Russia, and the United States, Korea never attempted to colonize a weaker nation or to plunder another's natural resources and riches. Korea did not send armies to Japan or China. It did not seek grand foreign conquests of land or power. For the longest while, in fact, it was an international outcast, like the school loner who sits off to the side and keeps to himself. I suppose this could be viewed as a collective lack of curiosity and sense of adventure. If every other nation engendered a similar inward-looking ethos, North America, Australia, and other major land masses might still remain largely unsettled. Historically, Korea's citizens rarely ventured past neighbouring China and Japan.

* * *

I was smitten with Korea. It would be a while, though, before I was aware of why I had an instantaneous attachment to the people and the country. My eventual conclusion: Chaos. Disorder. Energy. Koreans are hustlers. Not in the sense of Paul Newman in the classic film of the same name, but in a positive way. They bust their butts to succeed and rely on guts, determination, and sheer will.

After I read Bryson's books, I realized there wasn't a similar English-language travel book about Korea. Roger Shepherd, a New Zealander, penned *Baekdu Daegan Trail: Hiking Korea's Mountain Spine,* in 2010, but it was predominantly a hiking guide. British international travel writer Simon Winchester walked the length of the country and published *Korea: A Walk Through the Land of Miracles* in 1988. Without the benefit of a translator, though, the view seemed to be of Korea from the outside. Perhaps owing to the fact that from 1910 to 1945, Korea was a colony of Japan, and from then until 1987 it was ruled by a series of authoritarian military governments, there seem to be no travel books that I was aware of written during this period. One of the most thorough and accomplished travel adventures written was by British intrepid world traveller Isabella Bird, who after trekking through Korea's interior and conveying inland along the Han River by boat and on foot, riding on horseback along the east coast Diamond Mountains — and after four separate trips to Korea between 1894 and 1987 — published *Korea and Her Neighbours* in 1898.

Before her, in 1884, American George Clayton Foulk completed a nine-hundred-mile, forty-three-day journey being carried across the peninsula in a palanquin chair, and being one of the few Westerners to speak Korean at that time, gained an immediate and intimate knowledge of the people. He jotted nearly four hundred pages of notes, though it wasn't until 2007, when Canadian writer Samuel Hawley, author of the acclaimed book *The Imjin War: Japan's Sixteenth-Century Invasion of Korea and Attempt to Conquer China*, published two books about Foulk. Hawley had discovered the George Clayton Foulk collection at the Bancroft Library at the University of California, Berkeley, and had the American's notes and letters sent via microfilm to Seoul. Due to Foulk's truncated and messy handwriting, it took Hawley many months of poring over the pages to fully comprehend the content.

I somehow doubted that Bill Bryson would find his way to South Korea and write a bestseller. So it fell to someone else to explore and write about this uncut diamond of a country. Why not me? I had done a bit of writing. My university degree was in mass communication with an emphasis in journalism. I'd been a sports reporter at the *Tahoe Daily Tribune* in Lake Tahoe, California, in 1985. In 1997, I spent a year employed as a copy editor at the *Korea Herald* newspaper in Seoul. Yes, I'd do it, I decided. I'd devise a practical and assiduous long-term plan for a pan-Korea trip. But unlike my gritty, trekking predecessors — Foulk, Bird, Winchester, and Shepherd, among others — I'd use a car!

South Korea is smaller than thirty-seven of America's fifty-one states, including Florida, Kentucky, and Tennessee. Italy is three times larger. Slender Cuba and little Iceland are fractionally bigger. Yet I realized the preparations and the actual trip would not be so simple. Much of the country is mountainous. It also has 17,268 kilometres of undulating and indented coastline and more than three thousand offshore islands. Its long history was mostly a mystery to me, its culture and people puzzling.

I began to read up on my subject, and so began to frequent new and used English-language bookstores, buying up any titles I could find with information about the country and its history, geography, geology, culture, famous people, architecture, and wars. I joined the Korean branch of the Royal Asiatic Society (RAS) and began attending its twice-monthly lectures. Talks were presented in English by Korean and foreign professors, intellectuals, authors, and diplomats, and covered a diverse range of topics, from tea-making, traditional architecture, Buddhism and missionaries, to the Korean War, North Korea, Japanese colonization, and yangban (Joseon upper-class gentlemen). The lectures were highly informative.

I ordered home delivery of the *Korea Times*, the *Korea Herald*, the English-language edition of the *JoongAng Daily*, and the *International Herald Tribune*. Nightly, I clipped and chronicled articles about places and things I would be interested in seeing. I do not mean to disparage Korea — God knows the last century alone has been difficult enough — but it seemed that regularly the papers contained new and novel forms of social oddities and sometimes just plain weird stuff that I believe only happens in Korea. For that reason alone, I eagerly perused each issue.

The *Korea Times*, for example, for a time published contributions by an American doctor who practised in Seoul. The good doctor would describe snippets of his life, and, being single, he included stories about dating Korean women. In one piece the doctor wrote about his secretary, a young Korean woman who he described as pretty, intelligent, single, and seeking a marriage partner. He concluded that if any single men were interested in courting her, they were to contact him. A day or two later the secretary's lengthy remonstration appeared, in which she lambasted him for being a nutcase and implied that hell would freeze over before she would seek his assistance in this regard.

There was also the story of a thirteen-year-old boy, Kim Sung-ho, who was allegedly trapped for twelve hours in his bedroom under masses of test papers, notebooks, and text books. Sung-ho's mother had enrolled him in nine different after-school private academies (hagwons), and his room was stacked sky-high with books. One Sunday evening, the boy was standing up, memorizing facts for a test, when he accidently nudged the tower of books and the entire mass came crashing down around him. On Monday morning, his mother, unable to open his bedroom door, called the police, who needed an axe to break it down. It took thirty minutes to rescue Sung-ho, and fifty garbage bags to lug out all the paper.

There was more. I would see photos in the newspapers of seemingly annual National Assembly clashes, where the two opposing political parties squared off in the chamber, engaging in giving each other half nelsons and the occasional uppercut or left hook.

Sometimes the news was tragic. A man was arrested in Seoul for stabbing to death his former teacher. The student, now thirty-eight, had held a grudge since age seventeen, when the teacher struck him with a wooden rod for allegedly cheating on a test. The student had contacted the teacher to demand an apology. When it was not forthcoming, he stabbed him. Or the story of a sixty-eight-year-old priest in Seoul who stabbed a fellow priest from another church. Both priests were angry for reportedly being slandered by each other. The victim of the stabbing wrestled the knife from the perpetrator and proceeded to stab him! Luckily the injuries were minor. Priests no less!

Often it was close to midnight by the time I'd finished perusing all four newspapers.

I sought an English-speaking Korean national to accompany me, not just to translate, but to pose questions, so I could try to capture the unvarnished heart, soul, and spirit of the local people. Had I put in the time learning to speak Korean, I would not have needed a translator, but as it stood, I had only a perfunctory understanding of the language, for which I accept all of the blame.

Korean, like Hungarian and Finnish, belongs to the Ural-Altaic language group, the genesis of which is hazy, but thought to be central Asia. Though its grammatical structure is very similar to Japanese, spoken Korean bears no resemblance to spoken Japanese. And although it contains many Chinese words, Korean grammar and phonics are completely different. Clearly, the Korean language was invented by aliens. Chinese was Korea's written language until the twentieth century, despite Hangul, the Korean writing system, devised by scholars under King Sejong between 1443 and 1446. Hangul has twenty-four phonetic symbols that can be learned quickly. The Korean elite preferred writing in Chinese, however, to keep them distinct from the semi-literate masses who could not comprehend the complicated Chinese characters.

Patricia Bartz, author of the august 1972 book *South Korea*, which documented in excellent detail the country's geology, geography, and flora and fauna, wrote that it was not until 1945 that Hangul came into widespread use, and not until 1971 that the government ordered all documents to be written in Hangul.

According to the U.S. Department of State's Foreign Service Institute, Korean is one of the four most difficult languages for an English-speaker to learn, along with Chinese (both Cantonese and Mandarin), Japanese, and Arabic. To gain proficiency in Korean takes, on average, 2,200 class hours over eighty-eight weeks. To put that in context, learning French, Italian, Portuguese, or Spanish — languages similar to English — requires just 575 class hours over twenty-four weeks.

Korean language word-order is opposite to English. For example, the English sentence "I eat a hamburger" translates in Korean to "I hamburger eat" (*Hamburgeo meogeoyo*). In Korean, the verb usually comes at the end of the sentence. In theory, Korean shouldn't be that difficult for me to master, since my brain works backward. But after several years of making a quasi effort to learn, I felt overwhelmed when I realized that I had only acquired a mere handful of words and still had about 300,000 to go! At that point, I essentially jettisoned my quest to learn the language.

At the time I was undertaking my travels, my spoken Korean consisted of being able to change a handful of verbs to past, present, and future tenses, though my listening comprehension was pretty near nil, probably because I was never a very good listener, even in English, and to my ear, spoken Korean was harsh and choppy, as if an angry Russian was chattering at me in Arabic.

The only real choice for translator was my good pal of four years, Kim Heju, who I had met while I was travelling in Yeosu along the south coast. Sadly, six months before our encounter, Heju's Canadian husband, whom she had accompanied to Japan, China, Australia, and Korea, where he taught English, had died of cancer.

Heju had been raised in Daejeon, about 160 kilometres south of Seoul. She had been a tomboy as a kid, and liked to play outdoors with the boys. She marched to her own drummer. She had little ambition to accumulate wealth, did not automatically ascribe that Korea was the centre of the universe, and enjoyed getting away on her own. She was impulsive, impractical, gregarious, and bossy, and there was little I could do about the latter, because every Korean female I've met, from age three to 103, is headstrong and commanding. I believe it's in their genes, a Korean thing.

Heju was teaching English to Korean kids at a small academy in her hometown when I asked if she could join me on my proposed three- to four-month foray across the peninsula. She was noncommittal at first.

"You won't have to pay a cent," I exhorted, in an effort to convince her. "I'll pay all expenses — accommodation, travel, food." (It was not every day that the son of a Scottish mother and Dutch father acted so benevolently.)

She continued to hem and haw, so I unleashed my trump card, offering her a percentage of potential book royalties, though, of course, there was no guarantee that I would even finish the trip, let alone the manuscript. "If I sell a lot of books, you could become rich," I assured her with near-total conviction.

Despite her normally buoyant outlook, Heju, like many Koreans, was imbued with a healthy dose of skepticism. "So, how much money would I make from royalties?" she countered more than once, in jest ( I think).

It was not long before the excursion was set to begin that Heju finally agreed to accompany me. Without her as a conduit, as an intermediary into the world of Koreans, I would have been in the dark, a fish out of water. She arranged a four-month leave of absence from her teaching job, and with my one-year contract at a local elementary school soon concluding, we would be ready to begin in mid-March the first segment through Seoul — two and a half years after first reading Bryson's *In a Sunburned Country*.

March was the ideal month to begin. I wanted to complete the trip before the arrival of the brutally oppressive summer, when searing heat and humidity transform East Asia into a sauna. The unpalatable steam bath usually begins in May or early June, and lasts through August. It's not until late summer, in September, that the humidity abates and temperatures reach a moderate level, with lovely high blue skies. March is a transitional month, when winter's bitterly cold, dry air, conceived in Siberia and then sweeping south over Korea, finally loses steam, defeated by the warm air flowing north from the South China Sea.

We spent the first three weeks exploring Seoul on foot. The city had been the capital since 1394, the vortex of power and prestige, containing the Joseon Dynasty's royal palaces and Neolithic settlements dating back about six or seven thousand years — Seoul was an ideal place to begin.

Most days we rode the Number 5 subway line west, under the Han River toward Old Seoul in the downtown core. The subway system in Seoul is outstanding, by the way, with fourteen lines comprising 775 kilometres of track, and shuttling an average of 4.2 million passengers daily around the vast city. In fact, it is the world's third-largest system in terms of passenger numbers, behind only Beijing and Shanghai. The Seoul subway system is like a small self-contained underground city. Along lengthy subterranean corridors and halls that connect one line to another can be found all sorts of shops and itinerant purveyors offering myriad items for sale. I've even seen baby chicks being sold out of cardboard boxes. Subway cars are not impervious to salespeople, either, as sellers stride car-to-car, declaring with great gusto the merits of the flashlights, magnifying glasses, raincoats, or umbrellas they are offering for sale.

We predominantly took guided tours of palaces and historic sites in and around the city, not because we particularly relished such outings, but because they were the most efficient way for us to learn about the city's grand traditional architecture and places of interest.

One tour was of Seodaemun Prison, where, between 1910 and 1945, forty thousand criminals and political prisoners were held by the Japanese. Many were tortured and executed at the site.

We also took tours of various Joseon palaces and were led up Bugak Mountain — the dominant thousand-foot ridge that rises up behind the Presidential Blue House and Gyeongbok Palace (the largest and most impressive of the Joseon palaces) — where we were afforded a marvellous view over the crowded city core and the surrounding mountains.

One bleak, chilly afternoon, Heju and I wandered through the grounds of the small, desolate Yanghwajin Foreign Missionary Cemetery, which is located along the north shore of the Han River in Hapjeong-dong, in Mapo district, in the city's far western reaches (*Yanghwajin* translates as "dock by willow trees and flowers"). The land for the cemetery was a gift in 1890 from King Gojong to the foreign community, who at the time were mostly missionaries.

In 1866, an estimated eight thousand Korean Catholics were beheaded or strangled to death during a state-sponsored purge. One of two main execution sites in Seoul was along the Han River's north shore in front of this future cemetery. The spot is known as Jeoldusan Martyrs' Shrine — *jeoldu* means "to cut off heads" and *san* is "mountain" (referring to the steep embankment).

We crouched in front of each headstone, some worn, some of the engravings faded, reading the inscriptions from the approximately six hundred stones, many of which dated from the late 1800s and early 1900s, though there were also a few from the later part of the twentieth century. I scribbled names and dates into my notebook, the list forming a veritable who's who of missionaries, notable foreigners, and others who gave years of their lives to serving in Korea.

Arthur Ernest Chadwell's gravestone indicated he arrived from England in 1926, was named Assistant Bishop to Korea in 1951, and was buried here in 1967. Henry Gerhard Appenzeller's tombstone indicated he was the first Methodist missionary to arrive in Korea in 1885. Sadly, he drowned in 1902, at the age of forty-four, trying to save a Korean girl. His daughter, Alice Rebecca Appenzeller, born in 1885, was reportedly the first American born in Korea. She died in 1950 after spending most of her life teaching in the country.

In the far corner of the cemetery was the Underwood family plot: six black marble headstones representing four generations of Underwoods who have lived in Korea since 1885. The original patriarch was Horace Grant Underwood — brother of John T., the founder of the Underwood Typewriter Company in New York. Horace was the master of all Korean missionaries, and devoted his life to establishing schools, churches, and medical clinics and persuading Koreans to embrace Christianity on behalf of the Protestant Church.

While Horace wasn't buried in this plot, his wife, American missionary doctor Lillias Stirling Horton, was. She wrote the book *Underwood of Korea*, about the couple's life in the country. There is also a tombstone for Horace's grandson, also named Horace Grant, who was born in Seoul in 1917 and who died in the same city in 2004 at age eighty-seven. He was the author of *Korea in War, Revolution and Peace: The Recollections of Horace G. Underwood.*

The Underwoods have been in Korea for 120 years. Their original two-storey stone home, in use since the turn of the nineteenth century in Yeonghui-dong at Yonsei University, is now the Underwood Memorial Hall Museum.

Some inscriptions were grim reminders of how fickle life could be a century ago, with numerous children of missionary parents buried here, many the victims of diseases such as typhoid, cholera, malaria, and tuberculosis. After entering Seoul in 1887, The Church of England Bishop for South Tokyo, Edward Bickerstet, wrote derogatorily, "I thought when I saw it that the Chinese town of Shanghai was the filthiest place human beings live on this earth, but Seoul is a grade lower." Isabella Bird wrote of late-nineteenth-century Seoul, "For a great city and a capital its meanness is indescribable," speaking of a quarter of a million people residing in a labyrinth of alleys beside foul-smelling ditches, where solid and liquid waste from houses was emptied.

There were three headstones in a row on a slight knoll, for Kim Ok Ja, 42, Kim Hankaul, 16, and Kim Scott Hansol, 14, all perishing on August 12, 1985.

We were puzzled. Had the trio, likely a mother and her two sons, been in a car accident? Later, I did some digging and discovered that Japan Airlines Flight 123 from Tokyo to Osaka had crashed into 6,500-foot Mount Takamagahara that day, killing all but four of the 524 passengers aboard. The passenger list indicated there were three Koreans aboard. Were they the three Kims in the cemetery? The evidence seemed to point in that direction.

After three and a half hours, and with darkness upon us, I finally scribbled the last inscription into my notebook. I couldn't feel the fingers of my right hand; they were cramped from writing and the cold.

Cemeteries to me represent the end of lives. They weren't fun places for me.

* * *

After three weeks touring historic places in Seoul, Heju and I were itching to get out on the road and motor through the country. I had recently bought a used and inexpensive red 1994 Hyundai Scoupe. The car's most salient features were its bucket seats and ample leg room, the latter in short supply in most Korean compact cars. Granted, the car's shock absorbers were kaput, and if I drove up a mildly challenging hill, the engine would inevitably overheat and the temperature gauge would shoot up to "extremely dangerous" territory. But the Scoupe cost just 1.5 million won (US$1,250), and I only needed it for a few months anyway.

I didn't even want a car. There are already about twenty million vehicles on South Korea's roads. Comparatively, Ireland has just 1.5 million. Canada — one hundred times larger in area than South Korea — has just 13 million. Seven million vehicles are registered in Seoul alone. But if we wanted to travel to all the destinations we had planned to, trains and buses were not the way to go, particularly for those places located off the beaten path.

The month before we started out, I had to sit three separate tests to earn my Korean driver's licence. The first was a written one, followed by driving on a controlled course, and finally on the road. The second was conducted on a long, narrow swath of pavement next to a creek that fed the south shore of the Han River. The circuit had an S-curve, a stop sign, a traffic light, a crosswalk, and a parallel parking area. I was hustled into a little compact car at the start line. On the dashboard was a small electronic screen showing the number 100 in red. Suddenly, the car started blurting loud nonsensical Korean phrases at me.

I cursed. I had paid 60,000 won (US$50) to take the test, and I had the sinking feeling that I was already behind the eight ball. I craned my neck back and forth trying in vain to find the source of "The Voice."

*Beep*, I heard, as the number on the screen dropped to 95. I hadn't even stepped on the gas pedal yet. Then there was another voice coming from a loudspeaker outside the car; I guessed it was my cue to begin the test. I worked the clutch and slowly proceeded forward. *Beep*, the number fell to 90 at the S-turn. *Beep* again at the traffic light: 85. Another beep as I went through the lights. Now 80. Then I was suddenly accosted by a startlingly loud whining blast from a siren inside the car. I almost had a heart attack. I stopped the car.

I swore again, furious that my test was now doomed for sure. "What's going on?"

*Beep.* The red number changed to 75 and a young man suddenly ran across the track toward the car like a storm trooper. He flung open my door and told me to get out.

I was fuming. "I'm not going anywhere!" I retorted, refusing to budge, but the fellow practically pulled me out, then got behind the wheel and drove the car off the track.

I made a beeline to the track-side office, where I informed an official, in both Korean and English, that this was the most moronic test in the annals of world driving history! I looked out over to the track and noted a young Korean woman driver being unceremoniously pulled out of her car, too.

Not ironically, sometime after this, I came across a weekly *Korea Times* column entitled, "Seoul Help Center for Foreigners," and in it a Canadian complained about taking the same test on the same track. "I had a very bad experience today going for my driving test," he wrote. "I was thrown into the car with everyone knowing that I don't speak Korean, but during the test, the car spoke Korean to me. The examiner did not provide guidance, and no one told me I would have to wait for a Korean voice to go ahead. I have ten years of driving experience in Canada, and I know that I drive better than a lot of Koreans. I really hope something can be done about this terrible situation."

The Seoul Help Center had printed the reason why the Canadian had failed: he didn't use a turn signal, failed to fully stop at an intersection, didn't check the white line while parallel parking, and did not stop within two seconds when the emergency siren rang. Everyone is required to score over 80 to pass. "Please study Korean driving rules and try again." The article failed to address the fact that they fail to warn you that the test will be conducted in Korean.

A week later, I paid another 60,000 won to take the test again. This time I brought along my pal Moon ("Moonie") Seok-mo as a translator, and I passed. You'd think Koreans would be safe and circumspect drivers after all this rigorous testing. Yet, the moment they get onto the road, it seems many drivers, men in particular, miraculously transform into Formula One champion wannabes.

Heju and I loaded up the Scoupe's trunk and back seat with cardboard boxes containing hundreds of clipped newspaper articles, travel brochures, maps, newspapers, and books related to Korea. Into our bags we stuffed sundries and clothes (Heju's also seemed to contain a high percentage of skin creams, ointments, lotions, and potions, I noticed). I had with me my "Bible" — the trip's engine, the Holy Grail, which contained a summarized chronological list of hundreds of places we would stop at along the way. It had taken me two years to populate and organize "The Bible," and it was essential. Bryson may have driven more than nine hundred unfettered kilometres in a single day, from Daly Waters to Alice Springs in Australia's Northern Territory. That is equivalent to driving the length of South Korea, twice. If we attempted a similar marathon drive, not only would we complete the entire trip in two days, but we'd bypass everything worth seeing.

I would motor (Heju did not drive) slowly, purposefully, and assiduously as if I were a retired gentleman navigating a Winnebago across North America. This was not only for safety reasons, but because we didn't want to miss out on the local scenery and points of interest.

The plan was to first head northwest from Seoul, then move counterclockwise: south down the western flank of the peninsula, east along the south coast, north up the eastern shore, and finally west along the border back to Seoul. The country is not wide, so we figured we could sneak inland to visit places of interest without too much difficulty.

We had neatly packed the car to capacity. But for reasons I can't fully explain, when it came time to depart Seoul, stuff was lying unpacked around the seats and at Heju's ankles. We seemed to be travelling in a veritable market on wheels.

"We're finally ready to go!" I announced triumphantly.

Heju glanced at the overstuffed Scoupe and replied cynically, "It looks like we're homeless and living out of the car."

Her pessimism sometimes aggravated me. We were finally ready to rock 'n' roll though.

# CHAPTER 3

It was April tenth. The morning was nippy, overcast and grey. Heju and I got in the Scoupe to begin the drive to our first destination, Ganghwado (*do* means "island"), located about seventy-five kilometres northwest of our current location, Myeongil-dong in east Seoul. Off we headed northwest along Expressway 88 — named for the year Seoul hosted the Summer Olympics. The road hugged the south shore of the Han River and traced the great span of Seoul from east to west, a drive of more than an hour, in which time we passed more than twenty bridges that cross over the river to the north shore. Then, as the infrastructure and apartment buildings began petering out in the far western reaches of Seoul, we switched onto Road 48, which took us northwest across the wide expanse of the Gimpo Plain toward the coast.

I found the drive along the No. 48 a bit disappointing. Covering the plain was a combination of flat agricultural land and pockets of low hills, and along the weaving road was a haphazard assortment of spartan dwellings and light industry. We arrived at the coast by Ganghwa Bridge at the base of a thickly wooded mountain slope. Across the kilometre-wide Yeomha Channel we could see the northeast shore of Ganghwa Island.

Along the mainland and Ganghwa shorelines we could see nothing but muddy banks and woods. Except for the channel's dangerous looking, swirling grey-brown waters, nothing moved. Despite Ganghwa being the country's fifth largest island, we could see no cars, people, boats, or villages along its shore. It was as if time stood still.

The far shore rose slightly to a wooded knoll, desolate and tranquil. Unlike most of the inhabited islands of Korea, which have at least a small port to shelter a handful of fishing trawlers, I could see nothing in the way of a single vessel or harbour.

But perhaps the silence and tranquility were not so surprising. After all, North Korea lies just 1.6 kilometres north of the island across the narrow Han estuary, and boat traffic and commercial fishing is prohibited in these waters. Being in such close proximity to the enemy, the ROK troops stationed here are in a state of constant readiness.

We drove across Ganghwa Bridge, ripples and eddies swirling in the strong current. Twice daily, the Pacific Ocean pushes and sucks vast quantities of water in and out of the Yellow Sea basin, resulting in the world's second-highest tides. Here, along Ganghwa Island, high tide rises nine metres above low tide. The rapid rise and descent creates powerful currents that can sweep along at seven or eight knots between the islands as the tide sweeps in from the south and recedes in the opposite direction.

* * *

Ganghwa Island has been privy to some pretty remarkable history, due to its geographical location at the entrance to the Han River and its proximity to Seoul, just seventy kilometres upstream. During the last millennium, Ganghwa had served in times of trouble as a refuge for royal families, governments, dethroned monarchs, and disgraced officials.

Mark Napier Trollope, a British chaplain stationed in Korea who went on to serve as Bishop of Korea from 1911 until his death in 1930, trekked across Ganghwa Island and wrote that during the first eight centuries after Christ, it was considered a simple prefecture. Then, in the eighth century, its stature was raised to that of a fortress. Ganghwa was "the first outpost to be attacked and the most important to be defended in case of invasion by sea."

Over the years, the island has received the full brunt of foreign assaults. The Mongols invaded in 1231, and through 1258 attacked Korea seven different times in an attempt to dominate the Goryeo kingdom. The Goryeo king, Gojong, fled to Ganghwa in 1232 and established a government in exile and a mini fortified capital. The Mongols burned and pillaged towns and villages across the peninsula, including the ancient former capital city of Gyeongju in the southeast. In fact, Ganghwa was about the only area of the country not to be overrun, as the Mongols would not or could not cross the Yeomha Channel to land on the island. It would not be until 1270 that the royal court returned to the mainland. In the 1350s, the last of the Mongol garrisons were jettisoned from the country.

Paul Theroux wrote, in *Riding the Iron Rooster*, that the Mongols were then conquering on horseback half the known world, including Moscow, Poland, eastern China, Afghanistan, and Vienna.

Then, in 1636, the Manchu-dominated Chinese Qing Dynasty sent 120,000 soldiers overland to Korea. The Joseon king at the time, Injo, moved his entire court to Ganghwa, but this time the Manchus took Korean vessels to Ganghwa, and overran the island and set the fort and buildings on fire. Injo surrendered and Korea became a client state to the Manchus, whose army devastated parts of the country and plundered its cities.

In October 1866, the French Far Eastern Squadron — seeking retribution for the execution that spring of four French priests who had been proselytizing Catholicism in Korea — sailed up the Yeomha Channel and bombed Ganghwa's coastal fortifications, landing at the coastal village of Gapgot, near today's Ganghwa Bridge. They proceeded to burn much of nearby Ganghwa town to the ground. Five years later, the U.S. Asian Squadron anchored in the channel and pounded the island forts with shells before its soldiers moved to land and decimated the Korean soldiers in what's known as the Sinmi Invasion (*sinmi* means "year of the sheep" according to the Chinese Zodiac calendar).

Ganghwa has seen its share of death and destruction over its long history.

Just over the bridge, in Gapgot, a former historic town (though today, a four-lane main road runs through it), we drove to the Ganghwa War Museum. Over the winter, Heju and I had attended a national tourism exposition in Seoul, at which the Ganghwa Department of Culture and Tourism booth was represented by a youthful and friendly employee, named Gu Yun-ja, who spoke excellent English and insisted that we contact her when we visited her historic island. She had told us she would arrange for a tour of the museum. The appointment was for ten o'clock this morning.

We met Yun-ja, along with a museum guide who spoke only Korean, and the four of us moved slowly through the well-appointed and handsome interior of the museum. There was a glassed-in exhibit that incorporated G.I. Joe–type figures into a recreation of the battle between American and Korean soldiers that had occurred at Gwangseongbo (the suffix *bo* refers to a main citadel or garrison, where approximately 350 soldiers are stationed) on Ganghwa Island on June 11, 1871. In the exhibit, the Americans, decked out in blue uniforms and black leather boots, were curiously depicted in positions of submission. Six were supine and very dead; several others were on the ground, impaled by the swords of Korean soldiers. The Koreans wore baggy white pants and shirts of cotton — rather like judo attire — and straw shoes, and not a single one was injured or dead. The display would have been fine, were it accurate, but it was not, and visitors with no, or rudimentary, knowledge of Korean history, would wrongly conclude that the Yanks were walloped that day.

"What a bunch of BS," I whispered to Heju furtively, because I did not want our museum guide — a stern, serious woman who I thought would not take kindly to knowing her museum was being maligned — to hear me.

The fact is that only three of 759 U.S. soldiers were killed that day, but close to 350 Koreans lost their lives. You see, the Americans were equipped with lightweight carbine rifles but the Koreans had only swords, spears, and slow-loading matchlock muskets. It was a monumental mismatch. I have seen graphic photos of the slaughter that showed American soldiers standing over the bedraggled bodies of Koreans, lying where they had fallen.

An American, William Elliot Griffis, who lived in Japan in the 1870s, and was one of the first historians to chronicle Korean history, wrote in *Corea: The Hermit Kingdom*, that the U.S. Asian Squadron had sailed to Korea in 1871 to seek trade ties. America was already trading with Japan and China and was desirous to trade with Korea as well. But *Corea* — as it was then spelled — kept its borders tightly closed.

The accepted Korean perspective today is that the U.S. squadron, though, did not arrive only to seek trade and sign a treaty. They contend it was to exact revenge for an incident in which a U.S.-flagged ship, the USS *General Sherman*, had steamed up the Taedong River to Pyongyang in 1866 and, after hostilities, its crew members, including several Americans, were reportedly beaten to death.

The U.S. Asian Squadron had arrived off Ganghwa in May 1871. Their flagship was the *Colorado*, and there were two gun boats, *Monocacy* and *Palosa*, and two corvettes, the *Alaska* and the *Benicia*. The Commander-in-Chief was Rear Admiral John Rogers, and there were eight hundred infantry and marines aboard the ships as well as the U.S. minister to Peking, Frederick F. Low, a man wary of entering the "sealed country," believing Koreans to be "semi-barbarous and hostile people." Admiral Rogers seemed prepared for war.

The modest *Monocacy* and *Palosa* were the only vessels of the five suitable to head up the shallow Han River to Seoul. But when the two ships finally anchored just south of Old Seoul, only low-ranking Korean officials were sent to meet them. King Gojong, then nineteen, would not hold power until he turned twenty-one. His father ruled as a regent in place of Gojong, and he was known as Prince of the Great Court, or Daewongun (*dae* means "great," *won* "court," and *gun* "prince"). His foreign policy was simple: no foreigners, no Catholics, no treaties or trade with the West or Japan.

Rebuffed, the U.S. admiral informed the Korean representatives that his squadron would survey the land from the local waters by ship. Korean maps featured cities, rivers, and hills painted in generous and artistic detail, but were usually rudimentary, with little sense of proportion and no reference to longitude and latitude. *Monocacy* and *Palosa* moved downstream along the Han, then south through the long, narrow Yeomha Channel. Along Ganghwa's east shore was a twenty-kilometre stone wall, first erected (of earth) during the twelfth century. Along it were guard posts, armories, forts at regular intervals, and artillery emplacements for cannon. Surrounding the island's four coasts was a total of five garrisons, seven forts, nine gun battlements, and fifty-three minor posts. In short, it was well-defended.

As the ships sailed south through the channel, they suddenly received cannon and musket fire from behind the wall. "The water was rasped and torn as though a hailstorm was passing over it," wrote Griffis. "Many of the men in the boats were wet to the skin by the splashing of the water over them."

Amazingly, the ships were not damaged, due to a combination of lack of mobility of the Korean cannons, poor quality gunpowder, and bad aim. *Monocacy* and *Palosa* fired back with ten-inch shells.

The American ships anchored in the channel and demanded an official apology, and ten days later, on June 10, they received a letter, but no apology. They decided to launch an assault in retaliation and sent cannon fire toward Choji Fort, the southernmost of the battlements, destroying it. Admiral Rogers ordered 759 infantry — 105 of them marines — and seven howitzers to the fort.

Choji Fort was deserted when the Americans arrived and they decided to camp overnight there. The next morning they marched north for two kilometres along hills and ravines, dragging the howitzers to Deokjin Fort, which had also been abandoned. They destroyed it, too, before continuing on to Gwangseong Citadel, a few kilometres north of Deokjin. But when the Americans reached the citadel, a mass of Korean soldiers charged down from the embankment. The Yanks answered with the howitzers, which scattered the Koreans. The corvette *Palosa*, moored just offshore, poured a steady stream of shells at Gwangseong's stone rampart as American infantry and marines charged up the 150-foot hill to the fort, met only by sporadic musket shots. Matchlock gunpowder burned too slowly to allow for quick reloading.

The invaders gained easy entry through openings blasted in the walls. The first American through, Lieutenant Hugh McKee, received a bullet and died, but soon the American troops were decimating the natives. "Goaded to despair, [the Koreans] chanted their war-dirge in a blood-chilling cadence which nothing can duplicate," wrote Griffis. They fought with furious courage, using spears and swords and even throwing stones or dust into the Americans' eyes. "Scores were shot and tumbled into the river. Most of the wounded were drowned, and some cut their own throats as they rushed into the water."

Koreans at the rear of the fort retreated, and the Yanks attacked. There was more fierce fighting and another fifty Koreans were shot dead. Another coterie met the same fate. Griffis described the U.S. soldiers as "mowing them down in swaths. Moving at full speed, many were shot like rabbits, falling heels over head."

Around the fort lay dead 243 Koreans, an estimated one hundred more were dead in the water. Only twenty prisoners, all wounded, were taken alive. The Americans lost three men, and ten were wounded.

"It is said that even the commander of the American troops was much moved at the intrepid spirit of General Eo and his soldiers," we read in the war museum.

After a mere forty-eight hours on Ganghwa, the invaders re-boarded their ships, taking with them an almost fifteen-foot-wide beige and yellow cloth flag the Koreans referred to as "Sujagi." The flag featured two huge black Korean characters representing General Eo Jae-yeon, who had been killed in the battle.

The Americans interred their dead on a nearby island, but the Koreans who had been killed were left unburied. Wounded Koreans, however, were cared for by a ship's surgeon, but when Admiral Rogers sent word to Korean officials that he would return the injured, he was told, "Do as you please with them." The wounded were set ashore.

On July 3, after thirty-five days in Korean waters, the squadron set sail for China. The battle had garnered but a few paragraphs in American newspapers. The Daewongun, though, referred to it as a glorious victory for his country, having driven the enemy away.

Dr. Horace Allen, a Protestant missionary who arrived in Seoul from Ohio in 1884, and was employed first as a doctor with the U.S. legation, then as a diplomat at the legation until 1905, called the American attack an unfair and monumental mismatch, a "useless slaughter, one from which no good results ensued, and of which we have not since been proud."

In the museum, we paused in front of the Sujagi. The flag had been taken back to America and had hung in Annapolis, Maryland, until it was finally returned to Korea in 2007. As we moved along, I was taking copious notes and asking lots of questions, which had to be translated into Korean by Heju, answered by the guide, then translated by Heju back into English. When the guide didn't know an answer, Yun-ja would phone her tourism office to try to secure one for us. Thus, what normally should have been a two-hour tour ended up taking twice as long. It was close to three o'clock before we left.

We thanked the guide and Yun-ja, who had made a half-dozen calls on our behalf, and we apologized for taking up so much of their time. Yun-ja replied enthusiastically: "I loved so many questions — I learned so much today!"

After grabbing bowls of ramyeon (fried noodle soup) at the food hut by the museum, Heju and I drove the short distance west to Ganghwa town, which is located on a long bend in the island road that widens to six lanes through the town. On this tranquil island, the traffic here seemed incongruous, vehicles noisily motoring along at seventy or eighty kilometres per hour. Like many other towns and cities across the peninsula, this one was not what you would call pedestrian-friendly.

"If I was mayor, I'd reduce the number of lanes from six to two, and the speed limit to about twenty," I decried to Heju. "It feels like we're on a motorway."

The town looked dusty and worn. We parked and strolled along the main street, past nondescript old shops that looked as if they'd been slapped together quickly with aluminum and concrete. I had naively envisioned the town as an attractive, historic little place, like one of those two-hundred-year-old colonial villages you would came across in, say, Massachusetts or Maine.

In the 1960s and '70s, the country began modernizing and industrializing at a furious pace, transitioning from a primarily agrarian economy to one in which manufacturing played a major role. Sadly, the traditional rural villages of hanok dwellings constructed from wood, clay, tile, and granite gave way to inferior quality metal and concrete structures. In the cities, many of the hanoks and other one-storey homes were replaced with hastily built low-rise apartment blocks constructed of low-quality materials. Little attention was paid to aesthetics. Most communities were not well planned, and development happened haphazardly, particularly in big cities like Seoul, where millions had flooded to from the rural areas in search of employment. Seoul's population in 1966 was 3.8 million; four years later it was 5.6 million. There were no heritage buildings of any sort that we could see as we strolled along the main road in Ganghwa town.

When British chaplain Mark Napier Trollope explored Ganghwa town in 1902, he described it as having four pavilion gates, a bell and bell-kiosk, and a number of other public buildings, though he did admit that they were in less than stellar condition: "The empty and ruinous public buildings, for which there is no further use, present a sad picture of decay," he wrote. Except for the forts, which were for the most part constructed of stone, and the city gates, which are usually granite, almost everything in Korea's long architectural history was built of wood and clay, which is prone to decay and fire. Trollope added, "Monuments, in a land where the most usual material for architecture is timber rather than brick or stone, have a way of not lasting." He wondered why stonework — Koreans are excellent masons — had not played a larger role in their architecture.

For the trip, I carried with me the 1997 *Lonely Planet Korea* guidebook, among other guidebooks. It was quite uncomplimentary of the island, noting it was an "overrated" tourist attraction. "The tourist literature and some guide books to Korea go on at some length about Ganghwado's attractions, giving you the impression that the island is littered with fascinating relics and ruins. To a degree it is, but you have to be a real relic enthusiast to want to make the effort."

A tad harsh, I thought. The government had obviously spent time and funds to refurbish the forts on the island and establish the museum. There was real opportunity here to learn more about significant Korean history. I for one was content to absorb it in the short time we had on the island. It was getting late in the day, so Heju and I returned to the car and went in search of lodging, which we found in the town's west end, in the form of the West Gate Inn (Samungjung), a plain three-storey "love motel."

I had checked my parents into a love motel — the only accommodation available close to my Myeongil-dong flat — when they visited me in 2000.

"Why's our bed heart-shaped?" my mother had asked me.

"Because love motels are for couples," I replied simply.

In the West Gate Inn's lobby, the clerk — her face hidden behind a pull-down window shade — asked if Heju and I would be staying for two hours. (This is a standard first question asked of guests upon their arrival at love motels.)

"No, we're staying until tomorrow," was our stock reply.

Our room had the usual well-stocked assortment of toothpaste, toothbrushes, hairdryer, hairbrush, comb, razor, shaving cream, after-shave, cologne, moisturizer, shampoo, and soap. A small fridge offered complimentary juice, and TV cable programming provided oodles of channels. I appreciated all the amenities. The only drawback was that the room had no bedside reading lamp. Love motels never did.

At least the bed wasn't heart-shaped.

* * *

By late morning (we were slow-risers) we were back in the car. The sun was shining, a welcome reprieve from spring's grey and chill that had been dogging us for most of the previous weeks, and this substantially improved the look of Ganghwa town, though not entirely: to me it still appeared dusty and crumbly. Heju informed me she wanted to return to the war museum to visit the Catholic shrine that she had noticed there the day before.

Heju attended Catholic Sunday mass whenever possible and sometimes reminded me that her Catholic name was Catherine, which she adopted while attending the private and Catholic St. Mary's Elementary School in Daejeon with her elder sister. Few Koreans could afford such tuition in the 1960s and '70s, but Heju's father was a banker, a position near the top of the economic ladder, and of his four daughters and one son, he sent two to private school. "We had servants," recalls Heju fondly. "They walked with me to school and did my homework for me after school"

So we headed back to the museum, though a visit to a shrine did not seem terribly titillating to me. When we arrived, there were twenty-one school buses in the museum parking lot, and groups of noisy young students were piling out of them. We walked to the far side, behind the museum, then up a slight knoll that overlooked Yeomha Channel. There was a slight clearing in which stood a statue of Mary. Heju stood in front of it and bowed.

"Bow to Mary," she insisted sternly.

I was taken back. I wasn't religious in any way. "I'm not Catholic," I sputtered.

"It doesn't matter, it shows respect. Bow," she ordered.

"I won't," I said defiantly.

The modest Gapgot Catholic Martyr's Shrine honours the memory of Korean Catholics who were beheaded during different periods between 1801 and 1871. There were four major state purges of Catholics during this time. One of the first such executions occurred in 1801, after a Korean Catholic was discovered sending a letter to Peking, seeking Chinese soldiers be sent to assure freedom to practise Catholicism in Korea. The purges were frightening periods, equivalent perhaps to the reign of terror that befell the aristocracy during the French Revolution.

There were two main execution sites in Seoul along the Han River's north shore: Jeoldusan, in front of today's Yanghwajin Foreign Cemetery, and about eight kilometres upriver, at Saenamteo (*sae* means sand and grass, *nam* is south, *teo* is place) at Yongsan. The severed heads of executed Catholics were displayed on poles for all to see, including in Seoul and in Gapgot, then a ferry terminal for passenger travelling between Incheon and Seoul.

On a plaque near the statue of Mary it was written that a Korean Catholic duo of a father and son had gathered the remains of some of those who had been executed and buried them in proper graves. Paul Park, the father, did so in 1839, while his son Soonjib (Peter) Park, continued the practice during the 1866 extermination. Soonjib Park collected the remains of the French bishop Siméon-François Berneux, who in 1856 had been appointed head of the Korean Catholic Church. Berneux was tortured and beheaded on March 7, 1866, at Saenamteo.

In the 1840s, a handful of French Catholic priests from the Paris Foreign Missions Society began to stealthily arrive in Korea to minister to Catholics. The priests were left relatively undisturbed until the Daewongun, who assumed power in 1864, and who believed Catholicism to be a direct threat to his rule and to Confucianism, orchestrated the great purge of 1866. Six French priests met their deaths that year by execution.

The Anglican bishop Trollope wrote in early 1900 that of the three main foreign missions in Korea — American Presbyterians, English Anglicans, and French Roman Catholics — the last were the most aggressive in moving through the peninsula and preaching. The Korean court had restricted travel to within fifty kilometres of treaty ports without a special passport. Presbyterians mainly stuck to Seoul or took passport-conducted jaunts outside the city, said Trollope. But the French went anywhere, and made a virtue of their defiance. This adventurous spirit — risking life to preach — made the French priests a target of the Daewongun.

Soonjib Park witnessed 150 executions during his lifetime. He died in 1911, at the age of eighty-two, and was buried in his hometown of Incheon. In 1961, his body was transferred to the Catholic holy shrine at Jeoldusan in Seoul. In 2011, it was moved to where Heju and I now stood.

From the hill, we looked east out over Yeomha Channel and the long-abandoned Gapgot Bridge, its single lane still linking the island to the Gimpo mainland. The water in the channel appeared grey-brown and the far shore was a mix of pastoral greens and muddy browns that reached up the low mountain ridge. There was not a soul in sight, and the only sound came from the birds singing in the trees.

We saw a small cabin sitting on the edge of a patch of sparse woods and walked over to investigate. A plaque on the wall stated that a Catholic priest now resided there. We wandered around the building and noticed a skipping rope lying on the front porch. It was good to know that even a man of the cloth could have fun exercising.

When we returned to the parking lot, a group of ten young Korean marines in green fatigues had arrived and were standing motionless in marching formation. On the islands northwest of the peninsula and in proximity to North Korea, ROK marines have a discernible presence. We approached the young leader. His name, Samoon Song, was stitched onto the front of his uniform, and he sported four bars on his shoulder. From Samoon's implacable expression, I concluded that he did not suffer fools gladly.

"Excuse me, could you tell us how many soldiers are stationed on Ganghwa?" we put to Samoon.

He turned and stared at us icily. "About twenty thousand."

We decided to press our luck. "Would a North submarine be able to navigate the channel?"

"No, it's too shallow," he reluctantly muttered.

"Which areas of Ganghwa are guarded by soldiers?"

At this, Samoon looked chagrined. "Ganghwa's entire north coast and the west coast of Gimpo have barbed wire," he allowed. "There's no access to the coasts for citizens there."

Heju sensed Samoon was itching to march his troops off, and she tugged at my arm and whispered "Let's go."

We got the message. I may be a doughnut short of a dozen at times, but I was not permanently obtuse. I thanked the leader and he abruptly marched his platoon across the lot.

We drove along the island on a road that ran beside the channel, and stopped on the shoulder about halfway down the island. The map indicated that a dondae (sentry post) was located somewhere along the channel in this general area. Beside the road, on the inland side, spread a wide shallow pond sectioned by narrow raised earthen walking paths about a foot or two above the waterline. An elderly farmer was standing on one of these paths, so we strolled out and introduced ourselves.

He gave us a big smile, showing us his front teeth, which were generously lined with so much silver that if he melted them down he could probably take early retirement. "I've been farming here for fifty years," he told us. He explained that every spring he dammed the pond to form paddies. His water source was a local stream that flowed from somewhere inland to the channel. In the paddies he planted rice in May, and harvested it in late September or early October. He recalled how, before the first bridge was erected (Gapgot Bridge, built to connect Ganghwa to the mainland in 1969), the only mode of transportation to the mainland was via an oarsman, who rowed people back and forth in a large skiff.

We crossed back over the road and approached two men who had parked their van near our Scoupe and were preparing fishing rods.

"Fishing in the channel?" we asked, assuming that this was the only logical choice.

"No, over there," one replied, pointing to the pond.

"Oh. In the dammed water?" I remarked.

"No, it's the Han River," he declared assuredly.

But the Han, of course, flowed nowhere near here. "The farmer told us that the pond is formed from a little dammed stream," I said politely.

"No, no, no, no, no, it's the Han River!" he boldly insisted.

I could not in good conscience let such an egregious error slide. "But the farmer said for sure it was a local stream," I tried innocuously, because I did not want to appear overly didactic.

"You sure?" he asked breezily.

"Yes."

"I didn't know that," he said, not giving it a second thought.

"Why did you think it was the Han?" I queried curiously.

"I was just guessing," he said blithely. With that I present the quintessential Korean male: so absolutely confident in his abilities, so supremely sure of himself, so convincingly self-possessed that the mere thought he could be wrong, ever, about anything, would never enter his consciousness.

After Heju and I had a quick look at the dondae, we returned to the car and drove a few kilometres south to Gwangseong Citadel, where the hundreds of Korean soldiers had met their fate when they clashed with the Americans in 1871. We popped our heads in to the tourist hut by the parking lot and asked if we could get a short tour. It was already 4:30 and closing time was in a half-hour. An English-speaking guide, Lee Nam-suk, reluctantly agreed to take us around. She appeared weary and slightly aggrieved. "It's busy this time of year," she told us. "We get up to two thousand visitors a day."

She led us up the path to the fort, which was built on a high, broad, circular promontory, heavily wooded and overlooking the channel below. It jutted several hundred metres out into the water. The grand front gate of the fort was a massively thick wall of cut granite blocks with a tunnel through it. Atop was a heavy-looking traditional wooden arched roof that curved sharply upwards at the corners. The fort was originally constructed in 1656, and had been repaired in 1977. Unfortunately, our guide was unable to show us the fort, since we had so little time.

We walked up the dirt path that ran parallel to the channel It was lined with beautiful pine trees, their roots exposed from the erosive action of rain and wind. In a small clearing, seven gravestones honour the Koreans who died in the battle that took place here. They call this spot Sinmisunuichong, which translates as "A Tomb for Those Who Died Righteously During the Year of the Sheep." A small stone monument, Ssangchungbi, or "Memorial Stone for Loyal Twins," honours General Eo Jae-yeon and his brother

Eo Jae-sun, both killed during the battle. Their bodies were interred in their hometown, Eumseong, in North Chungcheong Province, but of the Korean soldiers killed by the Americans here in 1871, the ashes of fifty-three remain.

I was puzzled and asked Ms Lee why there were no names of the dead on the graves, only a reference on the plaque to "nameless heroes." Ms Lee replied that many of the soldiers weren't professional military men, rather, they were peasants or servants of the lower class who not only often weren't well-trained, but this segment of society often had no names. "Many of the bodies were too mangled to be identified, too" she added, "and families didn't come to search for the bodies because they probably lived too far away."

We continued down the path that led to the water and came upon a low stone rampart; behind it, three cannons faced the channel, weapons that were likely fired at the American ships.

When Ms. Lee returned to her office, Heju and I strolled farther out onto the spit, where pine trees lined the shore. We were the only ones there; everything was so still. The only sound was a flock of geese that passed low overhead, calling out as they flew northward in their V-formation. It was high tide and the murky brown water in the channel — only about half a kilometre wide at this point — flowed swiftly in the middle. Moss-laden boulders lay just off shore. The sky had turned grey in the growing dusk, and I trained my binoculars on the Gimpo mainland.

I scanned the heavily wooded shore, but nothing moved. A bit farther along, a small village appeared devoid of inhabitants. Then I noticed the telltale signs of military presence — barbed wire that topped the chain-link fence that ran along the shoreline was partially hidden by trees. At regular intervals tall floodlight posts and camouflaged guard posts poked up.

Dusk fully upon us, Heju and I returned to the car and headed back to town for some dinner.

Back in town, we stopped along the main road at a brightly lit chain restaurant, which, from its familiar name, I knew would offer modest prices. Inside was bustling, and a feeling of warmth and congeniality pervaded. This was common in many restaurants. You see, Koreans love eating out, whether with family, friends, or work colleagues. I contend it's a national hobby, along with mountain-climbing and drinking (the latter particularly with men). Young kids often accompany their parents to restaurants, and run and play, which can make for a hectic, lively, and noisy environment.

At the table beside us sat two older gentlemen. One wore a blue jacket. He reminded me of Larry King, if Mr. King were Asian. Sitting across him was his pal, about ten years his senior, who was decked out in a wrinkled green coat, listening to his companion with rapt, earnest attention.

The man's soliloquy must have been fascinating, so I whispered urgently to Heju. "Tell me what they're saying, please. Maybe I can use it in the book."

"I don't want to," she said. Understandably, she did not like to get involved in strangers' matters.

"Come on, please! What they're saying could be very important!"

Heju reluctantly acquiesced and sat quietly and unobtrusively, listening. Several minutes later she relayed their conversation to me. "One guy was saying: 'I'd like to live with a Japanese woman. I don't like Korean women. They're too tough. They try to control you all the time. Japanese women are softer.'"

I learned quickly when I first arrived in Korea that public displays of emotion — be it anger, impatience, happiness, joy, sadness, or surprise — often displayed with dramatic aplomb, can be part and parcel of Korean society. I'd watch as two *ajummas*, for example, verbally jostled in a market, or a female customer unhappily harangued a shop clerk, or a pair argued vociferously at a café. Public spats can be compelling theatre, like watching the final tempestuous act of a Shakespearean tragedy, though such occurrences seemed to warrant scant attention from passersby. It's a stark contrast to Canada, where public etiquette and politeness is a national trait.

The connotation *ajumma* in Korea usually refers to a housewife of mid-age or older who has jettisoned most proclivities to retaining youth, and whose demeanour can at times be aggressive. The word can also equate to a female of working-class distinction. When I'm at my local outdoor market, I'll ask the woman behind the fish stall, *"Ajumma, godeungeo eolmayeyo?"* (Ma'am, how much is the mackerel?), and she won't blink an eye. But at the bank, I once used *ajumma* to address the fortyish teller, and she rebuked me.

Dr. Horace Allen noted in his 1908 book, *Things Korean*, that when Korean women were "pressed too far, they will turn, and the fury into which they then work themselves is something awful to contemplate."

Heju explained that during the Joseon period, Korean women played prominent roles in the royal court and politics, and historically are known for their assertiveness. "It's not an insult to me," she added agreeably, about the scrappy nature of her female compatriots. "It's true — most Korean women like to argue," she added, in a matter-of-fact tone.

When the KBS (Korean Broadcasting System) evening news came on a few minutes later, I asked Heju, who was intensely absorbed in ingesting the noodles from her bowl, to please transcribe the lead story. "I can't," she said nonchalantly, not looking up, "I'm eating."

"Come on, please," I implored.

But she wouldn't budge and I was relegated to watching the screen and imagining my own plotlines for the accompanying news videos. When Heju wasn't looking, I added a sprinkle of arsenic to her noodles.

Suddenly, the phone on the cashier's desk rang. The manager, an ajumma, picked it up, listened for a moment, and then shouted angrily into the mouthpiece: "You brought me old seaweed. It falls apart when I roll it. Bring me good seaweed tomorrow!" She then slammed down the receiver and threw her plastic gloves onto the table in a pique. The restaurant's deliveryman was her next target: "What happened to the lid for the rice bowl?" she argued as the man slipped on his motorcycle helmet and made a hasty exit.

* * *

The next day, in the greyness of the late-morning mist, Heju and I returned to Gwangseong Citadel for another quick look around. Being spring meant that it was school field-trip season, and the parking lot was jammed with nearly forty school buses, streams of elementary school kids pouring off them in class-friendly, colour-coded tracksuits, carrying lunchboxes and being shepherded along by their respective teachers.

After a short sortie at the garrison, in which we entered the main citadel through the massive gate to find a circular earthen embankment with a low stone rampart on top, we drove to Ganghwa's southeastern tip to visit Choji Fort, where the U.S. infantry and marines first came ashore in 1871. Again, the parking lot was packed with tour buses and in a large square adjacent, masses of chattering elementary school kids were gathered. Gift shops offered tacky back-scratchers and toy bows and arrows.

We attempted to talk to some of the kids about what they had learned on their field trips, and several could not recall anything they had seen. Two veteran media-savvy kids defiantly refused to grant us their time and walked off. Others complained they were tired. One decried that the walk up to the fort at Gwangseong Citadel was a bit difficult.

Giving up on getting the student perspective, we strolled over to the hard-clay shore, which was strewn with rocks. The day was overcast but windless. Just south of us, the imposing Choji Bridge crossed over the channel. A smattering of visitors stood along the bank looking out over the water. I wanted to speak to a group of five senior women who had wandered over to the water's edge.

We introduced ourselves and asked the women where they were from.

"Seoul," they replied.

*"Gwangseongbo gabwasseoyo?"* ("Did you have a chance to visit Gwangseong Citadel yet?") Heju inquired.

There were puzzled looks all round. *"Gwangseongbo mwuo?"* ("Gwangseong what?") one asked Heju in a perplexed and indignant tone.

"Gwangseongbo … the citadel," Heju explained.

One shook her head and irritably announced, *"Urineun daehakgyo an gasseoyo!"* ("We didn't go to that university!").

A third interjected: *"Naneun Gwangseongbo an salyayo. Seoul salyayo."* ("I don't live in Gwangseong. I live in Seoul.")

We tried a new tack, suggesting there had been a battle here at Choji, during which the Americans had pounded the fortification with cannon fire from the channel.

They were not familiar with it at all. *"Urineun mollayo! Uriga eotteoke alayo? Uri yeogi an salyayo. Amado palsip neomeun saramdeuli museunili isseoneunji algyeoyo!*" ("We wouldn't know about that! How would we know? We don't live here. Maybe eighty-year-old people would know what happened then!")

Heju and I took our leave of the ladies and strolled back up the path to the fort, which had been built the same year as Gwangseongbo (1656) and had also undergone restoration work. On the path, we came across a large board displaying several black-and-white photos of American soldiers from the battle. In one photo, the soldiers were standing next to the fort, and the caption read: "On the afternoon of June 10, 1871, the U.S. ship fired cannon for two hours at the fort. The Americans reached shore but no shots were fired by the Koreans."

Throngs of school kids streamed by with their teachers. I could hear the latter exhorting *"Bali! Bali!"* ("Hurry! Hurry!")

*Bali* is a commonly heard word. This is an energetic, ambitious society where people want to get things done quickly. None of the classes stopped to check out the photos or read the information. The teachers simply rushed their charges along, likely to keep them on schedule.

It was not at all relaxing for us in the centre of this swirl of motion, so Heju and I retreated to the car and headed to our next destination: Mani-san (*san* means "mountain"), at 469 metres, is the tallest mountain in the island's five ranges. There was a trail that led to the top, to a reportedly five-thousand-year-old stone shrine. We headed west into a swath of agricultural plains, passing a few concrete farm shacks with galvanized tin roofs, a rusting apartment building, and smatterings of small industrial units.

We parked at the base of the broad Mani Mountain and got out. A wide path led onto the mountain and into the woods, past a souvenir shop, a small restaurant, and the public toilets. It was late afternoon, and it seemed we were the only ones setting out on the trail that day; we didn't see anyone coming down either, for that matter. We started off along the forested path, a small creek running alongside. It was very quiet and serene and the air was fresh.

After about twenty minutes we came to a small clearing where the path became narrower and steeper, though it was still quite an easy ascent. Only the sounds of chirping birds, gently rustling tree branches, and the distant barking of a dog reached us. There was a tranquility and harmony up here.

It's not hard to understand why hiking is so popular in Korea, what with so many mountain trails available across the peninsula. But despite the beauty and peacefulness, I must admit that Korean terrain is some of the most aggravating I have ever encountered. A preponderance of steep hills and mountains cover much of the country, and even the smallest ones are often rugged and steeply sloped. An officer in the U.S. military once referred to it as "dinosaur hump country" for its up-and-down terrain.

The west coast has its plains, of course. But to navigate them means traversing around a complicated patchwork of earthen banks that separate millions of little rice paddies and countless agricultural plots. And even country roads aren't always amenable to walking. Most don't have shoulders, requiring sometimes trudging alongside the pavement through weeds or briar. So it is to mountain trails such as this one on Mani Mountain that hikers, particularly adults, flock on weekends.

I gravitate toward easy rolling hikes like those Bill Bryson experienced while trekking in the Lake District in England. In *Notes from a Small Island*, he describes mile after mile of happily wandering along winding paths through undulating green meadows and fields lined with stone fences, and on coastal paths overlooking the sea. I prefer this type of topography, as you can move briskly. But it's a terrain you won't find much of here on this peninsula, and lugging my 250 pounds of flesh up Mani Mountain was not really my idea of a good time.

Heju and I came to a trail sign, which informed us that Mount Mani was one of the ten best energizing places in Korea, a reference to feng shui and geomancy, the Asian philosophy espousing the belief that the Earth produces a positive energy life force.

"I feel great from the mountain's energy — that's why I'm not tired!" enthused Heju. She was a big believer in feng shui.

"I feel like shit," I moaned despondently. "My thigh muscles ache." Mani Mountain is obviously capricious about who it dispenses fortuitous feng shui to.

Ironically, Heju was in a positive frame of mind physically that day, while I was the one complaining. It was usually the other way around, with Heju lamenting about various aches, pains, ailments, and things like blood clots, stiff muscles, palpitations, and headaches, of which no doctor could find any trace. Eastern medicine doctors that she visited, however, would prescribe expensive herbs and potions, which Heju steadfastly believed would alleviate her many symptoms.

"Hurry up!" Heju urged impatiently. "We better be off the mountain by dark. I can't see the path at night."

We were about three-quarters of the way to the summit when we were afforded a slim view north, out over a swath of alluvial plain, into which were carved out thousands of small, orderly, rectangular plots bordered on the north by a low wooded mountain. Today's Ganghwa was formerly four separate islands, but over time and after millions of tons of silt and mud have been washed along the Han and Imjin Rivers to the Yellow Sea, the space between the four was filled to form a singular island, thirty kilometres long and fifteen wide. Ganghwa's narrow plains, scattered between the low mountain ranges, contain rich soil. It was an arresting view. We pushed on.

About ninety minutes after starting out, we reached the summit. There was a helicopter pad there. We were met by a stiff southerly wind that whipped over the bending tree boughs. The view was south, and wow, what a vista! A haunting, deep purple sky rimmed by the setting sun's silvery outline. For thirty or forty kilometres a vast expanse of mud flats spread out until it met the grey, hazy islands and shallow leaden sea. Along the country's west coast, about 1,800 square kilometres of mud and tidal flats are exposed during low tide. They seem to stretch forever, and indeed they reach as far as thirty-five kilometres offshore.

As I looked through my binoculars, I spotted a Korean Airline passenger jet on its southbound approach to Incheon International Airport, located on Yeongjong Island, off Incheon's coast. The plane seemed to hang motionless, as if suspended in mid-air.

My thermometer read nine degrees Celsius, but the biting wind made it feel much colder. Exacerbating matters was the fact that light whispers of cold rain had begun to fall as the remaining streaks of twilight began to fade. The inclement weather didn't bother me: I was from Canada; today was merely a late fall day there. But Heju was cold and morose, and her exuberance had been replaced with silence. She removed a thin wool shawl from her backpack and wrapped it around her head.

"You look like an Afghan nomad," I kidded buoyantly.

Despondently, she said, "I'm going down. I can't see at night," and she started back down the trail.

"Hey, wait for me — we'll go down together," I called, but she was already disappearing behind a large boulder.

I walked along the ridge and found the altar, which Ganghwa guides claim was erected about five thousand years ago but some experts claim is of much more recent construction. It is called Chamseongdan, which roughly translates to "An Altar to Worship the Stars." It is the size of a small house; larger and more impressive than I had expected, it is constructed from thousands of small rocks that have been carefully piled up to form a circular wall with a roof. There is a graceful symmetry and beauty to it. A wire fence encloses it, but twice a year — on January 1 and on Chuseok, or Korean Thanksgiving — officials open the gate and permit visitors to enter.

As I turned and began to make my way down the path, my phone suddenly rang. I had to dig through my waist pack, which was stuffed with a wallet, notebook, mini tape recorder, camera, compass, and the kitchen sink, to retrieve it.

It was Heju. "Are you coming?" she asked, sounding exasperated.

"No, I'm going up," I told her facetiously.

"Be careful. It's slippery," she warned, ignoring my comment.

"I know."

"I don't care about you. I just don't want my camera to get damaged," she deadpanned.

"Don't worry. I tied it to my ankle. It's dragging along the path," I joked.

"Hurry up. I'm waiting," she demanded, brushing aside my attempts at humour.

*Yes, my lady. I'm a mere plebeian, at your beck and call, my life's mission to serve you.*

I trekked as fast as I could without slipping, and about a third of the way down, caught up to her in the dark grey shadows, as she sat on a stone step on the path waiting for me. We made it back at the car in about forty-five minutes, just as darkness enveloped us.

* * *

Back at the West Gate Inn, we watched TV and feasted on sandwiches. We had stopped at a small supermarket and a bakery and bought a long baguette and a package of sliced ham and processed cheese slices. This would be our standard diet on the trip. There was also bottle of orange juice and a couple of apples for dessert. It was much cheaper than eating out at restaurants every night, and saved us time, as we didn't have to stop for meals; Heju, though, preferred the long sojourns at restaurants.

We found ourselves watching an episode of *World's Most Shocking Moments: Caught on Tape 2*. One of the videos showed monks hurling items from a building at hundreds of riot police below. A cherry picker, with six men inside, was raised up beside the building. As the bucket got to the fourth floor, it suddenly flipped, sending the six men hurtling like limp rag dolls to the ground. When the host announced the video had been shot at a Jogye Buddhist temple in Seoul in 1999, I snapped to attention.

"We've got to visit that temple to find out what happened!" I announced excitedly.

After the show ended, Heju, who had been unusually sullen, launched a verbal barrage that caught me off-guard. I accepted the fact that, on occasion, Heju could be a bit moody. Mostly, I had taken her mini-combustions with a grain of salt (as most Korean men do if they hope to remain in a relationship with their wife or girlfriend).

"This trip's WORK. It's a boot camp. It's not travel!" she erupted.

I was gobsmacked. My immediate thought was that this could be highly problematic. We had only just begun the driving part of the trip, and still had about another hundred days or so to go. If she was upset now, what kind of mood would she be in three months from now? I also failed to understand exactly how being driven around in a car constituted "work."

Heju had seen me preparing for the journey and had scanned through "The Bible." She knew I planned to stop at a long list of places each day. I think, though, that she had erroneously envisioned us being on a bit of a semi-vacation, leisurely motoring through idyllic countryside and enjoying long, languorous meals on restaurant patios overlooking rivers and contently shouting "Tallyho" through the car window as we purred along in our Bentley. Instead, we were bogged down in long days.

Heju and I were a bit of a Yin and Yang. She was sociable and gregarious, and relished her leisure time. I was intense and driven, and was deriving satisfaction from checking off the list of places we were seeing and gathering facts and information. I didn't consider what she and I were doing to be work.

"Taxi driving is work. Construction is work!" I retorted heatedly, recalling short stints I had undertaken in both jobs in Toronto when I was younger. "Sitting in a car is NOT work … it's travel!"

"It IS work!"

"So, do you want to be carried around in a chair like a queen?" I shot back sarcastically.

For a moment I feared she might answer *yes*, because Kim Heju on occasion will proudly ascertain that she is the 34th generation descendant of King Gyeongsun, who from AD 927 to 935 ruled as the fifty-sixth and final king of Korea's Silla Dynasty.

Heju continued tersely: "And we're spending too much time in Ganghwa. At this rate we'll never finish the trip on time!"

She had a point. We had been on the island for three days and had yet seen only a museum, two forts, and ascended one modest mountain, which even my mother could have hiked up. Even I was mystified at our slow progress. But I was also royally irked. "If you want to pay for everything — motels, food, car, and gas — you're welcome to decide how long we stay in one place," I contested. "But since I'm paying, and since I spent two years preparing, it's my decision!"

Long after the trip was over, I realized that Heju was right … *sort of*. The journey wasn't as fun as it could have been. I hadn't intended it to be. My mission was to gather data, and I went about the task with resolute and efficient determination. In my "Bible," I hadn't included stops at pubs, or splurges on a good meal, or singing in a Karaoke room. Nothing about seeing a movie or sitting on the grass in a meadow and smelling the roses. Those were time-fillers. Heju would have enjoyed doing those things, but the trip was my priority. I should have provided a more balanced and relaxed ambiance for Heju. I feel bad that I didn't. Unfortunately, this profound clarifying moment of self-awareness hadn't yet occurred, and I was, at the time, angry about what I considered her childish behaviour.

I went out for a walk. It was nearly eleven o'clock and a light rain was falling. I strolled along the virtually deserted sidewalk, and passed a solitary elderly man pushing a large antique wood cart loaded with trash bags that he had been picking up from in front of the local shops and restaurants. Ironic, I thought. Korean multinational high-tech companies like Samsung produce silicon computer chips the size of a pinhead; yet here was someone collecting garbage using the same methods employed in medieval agrarian societies.

# CHAPTER 4

Heju and I were fine in the morning. We didn't stay mad at each other long. She did, however, continue to sporadically upbraid me in the weeks after, accusing me unflatteringly of being a slave driver and a drill sergeant, and continuing to insinuate that this wasn't a trip, but a boot camp.

In decidedly un-boot-camp style, we began our fourth day on Ganghwa by treating the exceptionally kind Yun-ja, the Ganghwa tourism employee — who had been phoning us regularly to ask if there was anything she could assist us with — to lunch at a little restaurant in town.

Seated at the table, Yun-ja remarked admiringly, "You've stayed on Ganghwa for four days. Most Koreans just visit for one day then leave."

"But there's so much to see here," I said, which was the honest-to-goodness truth.

After lunch, Heju and I drove along the town's main road, and, on a whim, stopped in front of the utilitarian Incheon Ganghwa Police Station. I wanted to ask about a tragic drowning of four young students that I had read about, which happened on the island.

Behind the station desk were two officers, Jang Bu-gun and Choi Kyung-ju. They recalled the sad event. "They were on a church outing to Dongmak Beach on the south shore catching shellfish out on the mudflats. The tide comes in very fast there. The water's very dangerous. No one's allowed to swim there. The girls panicked and got stuck in the mud. After the tide went out, people found their bodies. Locals don't go out to where the girls went. They use boards to catch shellfish on the mudflats."

I had seen on a TV program about how Korean coastal villagers collecting shellfish in particularly deep and soft mud flats must lean their weight on a boogie-board-size plank they thrust in front of them so as not to sink down into the muck. When Heju and I had been out on the tidal mud flats along the west coast in the city of Gunsan, in North Jeolla Province, I had sunk up to my shins in the soft goo, and it took me ten minutes to pry my legs out of the vacuum seal. Heju had thought it was hilarious.

"How do you get out of the mud if you're stuck?" I asked the officers.

"If you panic, your legs sink deeper," one said. "If you try to stand straight, it's easy to sink. Lie down, and when the tide comes in, let the water float you out."

*Easier said than done*, I thought.

After fifteen minutes, an officer entered the station accompanied by two gentlemen: a slight man and a much larger fellow, both with grim countenances. The smaller one as it turned out was a taxi driver, and the other had been his passenger the night before. They had been involved in a bit of a punch-up.

"They're here to work it out," the officer informed us, though they didn't appear overly conciliatory to each other. "The drinking culture's widespread here," he added. "When people get drunk, they become very emotional. It's easy to get in a fight." Drunken fights, minor thefts, and traffic accidents were the three most common issues on the island, he said.

Before fists started flying again we took our leave and drove up the quiet adjacent back street. In an unassuming little residential area we came to Goryeogungji (Goryeo Palace Site). Goryeo was the royal dynasty that ruled from 918 to 1392. The original Goryeo Palace was constructed somewhere near here in 1232 as a refuge for the royal court to rule from during the Mongol siege of Korea. That palace, though, was totally destroyed by the Mongols in 1259.

In 1636, the royal family again moved to the grounds, this time to escape the Manchu invasion. Several buildings were erected to accommodate them. But the next year, the Manchus captured Ganghwa town and took temporary occupancy of the palace. Since then, the buildings remained basically unused by the royal family and were later converted for government use.

In 1782, a royal library, Oegyujanggak, which roughly translates as "The Outside Building for Writings by Important People," was constructed on the site where we now stood. This structure held a surfeit of official royal Joseon books referred to as *Uigwe* (Royal Protocols). Uigwe recorded the annals of Joseon history, with hand-drawn illustrations of royal weddings and funerals, the construction and repair of palaces, court performances, costumes, musical instruments, and decoration. The approximately four thousand Uigwe volumes were stored at Changdeok Palace library in Seoul. In 1782, close to three hundred volumes were transferred to the Ganghwa library for safekeeping.

The French navy invaded Ganghwa in October 1866 to mete out punitive measures in response to the executions of French priests in Seoul the same year. The French set fire to the fort walls surrounding Ganghwa town as well as to the Goryeo Palace government buildings, including Oegyujanggak, burning them to the ground. The French reportedly carted off flags, cannons, eight thousand muskets, twenty-three boxes of silver ingots and several of gold, as well as lacquer ware, jade, and paintings in addition to the 297 Uigwe volumes. They stored the latter at the Bibliothèque nationale de France in Paris. The collection was largely forgotten until a Korean discovered it in 1975. Then, after decades of negotiations between the two countries, in 2010, presidents Nicolas Sarkozy and Lee Myung-bak signed an agreement that saw all the books returned to Korea between April and June the following year.

Goryeo Palace really has no connection to the actual Goryeo period, except for being on or near the same grounds where the large former palace once sat. Of the original palace, only a few foundation stones remain, and they are adjacent to this location. What was before us had been constructed much more recently, in 1977. A modest stone wall enclosing the interior, and a traditional but small front gate — two heavy vertical wood columns supporting a heavy arched tiled roof. We entered to find a small field of grass, and I was delighted, because grass is a rare sight in Korea. Almost every viable acre across the peninsula was long ago converted into agricultural farmland, and finding a natural grass meadow can be like spotting a rare bird.

Off to the side were several one-storey government buildings that had been rebuilt in 1977. The new incarnation of the library, Oegyujanggok, was erected in 2002. The wood comprising the low, modest buildings was so dry, its paint so worn and faded, their appearances and feel could have passed for hundreds of years old. One building was L-shaped, built on a foundation of several layers of flat cut granite, the black, shale-tiled arched roof extending far over the front walls. In front, a row of square wooden beams supported the roof, creating a protected porch underneath. The walls appeared to have a series of shutter-like doors painted green, though this colour, too, was badly faded. The courtyard was of dry earth.

Our guidebook said that Yongheun Palace (Palace of the Rising Dragon) was just a little way along the street. The name was misleading. It wasn't a palace either, but rather, a compound with a traditional home that had been renamed a "palace" to honour a Ganghwa lad who had grown up in it in the 1830s. The young man had been crowned King Cheoljong at the age of nineteen in 1849, after the heirless reigning king died. Cheoljong was a distant relative of a past king, and he was chosen to reign as the twenty-fifth monarch, more because he could be easily manipulated by a power-hungry court faction than for his sense of acumen.

Cheoljong's grandparents had been exiled to Ganghwa, due to their affinity for Catholicism, and his parents had farmed on the island. Apparently, little Cheoljong wasn't terribly studious, and the guidebook *Moon Handbooks: South Korea* politely referred to him as "uneducated and somewhat of a country bumpkin; he was definitely unprepared for his role as head of the nation." It was said he was living in terrible poverty and unable to read when he was chosen to be king — precisely the type of man needed to lead a country to prosperity. Heju recalled that during her school years, Cheoljong was one Joseon king that her teachers did not expand on. I suspect he was rather like poor old Chester A. Arthur or Benjamin Harrison — American presidents who sadly are consigned to presidential oblivion for eternity. Cheoljong died in 1863 at age thirty-two, reportedly a victim of foul play. His home, "Yongheun Palace," was reconstructed in 1974.

Heju and I drove from Goryeo Palace to a clearing nearby where there was a row of foundation rocks. Officials believe that these belonged to the original palace site.

And up a slight hill from the site of this place is the Ganghwa Anglican Church, built in 1900 under the direction of Charles John Corfe, the Church of England's first bishop to Korea (1889–1905). In an effort to try to integrate the Anglican Church into Korean culture, its missionaries, who began arriving in the late nineteenth century, built several churches in the traditional Korean architectural style. This was the first constructed.

Bishop Corfe apparently wasn't terribly enamoured with his posting in Korea. He was educated at Oxford and served twenty years as a chaplain in the Royal Navy before being sent to Korea at the age of forty-six. He spent sixteen years in the country, and recounted his experiences in his book *The Anglican Church in Corea*.

The one-storey building was a mix of Western and Korean architecture with Buddhist elements. Rust-coloured brick covered the lower walls, and above this was a narrow row of wooden shuttered windows, painted turquoise. Vertical wood beams painted deep red were inlaid in the walls. The roof was massive, constructed in the traditional Korean style, double-tiered with grey tile shingles and wooden rafters painted a light greenish-blue. The church had been refurbished in 1984, and it was indeed a beautiful work of architecture.

Along one end of the church were four faded turquoise wooden doors. We noticed one of them was ajar, so we popped our heads in. A woman was sweeping the floor. "Are you open?" we asked.

"No, only on Sundays," she answered.

It was Friday. "Is it okay if we come in and look around?"

"Yes, come in."

We took off our shoes and entered. Inside we discovered an architectural treasure. I felt as if I had been transported back to Victorian England. The basilica-like interior featured sumptuous polished dark red wood on the floor, ceiling, and rafters. The interior was bathed in a soft golden glow. Nine floor-to-ceiling vertical beams more than a foot thick ran along each side of the church, shouldering the weight of a second-floor wooden walkway and the heavy-looking roof. Across the high ceiling ran nine large beams. The walls were of white clay framed in wood. Above the walkway on each side was a row of windows, and several chandeliers, each with a set of six small delicate white ceramic shades, hung from the ceiling.

The aisle was flanked by ten rows of redwood chairs. We sat down and soaked up the ambiance. It really was an exquisite building, peaceful and calm. The artisans who refurbished it had obviously been master craftsmen.

"It's beautiful," said Heju, in a state of ecclesiastical bliss. "I love it here; I could stay all day."

Even I was imbued by a temporary wave of serenity.

Three women were cleaning the interior, so we asked one of them whether they had to polish the wooden floors, which would be quite an undertaking.

"We polish them twice a year," she told us, "but we don't wax them anymore. Our parishioners are old and they slip if we do."

I had a brief vision of Sunday morning worship service, with elderly churchgoers taking long runs in stocking feet, sliding briskly over the smooth surface, whooping and hollering in delight, then tumbling like bowling pins.

Noticing two portable gas heaters in the corner, we asked if it got cold in the winter.

"Yes, the church isn't insulated. We need to use heaters," she said.

Two men then entered the church and sat down. We exchanged pleasantries. One had a German accent, and when I inquired, he told me his name and that he taught choir composition at a university in Seoul. Like Heju, he preferred that I didn't talk, and was content to sit in a trance-like state and soak up the ethereal ambiance. Later, I discovered he had been the music director at the Spandau School of Church Music in Berlin, and was a composer too.

Heju and I stayed in the church for about an hour in order to properly receive blessings of good fortune from above. Finally, I suggested to Heju that we should get going.

* * *

Driving west from Ganghwa town along the north part of the island, Heju and I had stops at a roadside insect museum, a hillside crematorium, a millennium-old dolmen, and a "five-storey" pagoda — the latter, in actual fact, a five-rock pagoda the height of a small child. Back on the blacktop after a few hours, with evening settling in, we swung south along the west coast, though unfortunately a range of low wooded hills blocked our view to the sea. A short way south, in an area called Mangwol, we turned off the main road and headed onto a muddy and rutted side road that led to the coast. I turned on the headlights and illuminated a vast bleak stretch of muddy paddies. We soon reached the sea; it was desolate and grey. As we emerged from the car, we were met by a cold salty wind blowing off the water. About a mile out, a twinkle of yellow lights shimmered in the darkness from a small village on Seongmo Island. The tide was out, exposing a deep morass of brown goo and deep, wide, muddy moats and trenches that led from the shore to the sea and looked large enough to swallow a small house. I had never seen such treacherous mud flats before.

"No wonder people drown here!" I exclaimed.

We wandered along the shore to nearby Mangwol Dondae, a low sentry post constructed of small rocks. It had been built in 1679, and I found it exhilarating to imagine that more than three centuries earlier soldiers would have manned this now-crumbling structure and gazed out to sea, on the lookout for foreign vessels.

Back in the car, Heju and I continued south along the island road, and soon rolled into the small coastal village of Oepo, located about halfway down Ganghwa. We puttered through its "downtown" area, a short, narrow section of road with no sidewalks, lined with brightly lit restaurants with long aquariums full of fish on display outside. It was Friday night, but the restaurants were empty; the crowds from Seoul would arrive by the carload the next day.

We stopped at five different modern-looking motels within a stone's throw of downtown and Heju went into each one to check the room rates. She was informed by each one that they charged between 40,000 and 50,000 won, which sounded reasonable in comparison to Western prices, but was far more than the usual room rate of 25,000 to 30,000 won. "This is an Oepo Motel Cartel!" I charged in vexation.

The rates were unacceptable, of course, and having passed a castle-like five-storey motel along the road leading into town, we backtracked and pulled into the lot; Ganghwa Haesoo Sauna was quiet and dark.

Although there was no *motel* or *hotel* in the title of this establishment, it was indeed a motel that included a sauna (hot tubs, cold tubs, and a steam room) for customer use. In Korea, a sauna has tubs and steam rooms, and is typically used by Koreans for daytime use. But some saunas, also known as jimjilbangs (a Korean word meaning "hot pack" or "hot things room") are equipped for overnight stays with one or two floor areas available for customers to plonk down a mat to slumber on. Saunas evolved from pubic bathhouses, or *mokyok* (meaning "take a wash"). Up until the 1970s, before many homes had access to hot water, mokyoks were common, often being the only places where people could properly bathe.

"It looks closed," Heju said.

"Let's try it anyway," I said hopefully.

We entered the motel's substantial but utilitarian and dimly lit lobby, hoping a clerk might appear.

*"Annyeonghaseyo yeogi nugugyeseyo!"* ("Hello. Is anyone here?") Heju called out.

Moments later, a woman appeared behind the window. She was friendly and engaging and informed us that rooms were only 25,000 won, which greatly pleased me — Oepo's Motel Mafia hadn't gotten to her yet.

The basement sauna and hot tubs, she said, opened at ten o'clock in the morning. Heju was happy — she loved saunas. When Heju is home in Daejeon, on most Saturdays or Sundays she'll head with her mother to her local sauna, where they'll spend many hours. When not making multiple forays into the sauna and hot tubs to shrivel and burn, she'll rest, relax, and read in the common area. I suppose it's a bit like Westerners spending all day at the local tennis or country club.

Carrying our bags, we trudged upstairs to our fifth-floor room. There was no elevator. At each floor we paused and peered down a long, spooky hallway, high-ceilinged and in shadows with musty red carpeted floors. "This place reminds me of the haunted hotel in *The Shining*," I said. Had Jack Nicholson, as the crazed Jack Torrance, stuck his face, hideous, contorted and bug-eyed, out of a door and chortled evilly *"Hereeeeeeee's Johnnnnnyyyyyy!"* it wouldn't have surprised me in the least.

Our room was, let's just say, worth the 25,000 won ... well, maybe 15,000 ... or even 10,000. It wasn't that it was dirty or that there were stains on the walls. It simply felt very, very old, as if ten thousand people had slept in it before us. It was like one of those old rooming houses featured in a 1950s Hollywood movie, about a down-on-his-luck detective living in a seedy part of Los Angeles.

The room's only source of illumination was a single bulb hanging from the ceiling, the glass lampshade enclosing it the receptacle for a large number of long-deceased flies. The red curtains were bulky and dowdy. The bed was short and narrow and had the world's most pliable mattress. The ancient television wasn't hooked up to cable, though it did have the promised VHS player. The phone didn't work.

The room did have character, though, and it definitely wasn't a Holiday Inn. What more could we desire?

"What do you expect for 25,000 won?" said Heju cynically.

Well, clean sheets, no live bugs scampering about, and the couple next door not hollering all night in the throes of passion. On all three fronts we scored ten out of ten. Not bad.

* * *

At ten o'clock the next morning, Heju was ready to bound out the door, all set to luxuriate in the basement hot tub. Before she left, she translated a brochure I had picked up from the lobby, which explained the merits of the spa water downstairs: Water was piped up from three hundred metres underground because the local sea water was polluted, it said. Lithium, iron, zinc, copper, sulphur, chlorine, oxidized silicon, magnesium, calcium, sodium, and strontium were ingredients found in the water. Lithium was helpful for those suffering from manic depression and psychosis, and strontium benefitted bone fractures in older people. Now, I'm no scientist, but all these compounds we'd soon be immersing ourselves in seemed to me to be the same ingredients found in a bottle of multivitamin pills.

When I entered the men's sauna, I found three tubs: one with cold water, one with hot, and the last containing water guaranteed to leave you permanently bright red. Thermometers indicated the cooler of the two hot tubs was 105°F. I couldn't remotely contemplate sitting in the other. Yet, I have watched Korean men easily and quickly slip into such temperatures on many occasions. Obviously, over the millennia, they have developed a type of super-resistant skin cell that permits them to withstand temperatures that would boil most humans alive. Several men were already in the lava-hot one, submerged up to their necks. I sat on the edge of the hot tub meant for buttercups and dangled my legs in. It still took ten minutes to acclimatize my skin to the water temperature and I slowly eased in inch by inch. I scald easily.

After I felt I had been sufficiently stewed and shrivelled, I got out and dried off. A little while later, Heju and I checked out of the Overlook Hotel and drove the two minutes to Oepo's small harbour to take a stroll along the short concrete wharf. The sky was blue and a fresh warm breeze was blowing in off the sea. There hadn't been many days of sunny skies or warm temperatures of late, and it felt marvellous to absorb the warmth. Today was our fifth and final day on Ganghwa Island and Heju was happy to be moving on.

At low tide the immediate and entire offshore area is transformed into what looked like an expansive mud pudding, though now the muddy yellowish-brown sea was shallow and alive, bubbling with currents and tidal movements. About a mile out, Seongmo Island's steep forested mountain slopes ran parallel to Ganghwa's coast. A narrow ferry was docked at Oepo's nearby pier, loading a few cars to be shuttled across to the island. Being Saturday, the little harbour was beginning to spring to life with day trippers arriving en masse from Seoul.

Below us, several traditional wooden fishing boats were beached on the exposed mud flats. In the centre rear of each boat was a wood-framed wheelhouse covering the inboard engine. There was something quite graceful about the boats, with their flowing, smooth lines. To me they looked like larger versions of a Boston Whaler. A carpenter was on one of the vessels replacing several old wooden deck planks with new ones made of pine imported from Chile, he said, adding that Korean pine was too short and not strong enough.

Heju and I also chatted to a local police officer, who seemed to be patrolling the wharf, and he gave us a different take on the story of the four kids who tragically drowned on the mud flats. "Three boys and a girl," he told us. "They were out on the mud flats off the southwest coast. The tide was coming in and they were walking back to shore. The water was shallow, but there was a rift gulley four metres deep, and they stepped into it, literally just fell off and drowned." This seemed more plausible to me than getting stuck in the mud, an incoming tide sweeping over them.

Consider the shock of walking in knee-deep water and suddenly plunging off a ledge into a deep trench. I have no doubt panic could immediately set in. Koreans are also notoriously fearful of deep water, and it is common at beaches in summertime to see a long band of bathers floating on rubber tubes — no one really swimming — and all keeping within about four metres of shore. On a hot day, I'd take a dip in about any river, lake, or sea, but you couldn't pay me to swim in this goo off Ganghwa.

Now early afternoon, and with the island road already jammed with cars driven by Seoul city slickers, Heju and I drove along at barely a crawl, and it took us more than an hour to get to the day's main attraction, the Jeondeung-sa Buddhist Temple (*sa* means "temple"), located inland at the southern end of the island on Jeongjok Mountain. It is believed to be the oldest of the more than three thousand Buddhist temples in South Korea. Between the fourth and thirteenth centuries was the heyday of Buddhism in Korea. In 1392, though, with the adaptation of Confucianism by the Joseon Kingdom, the government began suppressing and relegating Buddhists to second-class status, and they even destroyed some temples.

We parked about a kilometre west of the temple and walked right next to the gridlocked road, tramping through the weeds that grew alongside (there is no road shoulder here).

At Jeongjok Mountain, a wide path led up the gradual slope to the temple At the base was a tiny old wooden stand in which a woman was roasting chestnuts to sell to visitors. The parking lot was full and we shared the path with many others. The branches of the massive centuries-old trees — including pine, cherry, and ginkgo — along the path stretched up and over us, a great green canopy.

As we passed a small café, three well-lubricated Korean gentlemen wearing identical grey windbreakers with "Incheon Airport" stitched on the front, came out. They greeted Heju and me with boisterous salutations.

"*Dangsindeul gonghwangeseo ilhamnika?*" ("Do you work at the airport?") Heju asked.

*"Ne hajiman urineun toegik haesseoyo,"* ("Yes, but we're retired,") said one. Then he asked me, *"Dangsinneun gonghwangeseo ilhamnika?"* ("Do *you* work at the airport?").

A strange question, I thought. "No," I answered.

He paused, and then announced with barely contained glee, *"Wae … dangsindeul haego deoeosseoyo?"* ("Why … were you fired? ").

The joke set the men off in convulsions of laughter. I was happy to contribute to the trio's merriment. We bid adieu to the standup comedians and proceeded up the path to the temple.

Jeondeung Temple was originally built in AD 381, under the auspices of a monk from China named Ado, who was travelling south to spread Buddhism in the southern Baekje and Silla kingdoms. In 1299, the wife of King Chungnyeol, Queen Jeonghwa, presented a gift of a jade lamp to the temple, then known as Jinjeong-sa. Henceforth it became known as Jeondeung-sa — "Temple of the Bequeathed Lamp."

The entrance to Jeondeung was through the stately and formal South Gate, a wall of finely cut granite stone about six metres high with an arched walkway through it. On top of the gate is a distinctive wooden structure painted dark red with teal blue trim. It is topped with a massive and very heavy looking arched roof comprised of a series of black shale tiles laid in vertical rows. Stretching out from the gate along the front of the temple grounds is a broad stone wall of piled and roughly hewn rocks that had once been part of the Jeongjok Sanseong fortress. South Gate and parts of the wall had been refurbished in 1976.

We walked east along the dirt path that ran parallel to and just inside the wall. There is history along this wall. Just weeks after the French naval forces, including the Far Eastern Squadron, came ashore at Gapgot on October 16, 1866, seeking retribution for the execution of several French-Catholic missionaries, French commander Pierre-Gustave Roze sent about 160 men to the island's south end to verify reports of an apparent buildup of Korean soldiers in the area.

But as the French soldiers patrolled along Jeondeung Temple's fortified outer wall on November 9, they were ambushed by a contingent of hundreds of Korean soldiers who had been lying in wait.

Korean bowmen rained a cavalcade of arrows down on the French, and spears and swords were wielded against the invaders. A Ganghwa guidebook puts the number of French dead at about sixty, though Korean history books more commonly state that three Frenchmen were killed and dozens injured. On November 12, three days later, the French Far East Squadron departed the island after almost a month of being camped out at Ganghwa town.

Korea counted this as a French surrender, a victory. To this day they are proud of having sent the French packing.

When Heju and I reached the far end of the front south wall, we followed the east wall back up the slope into the forest, then entered the temple grounds through the east gate. The area was also filled with families and kids. The compound was compact and contained a handful of small buildings, which were stately and finely built, with great graceful roofs. There was a beauty to both the grounds and the wooden structures, their typical rusty reds and greens now faded.

During the temple's more than 1,600-year history, there have been three main halls. The first was built in 381, the second burnt down during the Imjin War (1592–98), and the third and current one was completed in 1621. While not large, it had an exotic-looking roof that flared up into a graceful arch at each of the four corners. The underside had been skilfully constructed, comprising hundreds of round beams extending out from under the roof, taking the great weight of shale tiles above. There is also intricately-carved woodwork on the underside, and at each corner under the roof a small, wooden figure faces out, its shoulders and hands seeming to support the heavy roof.

We entered a large room called "Daeungjeon." Inside, the wood ceiling is carved in ornate and intricate detail with serpents and birds. A slow but steady stream of women was entering, then kneeling on the floor, offering prayers to the Buddha statue in front.

At the risk of being reprimanded for being nosy, we politely asked a woman exiting what she had prayed for.

"For my family and my kids," she replied.

"They always say that," said Heju. We had asked the same question of other worshippers at Buddhist temples.

It was late afternoon by the time we got back on the road, finally ready to leave Ganghwa Island. Due to traffic gridlock on the island and along the mainland in Gimpo, it was not until about four hours later, at nine o'clock, that we found ourselves in the three-million-inhabitant, blue-collar city of Incheon, only thirty kilometres south of Ganghwa on the west coast. We were sharing Incheon's six-lane downtown road with what seemed like a million drivers this Saturday night. The bumper-to-bumper traffic was going nowhere fast. Then the heavens opened up and a torrential rain pelted down furiously. The lights from bright blue, green, red, and yellow neon signs blurrily danced through the splattering rain that lashed across the windshield.

"Let's stay in Incheon tonight and leave in the morning," I suggested of our planned tour of a fort and palace in the city of Suwon, south of Seoul, the next day.

Heju agreed, and we took a room at a motel on one of the main city streets. With the rain abating we took a walk around the neighbourhood. As we meandered through the back lanes, we came to an outdoor market stall where cooked pigs' knuckles were being sold. With surprising gusto, Heju announced she was going to buy some, because she had never tried them before. They seemed to be all bone and bristles.

"You'll never eat them," I cautioned her.

"Yes, I will," she insisted resolutely as the ajumma placed the knuckles in a brown paper bag and handed it to her.

Nearby we found a small modern restaurant, where I opted for a more conventional meal of *guksu* (noodles in soup). On the restaurant walls hung handsome poster-size black-and-white photographs depicting

Seoul circa 1900. One was of passengers on a streetcar; another of hundreds of citizens sleeping in front of Seoul Station waiting to buy train tickets. There were ones of old clay homes with thatched straw roofs and another of forlorn-looking criminals, wood planks fitted around their necks, sitting on the ground.

"Great photos. You must be interested in history," I said to the well-dressed owner.

"No," he confessed, "my friend gave the photos to me as a gift when I opened the restaurant."

"How strange," I confided quietly to Heju when he returned to the front counter, "He has these amazing posters showing some of the fascinating moments in the history of Seoul, yet he's not interested in it."

# CHAPTER 5

Heju and I found ourselves in Suwon the next day, standing in front of Hwaseong Haenggung ("visiting palace"). A group of about fifteen Royal Asiatic Society members had just arrived by shuttle bus from Seoul with Joseon architecture expert and tour guide Peter Bartholomew for his annual spring tour of the palace and the surrounding Hwaseong Fort.

Peter was a past president of the RAS, and a well-known amateur expert on Joseon's historical and significant architecture. He leads RAS members on annual tours introducing them to grand Joseon architecture such as that here in Suwon. Peter arrived in Korea as a U.S. Peace Corps member in 1968, and had made the country his home. He speaks fluent Korean, and is charismatic, talkative, and easy to laugh. When he is leading a tour, though, he's also very intense.

Heju and I had taken Peter's royal palaces tour in Seoul. He had opened my eyes to minute and detailed aspects of architecture, which I had never previously considered. Now when I walk past a Joseon palace wall in Seoul, I can appreciate the five or six different sizes and patterns of brick used.

Although it was only ten o'clock, it was already oppressively hot, the sun bright and searing — and it was only mid-April. My mini thermometer read 27°C, though with the heated, moisture-laden air, it felt more like thirty-five, and as if a damp hot blanket was smothering me. (I don't do well in extreme humidity.) I removed a tissue from my pocket and wiped the sweat from the back of my neck. It was going to be a long day.

*Haenggung*, or "visiting palaces," were built both within and outside Seoul, and were used by the royal court for pleasure trips, relaxation, and as a home away from Seoul while travelling. Hwaseong Palace, built in 1789 but expanded several years later to include thirty-three different buildings, was the largest detached palace in Korea; however, it was still smaller than the five main palaces in Seoul.

Hwaseong Palace was constructed after King Jeongjo moved the tomb of his father, Crown Prince Sado, from Seoul to Suwon, so the king would have a place to stay when he visited the tomb. Confucian ethics required sons to visit the tombs of their fathers for extended periods each year. Seoul also could be highly malodorous during the summer, and having the palace forty kilometres outside the city gave the king the opportunity to escape the capital for a welcome respite. King Jeongjo had Hwaseong Fortress built to enclose within its walls Old Suwon and the palace. The king's ultimate plan was to move the capital from Seoul to Suwon. When he died in 1800, however, his successor opted against the idea.

What made this palace, and in particular the fort wall, unique and worthy of a tour, was that it was not only the last major construction project of the Joseon Dynasty, but Peter considered it the best example of architecture on a grand scale.

Due to Japan's intent to rid Korea of its cultural heritage, it razed most of the country's grand traditional architecture, much of it during the 1930s, said Peter. Hwaseong Palace was no exception. Japan destroyed all but two of its approximately thirty buildings after removing the contents, leaving, among the two, King Jeongjo's Memorial Hall, or Hwaryeongjeong (*hwa* is "flower," *ryeong* means "peace," and *jeong* is "big building"). The palace sits at the bottom of the eastern slope of the short, bulky, and wooded Paldal Mountain. The extensive landscaped gardens had once spread up the slope, but sadly the Japanese razed these, too.

Beginning in 1996, the Korean government had experts in traditional architecture construct palace buildings on the almost empty grounds. They had to start from scratch, though the placement of the buildings was extremely accurate, due to the fact that archaeologists in the 1980s and 1990s had unearthed enough of the original stone foundations to enable them to establish precisely where they had stood. The Memorial Hall was restored adroitly by artisans. As Peter commented, except for cleaning and mainly sandpapering and oiling the floors, which were in terrible shape, the experts left the structure virtually intact.

"That's why I like these buildings: they're the most original from Joseon with the least amount of restoration," he said. He was critical of past government attempts at restoration projects of Joseon architecture, contending some had been done poorly.

Peter led us to the grand front gate: a row of four massive swinging doors with eight rounded wooden posts supporting a wooden deck, and above that, the enormous black tile roof that despite its size swept elegantly far out over the doors in the Korean tradition. The structure was highlighted with turquoise green and was expertly detailed. Stretching along each side of the gate was a low stone wall made up of rows of small light-coloured bricks. Running along the inside of the wall was what looked like long barracks. This type of structure was common in the palace, used both for residences for numerous and varied members of the royal court, including servants, musicians, scholars, artists, poets, and gisaeng, or as a food storeroom, or *nusanggo* (*nu* means "attic," *sang* is "above," *go* is "storeroom"). The exposed top half of the nusanggo's wall was soft pink clay bordered with wood and what appeared to be small shutters. The roof was of a modest size and tiled with black shale.

Like the palaces in Seoul that we'd visited, the grounds here were stark and austere, reminding me more of a military camp. There was not a blade of grass. Once through the gate, we found ourselves in a large rectangular courtyard about fifty metres square. At the far end were two humble yet stately halls, with higher, heavier, and more dominating roofs of black shale tiles. As Peter led us through the grounds, we moved from one courtyard to the next, all of varying sizes, usually bordered by the simpler barrack-like structures. There were several bigger halls, too, which would have been for the king and royal family.

There were perhaps fifteen courtyards in total enclosed within the two-hundred-metre-long grounds. The open spaces and the buildings had been organized in a specific configuration, as if every space had a purpose. Unlike Goryeo Palace on Ganghwa Island, where the wooden buildings were dry and in critical need of paint, the wood and clay here was exquisitely kept up, with natural rusty red and earthy pink clay walls and the wood on the underside of the overhanging eaves painted a natural vibrant green. The overall effect of the colours was to produce a feeling of being in nature.

This rigid architectural order was, to me, akin to strolling through, say, a Dutch or German village, where every home, shop, and café was spotless, prim, and orderly. Joseon architects apparently were smitten with the same meticulous attention to detail. How I longed, though, to note something, anything, out of place, or something whimsical, perhaps.

As Peter painfully slowly led us through the grounds — detailing, for example, the various kinds of bricks used to create a certain courtyard wall — I knew, unequivocally, that had I been a Joseon king, I would have had one of the courtyards converted to a clay tennis court, and I would have been regularly leaving the palace to put back a few shots of soju (firewater) at the village pub. And I don't even drink. Courtyards and open spaces were required in Joseon palaces because ceremonies in which many hundreds of court-appointed singers and dancers performed were once a big part of royal protocol, so the common areas needed to be large enough to accommodate groups of performers and an audience. Ceremonies were numerous and frequent. Dancers, guards, servants, and musicians had to be in exact prearranged spots prior to the king making his heavenly appearance. During a royal birthday, for example, it was common for up to one thousand singers and dancers to perform.

King Jeongjo would be transported in a royal palanquin the forty or so kilometres from Seoul to Hwaseong. Kings and queens during Joseon were considered mythical, intermediaries between heaven and earth. Such divine figures rarely ventured into public, and when they did, civilians were forced to avert their gazes from the king and queen. On a rear wall Peter pointed out a mural about forty metres long; an artist's account of one of these royal processions from Seoul to Suwon. In it were thousands of participants, including soldiers, horseman, banner-men, musicians, dancers, guards, and servants. Every horse and flag in the cortege was recorded in colourful detail.

Isabella Bird wrote in *Korea and Her Neighbours* about King Gojong making an extremely rare public appearance, departing the royal palace in Seoul in a palanquin and being carried across the city to his ancestors' graves. Bird referred to this as the *kur-dong* (*geodung* today — *geo* meaning "lift," *dung* "to move"). Geodung was "one of the most remarkable spectacles I ever saw," Bird wrote. The procession, no doubt, would be similar to the type King Jeongjo had led from Seoul to Suwon.

On hand to witness Gojong's entourage that morning in Seoul were perhaps 150,000 citizens, estimated Bird, and all were crowded along the dusty road leading away from the palace. The sounds of trumpets, flutes, cymbals, drums, and baying donkeys filled the air, and the procession was a visually stunning smorgasbord of colour — beautiful silk garments and banners in every shade of the rainbow. Bird noted about five thousand officials and servants were affiliated with the palace, and the same number of soldiers.

Bird was so impressed with the spectacle that she devoted eight pages of her book to describing it.

> Waves of colour and Korean grandeur rolled by, official processions, palace attendants, bannermen, with large silk banners trailing on the stiff breeze, each flagstaff crested with a tuft of pheasant's feathers, the King's chief cook, with an enormous retinue, more palace servants, smoking long pipes, drummers, fifers, couriers at a gallop, with arrows stuck into the necks of their coats, holding on to their saddles and rope bridles, mixed up with disheveled ponies, with ragged pack saddles, carrying cushions, lacquer boxes, eatables, cooking utensils, and smoking apparatuses, led caparisoned ponies, bowmen, soldiers straggling loosely,

> armed with matchlock guns, till several thousand persons had passed.

Peter led us along an extended porch in front of the residences. Dark grey tile covers the heavy roofs, which arch gracefully out over the buildings' red walls. This creates a covered walkway several metres wide around each structure, which would have provided shelter from the summer monsoon rains. The walls are smooth red clay, the lattice shutters painted a lovely green. Large heavy shutters designed to be swung up and attached to hooks under the eaves allow a welcome breeze to flow through the buildings during the hot summers. With the vertical wood beams painted a dark red, the granite foundations white, and the dark-coloured roofs, it creates an altogether natural look, very pleasing to the eye — precisely the effect the original Joseon designers had sought, I imagine.

The buildings are situated in such a way that they faced away from the winds that bear down on the area during typhoon season, so the delicate swinging doors across the front side won't be destroyed. In traditional Joseon architecture, locally sourced red clay was used to insulate the walls and even the roofs, as it was laid under the tiles. Mixed with water, the dense, viscous clay forms a hard layer and is a superb insulator, blocking out cold air in winter and stymieing the hot, humid air from seeping in during the summer. It is also an excellent absorber of sound.

To stay warm during the winters, a refined heating system called *ondol* (hot stone) was used, in which a fireplace on the outside of the wall produced hot air that was then forced through stone flutes under the structure's floor, which was covered first with clay, then flagstone, and finally a layer of thick paper coated with oil and lacquer to make it watertight. The stone floor stayed hot for between twenty-four and thirty-six hours. Highly efficient, this form of in-floor heating has been used in Korea for more than two millennia.

After a couple of hours, we were all ready for a break. So we hopped on the shuttle bus and were delivered to a nearby restaurant for lunch. Finally, some relief from the hot sun! After the welcome interlude, we were back into the broiler, so to speak, for the second half of the tour, which involved a six-kilometre trek around Hwaseong Fortress.

The fortress wall is palatial and grandiose, and varies in height from four to nine metres, depending on the terrain. Originally an earthen fort, the walls were rebuilt using stone in 1794. Sadly, over time, the walls fell into a severe state of disrepair. All of the sentry posts were demolished by the Japanese in the 1920s and 30s and after President Park Chung-hee's military government came to power in 1961, it ordered long sections of two walls to be torn down, because "they weren't needed," in Peter's words. The Korean government then had a change of heart, and undertook a massive repair and reconstruction project in the late seventies. They did a superb job, our guide added.

Almost the entire length of the west wall was built up and over and down Paldal Mountain. We began walking north along the path, from the south end of the wall, tracing it up along the long, gradual slope of the hill. The closest thing I can compare this wall to in scope is the Great Wall of China. The height and breadth were prodigious. It was built onto the hill's natural slope. Its thick granite blocks — many irregularly shaped — were cut to fit together without the use of cement. Atop this battlement were more modest-sized granite blocks forming a parapet with crenels from which to fire weapons. Along the entire length were turrets, and more small square openings or portals from which to aim weapons.

At the rounded crest of the mountain was a command post and fire beacon. Looking west from our heightened vantage point afforded an expansive airy view over west Suwon. The large plain in the distance was dominated by myriad and orderly agricultural plots.

Descending the hill on stone steps toward the fort's northwest corner, we entered West Gate Pavilion, where heavy vertical wood beams support the massive weight of the roof.

"It's so cool in here," I said, collapsing on a seat.

"That's because clay is a great insulator," Peter said of the approximately one-metre-thick layer of clay above us.

Too soon we were back outside strolling past the mammoth Northwest Military Post, or Seobuk Gongshin-don. It reminded me somewhat of the vertical stone structures on Tower Bridge in London.

This imposing structure is rectangular and tapers slightly as it rises up, as tall as a four-storey building, with the base of large granite blocks giving way to smaller stones farther up. The parapet at the top is capped by a weighty wood and tile roof, and there were numerous openings in the outer wall from which weapons could have been fired.

We continued on, turning the corner to walk along the imperious north wall to the amazing Janganmun, or Longevity and Peace Gate, which was not so much a gate as a testament to architectural domination. (I thought it would have made the perfect film locale, perhaps as Hogwarts School from the Harry Potter films). At close to five storeys high, it is the largest gate of this type in South Korea. The large grey granite blocks that make up the soaring arched entranceway are topped with a long section of granite and brick, and finished off with a long, ornately carved two-storey pavilion with a black shale roof.

North Korean soldiers took refuge here for a short while at the start of the Korean War, with U.S. troops firing a barrage of artillery shells at the north gate and walls. "They blew the wall to smithereens to dislodge them," said Peter, pointing out the pockmarks and gouges in the stone gate. "That's where the shells hit."

Walking south outside the east wall, more architectural richness awaited us. There was East Gate, smaller than Janganmun, but equally splendid. The Eastern Command Post was a huge open-air pavilion distinctively alone in the centre of a granite promenade, with numerous round wooden posts supporting its enormous arched roof. Along the wall on a steep grassy hill overlooking a pond fringed by sweeping willow trees was a lovely open pavilion, regal wooden beams holding up its large shale roof. We walked along Gwanggyo Stream, which flowed under seven arched granite floodgates. Farther south was a forbidding dark-bricked oval watchtower.

It wasn't until late afternoon that our group finished circumnavigating the fort and we wearily trudged back to the south wall. It occurred to me that while King Jeongjo established this state-of the art city/fortress more than two centuries ago with the aim being to transfer the capital from Seoul to Suwon, for all practical purposes, the fortress was a white elephant; it was never used for defence or protection.

Peter and the RAS members boarded the shuttle bus for the trip back to Seoul, but Heju and I would be staying on in Suwon for another day, as we planned to visit the Korean Railroad Museum in Uiwang, just north of the city.

We decided to explore the area around the fortress. At the nearby Jidong Market we spent an enjoyable hour wandering around the outdoor stalls, where all sorts of meat, seafood, and produce were for sale. We then drove the short distance to downtown Suwon to the combined Suwon Station/department store complex. The street in front was impossibly busy and vitally energetic on this Sunday evening, with innumerable pedestrians crowding the sidewalks and multi-storey buildings ablaze in the darkness with a rainbow of bright neon lights. Hoards of cars, taxis, and buses jockeyed for position on the chaotic street.

We parked across from the station and snuck back into a confusing network of old lanes with brightly lit store fronts. The "goods" on sale here were women — the red-light district. Along the back lane we chatted with a group of well-tailored young Pakistani men who were employed as labourers at Suwon factories. They informed us there was a Pakistani restaurant nearby.

Two of the young men escorted us to the busy main street and showed us to a small door in an otherwise nondescript brick wall. Once on the other side, we found ourselves in a Little Pakistan of sorts — a noisy restaurant crowded with mostly young Pakistani men. There were no Koreans and no women at all in the space, which consisted of a long, narrow room with a concrete floor and long communal tables. Dishes of lamb and rice sat in front of the voluble men, all of whom were moustached and bearded. Cigarette smoke hung thick and acrid and stung our eyes. We were shown to a small table at the rear, where a chef was manning the semi-open kitchen immediately behind us.

We both opted for the Basmati rice and lamb in sauce with pita bread, then waited patiently with hungry bellies. It wasn't every day we dined out, and we were excited to be on the receiving end of some decadent lamb.

"I love lamb!" Heju announced, as happy as kid at a birthday party, her mood always suddenly elevated when we dined out. Then she said, somewhat accusingly, "We never eat out!"

"Of course we don't," I replied in mock alarm. "The trip's costing a lot of money. I need to be careful." As the lone son of a generous but parsimonious Scottish mother and a spendthrift Dutch father, I had a mandate to uphold, after all: the old-world family tradition to be circumspect with money.

As we waited, we observed a rather touching ritual as pairs or small groups of men arriving and departing engaged in a lengthy process of shaking hands, hugging, cheek-kissing, and waving to almost every other man in the place, so that it took quite a considerable time for each party to get from their table to the door and vice versa.

In the kitchen behind us, I suddenly noticed that the chef's dark eyes were locked in on me with a penetrating and hostile glare. *Was he upset for some reason that we were here?* I wondered

"Heju, don't look now," I whispered stealthily, "but the chef in the kitchen ... I think he —"

Heju turned to look.

"Not now!" I muffled a cry.

A few moments later I gave her the green light: "Okay, slowly ... take your time ... look!" She cast an unobtrusive glance in his direction.

"I think he wants to kill me," I squeaked. "He keeps staring at me."

Heju thought for a few seconds before asking me, with a straight face, "Can I have your plate of lamb and rice if he does?"

*Ha ha!* Throughout dinner I snuck frequent furtive glances back at my nemesis, who continued to eyeball me. I sat poised and alert, ready to leap from my chair and through the front door in case he rushed at me with a carving knife.

The food was marvellous, though: succulent, tender lamb and sweet, fluffy Indian rice (much different from the sticky, glutinous rice grown in Korea), and delectable naan bread. My only complaint was that there was a paucity of food, which was a fundamental problem, it seemed to me, when eating out. I was often relegated to begging for scraps from Heju, who thankfully usually couldn't finish what was on her plate.

I thought how strange it was that there wasn't a single Korean here, other than Heju. When I've dined out at American chains in Korea — Outback Steakhouse or T.G.I. Friday's, for example — where food is overpriced and run-of-the-mill, the premises are often absolutely crammed with Koreans.

Only partially satiated, and with our clothes reeking of cigarette smoke, we found ourselves back out on the bustling sidewalk. I looked warily back at the restaurant. "Just making sure the chef's not following me," I told Heju, who thought I was bonkers.

* * *

Two days later, after some sightseeing just outside Suwon, we arrived at the Korean Rail Museum in the late afternoon. About half a dozen old diesel and electric locomotives and passenger cars that once plied Korea's rail lines were on display in the large compound out front. A plaque on a luxury passenger car informed us that U.S. President Lydon [*sic*] B. Johnson had ridden in it on November 1, 1966, during his visit to South Korea. At the rear of the compound sat a mangled and rusted train engine, which had, before the Korean War, puffed back and forth along the sixty kilometres of track that ran between Seoul and Gaesong. Both the line and the engine itself had been bombed during the war.

Next to this was a short section of track less than a metre wide, like one might find at a kids' amusement park. In 1937, the Japanese had constructed the narrow-gauge Suin Rail Line, which ran for forty-seven kilometres between Suwon and Incheon and on to Yeoju, another sixty kilometres east, though this latter section of track was dismantled in the 1970s. The following week, when Heju and I were in Incheon, we spoke with a couple of local old-timers who fondly recalled riding the Suin Line. Up until the 1970s, only a dirt road connected Incheon to Suwon, they said, and the rail line was popular with locals. Each car was only about eight metres long. The train's wheels caused a racket as they bumped and clanked slowly over the track. Inside, the cars were crowded, noisy, and smelly, as farmers and merchants brought aboard pigs, chickens, and dogs to sell at outdoor markets located at each station stop.

"Even a cow staring at the train could tip it over," one fellow joked.

We spoke with a rail historian, who said that, during colonization, many narrow-gauge lines were built by the Japanese, though they were later torn up or altered to standard gauge. In 1995, the government demolished the Suin Line. This seems a shame. How much fun would it be for tourists to ride that rail today, to experience the short, bumpy, and rattling trip.

The spacious museum was devoid of visitors (which didn't surprise us, due to the fact it was located in a vast industrial park behind factories and virtually impossible to find) and apparently staff, too. As we wandered through the building, we saw the occasional movement in the shadows that we thought could be an employee, but no one materialized.

The history of rail travel in Korea is quite fascinating. The first rail line in the country was constructed in 1896–1897 by an American company, and ran from Incheon to Seoul. In 1900, the Japanese began building a line north from Busan. It reached Seoul in 1905. (A photo in the museum depicted the inauguration of the line in Seoul, with Japanese officials and soldiers and thousands of curious Korean citizens standing along the track looking on.)

By 1911, a line ran northwest from Seoul into Manchuria to Mukden (today Shenyang). The Japanese wanted a line from Busan into China for their planned future conquest of the nation to the north. At Mukden, the Chinese Eastern Railway intersected the line that ran up from Seoul. The Chinese line ran from Beijing to Harbin, where it connected to the Trans-Siberian Railway.

Subsequent rail lines were constructed in Korea by the Japanese, most on a north–south axis. Because of the mountainous terrain, it was not easy to build tracks, and a large number of rail tunnels had to be constructed through the mountains. The Jungang Line, which runs from Seoul to Gyeongju in the southeast, required the building of forty-two tunnels. The line's longest is the 4,500-metre Jungnyong Tunnel.

Up until the 1960s, rail travel was the only real option for Koreans. Bus transportation was in its nascent stages, and very few roads were paved. Besides, there were only about twenty-five thousand cars in the entire country as of 1964. Hence, more than 150 million passengers rode the rails annually. Prior to the availability of rail travel, Koreans relied for millennia on strong legs to trek through the country. Goods were often carried on *jigye*, wooden A-frames which men strapped to their backs, and on which supplies could be piled up to two metres high. Foreign missionaries arriving in Korea, disembarking from ships onto the tidal mud flats at Incheon, must have gazed in wonder as the Koreans thrust up to three hundred pounds of bags and cargo onto their jigye, then lugged it forty kilometres to Seoul. Ponies and oxen were used to haul heavier loads.

A millennium-old traditional trekking route conveyed the length of today's South Korea, from Busan to Seoul. This essentially straight-line path followed the wide Nakdong River valley north to the Sobaek Mountains, then cut northwest through a mountain pass and traced the narrow route of the South Han River valley to Seoul — a total distance of about 360 kilometres. In George Foulk's epic 1884 account of his pan-Korean journey, he mentions the names of the towns he passed through as he travelled north on this trail — Busan, Miryang, Daegu, Sangju, Mungyeong, Chungju — before continuing on to Seoul.

The Seoul–Busan rail line basically followed the traditional walking route from Busan to Daegu, but instead of continuing northwest and shadowing the trail, it made an abrupt divergence almost due west, to Daejeon, moving partway through a long, narrow pass in the Sobaek Mountains before finally reaching north to Seoul — in all, a distance of approximately 440 kilometres. Formerly bustling towns north of Daegu along the walking path, such as Sangju and Chungju, were far from the rail line and relegated to obscurity. I had been to Chungju, which is today a slow and peaceful town off the beaten path in a pretty rural area beside the wide Han River. As for Sangju, I didn't know where it was, and needed to consult a map to find it.

Conversely, formerly minor and inconsequential outposts along the new Gyeongbu Line prospered. Daejeon is a prime example. Formerly a mere hamlet not even warranting a name on a map, the town soon developed into a major rail cog, and in the south, rail lines from Mokpo, Masan, and Busan were connected to it. Daejeon is now the fifth-largest city in South Korea with 1.5 million citizens — not to mention being the home of the world-famous Kim Heju. When Gyeongbu Expressway, the country's first highway, was completed in 1970, joining Seoul and Busan, it also followed the path of the rail line.

The museum had on display scores of interesting exhibits and photos depicting the history of Korean railways. One photo taken in 1963 showed a section of track located in the Tabaek Mountains along the east coast in which the rail cars were being winched up a low but steep mountain slope. In the photo, passengers were walking along the track. This section was on the Yeongdong Line, located between the east coast city of Donghae, and Simpo, just to its southwest. In the 1970s, a series of switchbacks supplanted this short section of steep track.

After two hours in the museum, and just before six o'clock, a sleepy-looking college-aged fellow wearing a blazer suddenly and conveniently materialized. He approached us on the second floor, and announced that it was closing time.

*Good*, I thought. I had been hoping to meet a staff member who could answer a few railroad queries I had. But to each of my questions, he replied listlessly "I don't know." Continuing to throw questions at him, he then suggested that we go look on the museum website to get the answers. Excuse me, but I think that a rail museum employee ought to know at least a thing or two about railroads.

From Uiwang, Heju and I headed back toward Seoul. Over the next couple of days, we had several tours lined up, including the one to Panmunjeom. We moved north along the main six-lane artery from Uiwang toward Seoul, passing the satellite cities of Anyang and Gwacheon and a seemingly never-ending string of tall white apartment buildings. Most of Greater Seoul's seven million vehicles seemed to be sharing the road with us, a sea of red tail lights in front of us in the fading light. At about nine o'clock, having taken about three hours to cover a mere forty kilometres, we finally arrived in Amsa-dong, close to my place in Myeongil-dong.

We checked in to the Bali Motel, because I had sublet my humble flat while I was away. The clerk, who was sitting behind a narrow pane of glass at the front desk, asked, "Will you be staying two hours?"

"No, for the night," we answered.

*"Samman won,"* ("Thirty thousand won,") she said.

A couple who looked to be in their forties entered and waited behind us in the lobby. The man was wearing a suit, and his female companion, trying hard to remain incognito, lurked in the background with her head bowed. I assumed that these were the two-hour customers who patronize such facilities.

Our room was barely larger than a jail cell. On the ceiling were dim green and red fluorescent lights, a throwback to the 1960s hippie era. Settling in, we heard the muffled but unmistakable sound of a woman's passionate groans emanating from the adjacent room.

"Are those real or from the TV?" I asked Heju, because love motels offer porn channels. I thought perhaps that was the source of the impassioned noises.

Heju paused and listened. "I'm not sure," she said.

So I turned on the TV, tuned in the porn channel, and turned up the volume.

"They don't match. It's a real person next door making the sounds!" I declared triumphantly.

Heju shrugged; she didn't share my enthusiasm for having cracked the case.

# CHAPTER 6

Heju and I decided our room was too small to stay in it for another night, so we conveyed ourselves and our luggage across the street to the Casa Motel the next morning. In the Casa lobby we found a small office, and against the inner wall was a bank of video monitors. The screens showed closed-circuit live feeds of the hallways on each of the floors, the male and female managers keeping a close eye on the goings-on.

"You staying for two hours?" the man, a short, aggressive character with the disposition of an aggrieved used car salesman, asked us brusquely.

"No, just for the night," we said.

He didn't look pleased. "Where are you going to park?"

"In the motel lot."

"In the garage?"

"Yes."

"You can't!" he insisted unpleasantly. "If you do, customers [the two-hour kind, I presumed] can't get in and out with their cars during the day. If you keep your car in the garage, it'll cost you 30,000 won," he concluded, tacking 5,000 won on to the room fee.

"Okay," I answered.

I parked the car in the lot, then Heju and I did what we always did on the trip when we arrived at a motel, and proceeded to unload our bags containing clothes, books, camera, binoculars, and newspapers. Granted, it did appear as if we were moving in long-term.

When the man saw all our stuff, he declared tersely, "What are you doing with all that in here?" (Two-hour customers didn't bring luggage.)

"We're journalists touring Korea. We've got valuable equipment in the bags," I replied.

"Well, don't leave it in the room when you leave!" he demanded uncharitably.

Like I was about to leave it all in the room for him.

I waited expectantly at the office window, but he ignored me. "May we have the key, please?" I asked, finally.

"There's no key," he barked. "What do you need a key for? Customers only stay two hours!"

The poor man couldn't grasp the fact that there existed patrons other than those on short trysts. He was upset because he would only be making 30,000 won from our twenty-four-hour stay, rather than 20,000 won for a two-hour rental.

Finally, he grudgingly handed us the key. A real joy of a man.

When we entered our third-floor room (first and second floors were reserved for short-termers, of course), I went into the bathroom and promptly banged my forehead square on the top of the door frame. I cussed and rubbed my head. It wasn't the first time I had thumped my noggin on a low door frame in Korea. "Why do they make such low doorways in this damned country?" I bellowed, digging through my bags to find my tape measure. "Five foot seven inches!" I announced to Heju. "What kind if idiotic motel is this?"

When Bishop Corfe first arrived in the country from England in 1890, the tall man hit his head on the low overhead beams inside the traditional Korean home he resided in at Incheon so often that he nailed socks to them.

After throwing our stuff in the room, Heju and I departed Casa Motel and walked to the nearby Amsa subway station, as we needed to be at Bugak (North) Mountain for a two o'clock guided hike. Once downtown, we transferred onto the No. 4 line to head north to Hansung University Station, where we exited and walked west through a busy outdoor market toward the east slope of Bugak Mountain. On the way, we passed by the quiet and stately residential neighbourhood of Seongbuk, surely the toniest and priciest in all of Seoul. The magnificent multi-million-dollar homes here belong to the fabulously rich, the titans of Korean industry. Soon, we arrived at the base of Bugak's moderate north ascent, where we waited at a tourist hut with a couple of dozen Koreans for a prearranged tour that would take us up the hill.

In 1968, Bugak's popular hiking trails were made permanently off-limits to citizens, when the area became a patrolled military zone. On January 21, 1968, thirty-one elite North Korean commandos sent by North Korean president Kim Il-sung to assassinate the South's right-wing president, Park Chung-hee, made it to within two hundred metres of the Blue House in an attempt to carry out their plan. The armed commandos had snuck over the border into the South and approached Seoul clandestinely through the Gwangju Mountains, which run southeast from the Taebaek Mountains and surround Seoul. North of the city lay the distinctive and rugged granite ridges belonging to the Gwangjus.

Near the Blue House, the enemy donned disguises to avoid detection. The ploy worked at first, but then a local police chief on duty, Choi Gyushik, grew suspicious of the coterie and demanded to see their identification. He was shot dead by the infiltrators. Their cover blown, they opened fire and threw hand grenades. The South military guards and police returned fire, and a prolonged firefight ensued in which as many sixty-four South Koreans were killed. Three U.S. soldiers also lost their lives.

The enemy fled into the mountainous woods, and over the next nine days, twenty-nine of the North Koreans were hunted down and shot dead. One, Kim Shin-jo, was captured, and went on to reside in Seoul and became a preacher at a church in west Seoul. (Heju had contacted Mr. Kim's church in an attempt to meet with him so we could get an eyewitness account of the incident, but he declined.) One commando presumably made it back to the North.

Bugak Mountain would not open to the public until 2007. To hike it these days requires pre-registration for a guide-led tour. Non-supervised or individual hikes are still not permitted. Heju and I had emailed our identification information to the military in advance, and despite my dodgy youthful past, which included consistently being late for Wednesday night Boy Scout meetings (which I saw as a terrible nuisance), and encouraging my younger sister to touch an electrified cow fence on a country outing, for reasons I cannot explain, Seoul authorities officially okayed me for the tour.

Our group included about twenty mostly middle-aged and elderly Koreans, and our guide was a dour, officious, retired Korean man who gravely explained the rules: "No smoking. No throwing garbage. Stay together at all times. ID cards must be worn around your necks and can't be removed until the tour is over." Accompanying us was a young, glum ROK soldier carrying a rifle.

The mid-April weather was warm and pleasant as we headed up the dirt path through the woods. Within fifteen minutes, we arrived at the imposing granite-stone North Gate, one of four main gates that permitted entrance to Old Seoul during the Joseon Dynasty. This entrance is most commonly known as Sukjeongmun: The Gate of Dignity and Tranquility. It was enormous, and loomed up in front of us out of the woods. During more than five hundred years of Joseon rule it was rarely opened or closed, as it was considered more an emergency exit if a king needed to quickly escape Old Seoul. South of the gate, the land drops in a long sweeping descent through the grey woods; Gyeongbok Palace, unseen, lies far below.

The wall enclosing Old Seoul ran in an imperfect circle for 18.6 kilometres. As I looked along the broad wooded ridge line, I noticed that little remained of the portion of the wall that once stood along this section. In 1392, when the Joseon Dynasty was established, a capital was needed. Goryeo, the previous dynasty, had its capital in Gaseong, located just north of Panmunjeom. Seoul was chosen, and during the first months of 1396, Taejo, Joseon's first king, conscripted 120,000 commoners to construct the first half of the fifteen-foot-high wall around Old Seoul in just forty-nine days. Later the same year (as an agrarian society, most of the men were farmers, so they required the spring and summer off to plant and harvest crops) 80,000 men completed the wall and built four main and four smaller gates in just forty-nine days.

It must have been quite a scene: 100,000-plus labourers congregating in Seoul, then a mere village with a population of only about 10,000. Lugging the large amounts of granite, stone, and mud (mud was used for two thirds of the wall, stone for the other third) needed to construct the wall several hundred metres up the formidable ascents would be back-breaking work. The wall was constructed up and along four mountains: Nam to the south, Inwang to the west, and Bugak and the minor Nak Mountain to the east. Eight hundred and seventy-two men died during the construction, from exhaustion, ill health, or disease. Years later, in 1422, about 320,000 labourers were tasked with replacing the wall's mud ramparts entirely with stone in just forty days.

Our tour group was ushered a few hundred metres west along the ridge to the high point, which stood at 340 metres elevation. We congregated at a flat granite clearing crowded with other, mostly Korean, tourists busily snapping photos of the expansive views. I had not been up here before, and was impressed. A few miles south, beyond the city core with its myriad glass and steel office towers, stood the stalwart and heavily wooded Namsan (South Mountain). At its crest was Seoul Tower, rising to the highest point in the city.

Far below us was the massive Gwanghwamun (Gate of Radiant Transformation) of the walled Gyeongbok Palace. The sixteen lanes of Sejong Street in front of the palace were clogged with innumerable cars, taxis, and buses, which crawled along like ants. Behind the palace's rear wall is Cheong Wa Dae, popularly known as the Blue House, which serves as the presidential residence. To the west was the low, steep Inwang Mountain ridge, with its bald patches of smooth white granite. To the north, a long block of rugged and rough granite peaks and ridges, the Gwangju Mountains, stretched to the border.

In 1392, when the first king of Joseon chose this village as the new capital, there were no walls, palaces, buildings, or roads. But the location was selected for several reasons. It lay close to the Yellow Sea, yet it was far enough upstream along the Han River that it was well-protected from the threat of Japanese pirates, who were the scourge of coastal regions, particularly during the thirteenth and fourteenth centuries. The Han River basin was also extensive, so large numbers of people could reside there. And to the north, west, and south were the fertile agricultural areas of Paju, Gimpo, and Pyeongtaek, which would sustain the growing population.

Prior to Joseon, the inhabitants of Korea obviously thought Seoul a favourable location, too, and dug-outs or pit houses and utensils and other items dating from the Neolithic Age to about 5000 BC, have been discovered along the shores of the Han River in Amsa-dong in eastern Seoul. It is the largest settlement of this type ever excavated. And for about the first seven hundred years of Christianity, three kingdoms: Goguryeo, which ruled the entire peninsula north of the Han River well north into today's China; Silla, which commanded the southeast; and Baekje, ruling to the southwest, all tried to control the strategically critical Seoul area. Today, evidence of earthen fort walls erected by those dynasties can be found in Seoul.

The Han River was also a seminal waterway. Rice and other goods were transported in flat-bottomed hanseons (*Han* means "Korea," seon is "boat") up the west coast of the peninsula to the Han and then on to Seoul. Smaller hanseons conveyed goods such as salt from the city to points farther inland. In exchange, items such as firewood and charcoal were brought downriver from villages far upstream. Seoul officials also travelled up the river to collect taxes from the villagers; in most cases, taxes were paid not with money, but in staples such as rice, grain, or cotton.

King Taejo ordered construction of Gyeongbok Palace in 1396. Combined with the previously erected country palace (today's Changgyeong Palace) and Changdeok Palace, built in 1405, the triumvirate formed a row.

Still, an entire city of roads, shops, markets, residences, and government offices needed to be created from scratch. In 1412, Taejo's son, King Taejong, who had reigned since 1400, ordered construction to begin. The main earthen thoroughfare was built in front of the palaces from East Gate to West Gate, through today's Jongno District. From the main roads radiated a series of minor roads and alleyways, some as narrow as a metre wide, along which commoners (the majority of the city's residents) constructed their clay hanoks and mud hovels. Stores, which sold textiles of silk, linen, and hemp, as well as fish, rice, paper, straw-ware, and ironware, popped up along the thoroughfares, all regulated by the government and taxed.

By 1420, Old Seoul had its essential framework in place, its population was now over 100,000, and it had become the heart and soul of medieval Korea. While political power was countrywide, wealth converged here and the educated and talented moved in. It was the place of opportunity. Yet, despite the natural beauty of the surrounding granite mountains and the Han River, there was litle if any *grandeur* — the city was simply functional.

By the 1550s, however, five major palace compounds and detached palaces and service compounds stretched almost unbroken along the west and north sections of the wall. The palaces and their adjoining buildings were virtual cities within a city. The compounds held hundreds of structures, and the grounds were laid out with buildings separated by corridors, gates, and alleyways.

Myriad compounds, usually square, housed facilities for food preparation, textile design, tailoring, herbal medicine, acupuncture, and all sorts of craftmaking involving wood, stone, mud, clay, plaster, metal, paper, and leather. Principal palaces also had a kiln and housed potters for creating ceramics and pottery. Outside the core palace area of the throne hall and royal residences was a virtual maze of courtyards and canyon-like walkways that linked them; hundreds of rooms housed servants, artists, artisans, calligraphers, painters, poets, musicians, and scholars. Each group had their own separate compound. Rooms were also available for visiting guests and officials.

Over the years, the number of compounds, courtyards, and rooms increased in number as more services were introduced. Kings added more internal walls and gates in case a quick escape was needed, and sometimes they added new compounds for a particular son or grandson. In the 1700s, both Changdeok and Changgyeong Palaces were greatly expanded. By the nineteenth century, Gyeongbok Palace comprised 150 courtyards and 450 buildings.

Yet when Isabella Bird arrived in Old Seoul in 1894 — with 80,000 citizens living within its walls and about 70,000 outside — there were no trees, parks, or green spaces, and "not a work of art to be gazed upon," she wrote. Bird said her view was of a sea of one-storey dwellings with straw or tile roofs.

Foreign missionaries in Seoul during that time recalled the city being eerily quiet within the walls and almost completely dark as there were no street lights. At about eight o'clock each night, the great bronze bell on Jongno Street (*Jongno* means "Bell Street") would be rung twenty-eight times, signalling that it was time for women to leave their abodes, free to walk the streets, while men were to be indoors. About two hours later the ladies had to be back inside. In the morning, the bell would clang again, thirty-three times, to coincide with the reopening of the city gates. The bell is still located in Jongno, inside the Bosingak bell pavilion.

But, of course, Seoul didn't exist in a vacuum, and Joseon artisans had been busy across Korea erecting structures, which included provincial walled towns, administrative centres, military compounds, fortresses, detached palaces, and Confucian academies. There were about 350 provincial walled towns, each with an administrative centre containing between forty and eighty buildings. There were about one hundred military compounds, each with scores of buildings. In all, there were more than four hundred different compounds containing, collectively, between 17,000 and 20,000 structures. Peter Bartholomew refers to this grand architecture as "monumental; well-designed and constructed to last many hundreds of years. Joseon architecture is unsurpassed in Asia," he told us. "It's significant, highly sophisticated, multi-layered and developed over two-thousand years."

But here's the tragedy: nearly all of these monumental Joseon structures, which just over a hundred years ago spread far and wide across the land, are now gone. The Japanese authorities engaged in the purposeful destruction, or mutilation beyond recognition, of virtually every Joseon-period secular compound of significance on the Korean peninsula, according to Peter. As many as 95 percent of the structures were destroyed by the Japanese, he added.

The colonizers also razed 85 percent of all of Gyeongbok Palace's buildings — more than three hundred of them — including its front south wall and its main gate (Gwanghwamun). The gate was rebuilt in its full monumental splendour in 2010.

Many priceless Korean treasures of obvious royal quality today appear in Japanese museums and private collections, owned by descendants of Japanese officials from the occupation period, reports Peter. And Shinichi Arai, a historian at Ibaraki University in Japan, who has studied his country's plundering of Korean cultural assets during colonization, has said that while many artifacts have been returned to Korea, there were still 67,000 known Korean pieces in Japan, though not all had been stolen.

During the occupation, the Japanese destroyed Joseon government buildings along Sejong Street south of Gyeongbok Palace and Japanese residences were erected in their place. Much of Seoul's wall, with its eight arched gates, was flattened by the colonizers between 1910 and 1919. They reduced Seoul's Deoksu Palace to less than a quarter of its original size. And in the 1930s, they converted Changgyeong Palace into a zoo and amusement park, demolishing all but five of the original buildings and levelling all its parks. In fact, Heju recalls visiting the Changgyeong zoo and amusement park as a child with her family in the 1970s, and it wasn't until 1983 that the animals and rides were relocated, and parts of the palace grounds restored.

But the Japanese were not solely responsible for Seoul's architectural losses. In 1945, Seoul began a period of vigorous expansion after liberation, bulldozing new thoroughfares through the rubble and hovels of the old city. As well, bombs dropped and artillery fired during the Korean War resulted in more destruction, and Korea's own government in the twentieth century razed parts of some palaces and traditional compounds in favour of modern development.

Since 1960, about 90 percent of Seoul's hanok have been destroyed, Peter said, and he has been opposing the Seoul government in court for years in an effort to stop developers knocking down the traditional houses: "There were somewhere around 250,000 hanok in the 1960s; now there are about three thousand left. Those are disappearing, too."

A hanok is uniquely Korean. It is constructed from natural materials: earth, rock, wood, and, earlier, straw. The walls and roof are a mixture of clay and wood. While commoners typically resided in simple mud or clay dwellings with earthen floors and a straw roof, the better-off resided in hanoks with flat granite-based foundations, with vertical wood beams inserted into the granite to form the frame of the house. Clay was then applied between the beams to form the walls. Narrow support beams formed the frame of the roof and a layer of clay was applied over this. The roof was finished off with baked tiles.

The roofs extended well over the buildings to create a covered walkway that provided shelter from summer monsoon rains and blocked out the heat of the sun. Wooden shutters or swinging doors allowed the summer breezes in. The buildings were situated so that a delicate lattice door faced away from the windward side; the units often positioned in an L shape to block out the gusts. Rural villages were typically built clustered along the V and crook of mountain bases, with the hill situated immediately north to block the cold winter winds blowing in from Siberia.

Soon after I arrived in Seoul in 1995, I was walking through the neighbourhood around Deoksu Palace — about a mile south of Gyeongbok Palace — and was pleasantly surprised to come upon a narrow alleyway abutted by dry, crumbling red clay hanok homes. On the wall that faced the laneway was a small opening that would have served as a window. I suspect people still lived in these utilitarian homes, but in keeping with Seoul's quest to modernize, I'm sure these hanok have since been razed.

It took time for foreigners arriving in the late 1800s to adapt to the hanok. When the first U.S. minister to Korea, Lucius Foote, came to Seoul in 1884, he purchased two old hanok from two members of the queen's Min clan for use as an embassy. The United States was the only country in Seoul then to use existing housing rather than build its own legation. (Washington deemed Korea unworthy of a new building). The U.S. legation's beamed ceiling was quite low, resulting in future minister Horace Allen, who was over six feet tall, to complain to Washington that when he stood with his hat on, it hit the beams.

Take off your hat when you go inside, was Washington's reply.

A hotel was a rarity in Seoul at that time, so when Americans visited Korea, they would reportedly request to stay at the U.S. legation. Even a guidebook published in Europe at the time listed "Guest House — American Legation," under "Seoul Hotels."

As Koreans' earning power increased in the 1970s and '80s, there was an inexorable decrease in the number of hanoks. In the *JoongAng Daily* newspaper, writer Ines Cho wistfully and poignantly summarized the plight of the traditional home:

> Decades before high-rise apartment buildings colonized the horizons of Koreans, what they called home was the hanok, a traditional Korean house, whose bluish-gray roof tiles spread like a sea of rippling waves across most of Seoul. These low-rise houses on a bed of stones were environmentally-built of pine, granite and clay. As society fast forwarded in a frenzy of democracy, however, they were considered embarrassingly backward with kitchens that used coal and wood, outdoor toilets without septic tanks and water pumps in the atrium that froze in winter. By the early 1980s, most homeowners had long abandoned hanok, happily settling for westernized living quarters.

When I arrived in Korea in June 1995, my English-language academy put me up for three months in a close cousin to the hanok, a yeogwan, or traditional country inn. It was located along a back lane next to the Cheonho-dong outdoor market, by the south shore of the Han River, near where I have lived for years in Myeongil-dong. The exterior of the yeogwan was surrounded with a low stone wall, and its heavy swinging wooden entrance doors led to an inner outdoor courtyard encompassed by rectangular four-sided wooden verandas. Along each veranda was a row of three or four rooms as narrow as jail cells and with paper-thin walls. At the entrance to each room was a lightweight paper-covered lattice sliding door. I estimated the yeogwan to be a century old.

The rooms weren't wide enough for a regular bed, so after I returned from my last class in the evening, I would unroll a well-padded mat, or *yo*, onto the yellow linoleum floor. I'd turn on the small, battered, old portable TV that sat on the low table and surf to *The Late Show with David Letterman* or *The Tonight Show with Jay Leno*, programs broadcast on the local United States Forces Korea network, picked up by the coat hanger antenna on the top of the TV.

Tucked in the far rear corner of the courtyard, was a threadbare and grubby communal bathroom and washroom with a pit-style squat toilet behind an old wooden door. Across from it, in a small barnyard-like shed, was the "bathing room." A single bare light bulb hung from the ceiling. In the room, I'd fill a big plastic tub with hot water, sit on a little plastic stool next to the bucket, and scoop water over myself, quite delighted to take a bath in the way they did in the nineteenth century. I would feel thoroughly refreshed and invigorated.

To wash my clothes on the weekends, I filled a big plastic bucket with water from a garden hose in the courtyard, threw the garments into the bucket, stomped on them with my feet, then rinsed and hung them up to dry on the clothes line. I recall my hands would turn red after wringing the water out of so many pieces of clothing.

The yeogwan owners were a delightful old couple, but I don't think that they had cleaned the unkempt, musty place since about 1950. But it was as close to nature as one could get in a city, shut off as the courtyard was from the outside world of rushing motorists and pedestrians; my own little private Shangri-La.

I'd wake late in the morning (my teaching job didn't begin until two o'clock) and open the sliding door, feeling the summer sunshine and a light breeze enter the room. Sadly, though, after several months, my academy transferred me to a cramped basement flat in Myeongil-dong, which I didn't like at all.

Afterward, if I was strolling through Cheonho-dong, I'd go past the old inn, recalling my time there. But a couple of years on, I was disappointed one day to find it gone, replaced with an ugly, boxy, nondescript three-storey townhouse unit. How sad. With a little elbow grease and some vision, it could have been refurbished into an appealing inn, testament to the city's traditional architecture and culture. Likely, its owners had been offered good money by developers to sell up. Unfortunately, money often wins out over heritage.

* * *

On Bugak Mountain, our tour guide permitted our group about thirty minutes to shoot photos and relax. There were two young armed ROK soldiers patrolling the peak, so Heju and I approached one, and I masqueraded as a newbie visitor to Seoul, and asked, *"Sillyehamnida, eodiiga bukjjokimnikka?"* ("Excuse me, could you please tell us which direction is north?")

We already knew which way was north, but during my years in Korea, I had been consistently gobsmacked when I asked for directions (a common occurrence during my first few years) and strangers would point in seemingly random directions. The soldier silently gazed north, then west, then south, and finally east. He scrunched his face in thought. Before he could offer a response, though, an older Korean hiker on a tour who was nearby and had overheard our question, announced in English: "Nam Mountain's south, over there. So north is the opposite way."

*Damn!*

We sauntered over to the second young soldier and asked him if he knew which way was west. He was silent at first, then glanced at his left hand, as if trying to get his bearings, then at his right hand. Finally, he correctly pointed west. Now, bear in mind that these are trained military men, and at a moment's notice could be put on high alert to respond to a possible threat from North Korea. Should the North ever foolishly decide to launch an attack, my main concern would not be if our ROK boys were prepared, but if they knew which direction to aim their weapons. If the entire ROK military was as unsure about directions as these two, and mistakenly aimed their missiles and rockets, say, west to China, South Korea could end up in a very sorry mess.

Our group trekked west down a steep set of stone steps along Bugak's west slope. Back at street level, we exited through a former minor gate, Jahamun, and walked east along the lush base of the mountain. We passed a statue of Captain Choi Gyushik, the officer shot by North Korean commandos in 1968. About two kilometres farther on, we arrived at the busy main street in front of Gyeongbok Palace. The distinct blue shale roof of the Blue House peeked up behind the palace.

During our extended tour of Seoul three weeks earlier, Heju and I had wandered north along the fashionable boulevard paralleling Gyeongbok's west wall. As we passed by the white multi-storey National Intelligence Service (NIS) building, we noticed a number of fit young men wearing dark pants and jackets and sporting earphones who were standing at set intervals along the street.

We arrived at a traffic circle at the rear of the palace that connects to a pedestrian-only street that runs in front of the Blue House. There were several agents standing or walking through the area, but on the corner of the traffic circle stood Korea's most beautiful female police officer. Probably in her late twenties, she surely thought me bonkers.

"She looks dry-cleaned," I whispered to Heju, of the immaculate woman.

Her police uniform comprised polished black shoes, black tapered pants, white collared shirt, blue tie, black jacket, and black police bonnet. Her face was absolutely creaseless and liberally awash with foundation and pale blush, her eyebrows penciled-in, her lips painted red, her long, shiny black hair held neatly in place in a bun with bobby pins under her hat. Her expression was frozen in a permanent wry Mona Lisa smile, as if moving a facial muscle might crease her mascara. She was so starched, crisp, and neat; I suspected she had been wearing the uniform when it was dry-cleaned. We left Ms. Police Officer South Korea and continued along the sidewalk to the east end of the palace, where we encountered Korea's second-most-beautifully-starched -policewoman, the twin of the original. Without a doubt, the hiring manager for Blue House security was male.

But this was three weeks earlier, and today, dusk upon us, Heju and I moved along in front of Gyeongbok Palace, with the street locked in rush-hour traffic, car horns beeping. Heju by this time was walking at a maddeningly slow pace.

"Come on, Heju. Why are you so slow today?" I grumbled.

"My legs ache," she replied in a desultory tone. "We walked *a lot* today."

I suppose we had — from Hanyang University subway to the rear of Bugak Mountain, along its ridge and to Gyeongbok Palace, a total of perhaps six kilometres. We arrived back at the motel in mid-evening, and Heju was soon asleep. She was exhausted.

Despite Seoul's rapid modernization, it is a marvellous city. It has a compelling, rugged beauty, the only city I'm aware of that within a fifteen-minute walk from its core one can be hiking one of several mountain trails and ridges. The Han River is striking, particularly during placid evenings when apartment lights from both shores glimmer off the mirror-like water's blackness. It's an exciting, crowded, bustling megatropolis that never sleeps. Seoul was the place to be in Korea in 1400. Six hundred years later, it still is.

* * *

The following afternoon we were downtown again, this time in Jongno at the Jogye Buddhist Temple, the same one we had seen on *World's Most Shocking Moments* while at the motel on Ganghwa Island. The temple is located off a quiet, handsome back street called Ujeongguk, which is lined with small upscale shops that sell an amazing variety of Buddhist paraphernalia.

On a bright, warm afternoon, we entered the grounds. The grand temple is set back. Constructed in 1910, Jogye is the only temple of the thousand or so in and around Seoul that is located in the centre of the city.

Its main hall (there didn't seem to be other Buddhist structures around) looked like one of those square modern "box" houses one would find in the suburbs and which takes up every inch of the property it sits on. Jogye Temple, of course, was infinitely grander and more aesthetically pleasing than that. It walls were lined with a series of immense wooden turquoise doors. Above these was a grand display of carved wood — the underside of an upturned, massive arched roof — also turquoise.

When we arrived, temple workers were busy stringing up thousands of candle lanterns in preparation for Buddha's birthday, which would be celebrated on May 19. People were coming and going from the temple.

There are approximately ten million Buddhists in Korea today. During national university entrance exams, mothers mass in front of Jogye Temple and other temples across the land, bowing and fervently praying for their sons' and daughters' exam success. In 2006, Jogye Temple was the site of a mass gathering of people, mostly women, who were being led in prayer by monks, all collectively willing the country to be selected to host the 2014 Winter Olympics. As it turned out, they were five years too early: South Korea won the right in 2011 to host the 2018 Games in Pyeongchang.

Heju and I weren't at Jogye, though, to pray for better grades or to bow to Buddha in the hope of qualifying for the 120-metre ski jump in 2018. No, we were here to inquire about the video we had seen on TV of the cherry picker that had tipped in 1999, sending the men inside plummeting to the ground. As we headed across the compound to the administrative centre, a trio of bald monks wearing light grey cloaks came toward us along the path. We stopped them, introduced ourselves, and asked them about the incident.

They looked back at us bemused. One cheekily joked, "Because we have so much energy, and because we're single and can't marry, we use our energy to fight. But only during days, since we have no wives to fight with at night."

*Good one, little grasshopper!*

We entered the building, which was headquarters for the Jogye sect of Korean Buddhism. The Jogye sect comprised the largest number of monks in Korea, and its website noted there are 3,298 Buddhist temples registered to Jogye in South Korea. When Japan colonized Korea in 1910, though, it brought with it its own Taego sect, which permitted monks to marry (Jogye monks could not). Taego is still a viable sect in Korea.

Standing in the lobby, we must have looked somewhat befuddled, because a monk soon approached us and spoke to us in excellent English. He told us he went by the name Venerable Jae-An, though the official title on his business card read Jogye Order of Korean Buddhism — Bureau of Missionary Activities — Deputy Director, Office of Lay Buddhist Affairs. Befitting such a grand title, Jae-An was charismatic and confident, and boyish despite his forty-one years.

We asked the Venerable One about the 1998–99 conflict. He told us that violence within the Buddhist sects was cyclical — one thousand years of peace followed by short periods of fighting, then another thousand years of peace and more fighting. I suppose Korea in the 1990s represented a brief interlude of pent-up monk frustration released after millennia of tranquility.

Jae-un obviously was sensitive to belabouring past Jogye issues, though later I was able to cobble together the narrative. The strife we saw on TV had been an escalation of a rivalry within Jogye apparently pitting one group of progressive monks against the entrenched monks, the latter controlling the organization's ample purse strings. When hundreds of riot police were summoned to headquarters to deal with the conflict, they were pelted with debris and projectiles from the senior monks holed up in the building. Six police officers were sent up in the cherry picker, which was not meant to hold so much weight. Overloaded, it overturned as they attempted to reach the upper floors. Luckily, none of the officers died in the accident. Hundreds of monks in the building were eventually arrested.

There had also been a bitter Taego-Jogye feud in past decades. When Heju and I hiked minor Acha Mountain, located across the Han River from Cheonho-dong in Seoul, several weeks earlier, we had spoken with the administrator at Younghwa Buddhist Temple. He recounted how, in the 1970s, Taego was in possession of the temple but Jogye wanted them out. There had been at least fifty clashes involving the two sects over the years, he told us. Sticks and clubs had been used, sending injured monks to hospitals. A court eventually ruled that Jogye could reside in the temple and the Taego monks were forced to depart.

Korean monks are not averse to battle. During the massive invasion by Japanese soldiers on Korean soil between 1592 and 1598, during the Imjin War, Korean monks were called upon to bravely fight against the invaders. Today, Taego and Jogye coexist in brotherly monk love.

"There are no more problems or fighting," Jae-An insisted proudly.

The conversation then somehow turned to my stomach. "It's too big, Mark!" Jae-An announced brightly, without a hint of malice or self consciousness. "You should meditate to lose fat. When I came here in 1992, I was fat and had big legs. But we had to kneel two hours a day. It was very painful, but I lost weight. Now I can kneel all day. Some of our monks can stay awake for twenty-one straight days."

*My stomach isn't that big*, I thought, as I sucked it in. Back in Canada, when I went into any mall, I saw many guys with huge bellies. But here in Korea I could count on one hand the number of obese citizens I've encountered during my years here. It's all relative.

I sidestepped the comment and asked why someone would want to stay awake for twenty-one days.

"For enlightenment," said Jae-An enthusiastically.

"What's enlightenment?"

"Your eyes become brighter, your skin becomes shinier, your body can fly," he announced.

But I was satisfied that my eyes and skin weren't bright and shiny, and that only in my dreams did I occasionally soar like a bird.

Jae-An then insisted that my calling was the monkhood. "You were a monk in your former life, Mark!" he declared with alarming certainty. "You're here today because it's your destiny. You need to live here with me. You can't work anymore. No more work, Mark!"

But I wasn't ready to be imprisoned at Jogye Temple. There was no way I could sit cross-legged for eight hours a day or bow to Buddha on sore, wobbly knees, or shave my head bald, or wear grey robes each and every day. I certainly wasn't ready to jettison my current lifestyle and freedom and commit to a life of monastic ascetics.

"But I need to work to earn money for retirement," I stammered weakly.

"No, your work's over," he insisted resolutely.

"Can I get back to you?" I squeaked.

The Venerable One nodded, and before he had a change of heart and ordered the monks who were veterans of the 1998–99 clashes to detain me, Heju and I scampered off the temple grounds and into the security of the secular world. I made a note not to visit Jogye Temple again.

# CHAPTER 7

The day after our visit to the temple, I took my solo tour to Panmunjeom and the Joint Security Area. Heju and I then spent the weekend relaxing at a Myeongil-dong motel in Seoul and playing some tennis. But there was a disquieting time when Heju disconsolately complained to me that she wasn't enjoying the trip and wanted to quit. We had only been on the road for two weeks. Late that afternoon, she strode off alone and headed downtown, returning about midnight. We didn't speak again on the topic.

On Monday, we headed to Incheon. We spent three days in the industrial, blue-collar port town. We ate noodles in black bean sauce (*jajangmeon*) at Incheon's surprisingly modest and quiet Chinatown, and we toured the Incheon Landing Memorial Museum, devoted to General Douglas MacArthur's surprise amphibious landing in September 1950, which turned the tide in the early stages of the Korean War in South Korea's favour. We embarked on a ferry cruise along the industrial waterfront, and were invited to the Incheon Coastguard headquarters on Yeongjong Island, where we spoke with the commander.

From Incheon, we headed east to Yongin, about fifty kilometres southeast of Seoul, and spent a fun but long and hot day at Everland

Resort theme park, Korea's version of Disneyland. We stayed that night not far from the park, at the pedestrian Everpark Motel in a nondescript little roadside area in Jondae-ri (*ri* means village) in Yongin County.

In the morning, which was already fabulously bright, we strolled across the street to the Seoun Fruit Market — a large, covered outdoor stall — to purvey some tasty fruit for breakfast. A short, wiry, man in his fifties, with a brush cut and a scar on his face, who seemed to be the owner, was sorting fruit. He looked Korean, but I couldn't help but notice that he had green eyes. Koreans don't normally have green eyes; theirs are uniformly brown or black. He was the only Korean I had ever seen whose eyes were green.

"You see his eyes?" I whispered to Heju, out of his earshot.

"Yah."

"He's Korean, right?" I asked for confirmation.

"Yeah," she said, nonplussed.

"Why does he have green eyes, then?"

"I don't know."

"Maybe one of his parents is Caucasian. Let's ask him!" I added enthusiastically

"I don't want to," she protested.

"Come on. How are we going to know if we don't ask? Just inquire real polite. Say 'Excuse me, sir, but I couldn't help notice your green eyes.'"

"It's not a good idea," she dissented, skeptically.

I admit that inquiring about the colour of a stranger's eyes isn't the most sensitive thing, but with a little tact and guile, it could be done innocuously. The man was still tending to the fruit when Heju approached. She spoke a few words to him in Korean. Immediately, his entire demeanour changed, his expression turning dark and angry. He spat out a litany of words at Heju that I didn't understand.

*"Sipal nahante mutjima! Sipal wae mulea? Sipal oneul jasu ombute-one!"* he spat. Then he turned his back to her.

"What did he say?" I asked Heju a few moments later. She replied stoically: "He said, 'Don't ask me that fucking question Why are you asking me that fucking question? You ruined my day with that fucking question,'" adding resignedly, "I told you we shouldn't have asked him."

Obviously not. But I'm still curious.

We drove east from Yongin toward the city of Icheon to visit the Chungkang College of Cultural Industries, where I worked as an English conversation teacher for two years between 1999 and 2001. I wanted to show Heju the campus.

We leisurely motored into the peaceful countryside and through an outlier of the broad green Charyeong mountain range, which branches off from its mother range, the Taebaeks.

Not far from Yongin, we spotted a small roadside sign that read, in English, A GROUP OF MONOLITHS AT SAAM-RI. THESE MONOLITHS DATE BACK TO THE NEW STONE OR BRONZE AGE.

If I wasn't mistaken, a monolith was a singular rock of noteworthy proportion, which had generally plunked down in the middle of nowhere, like massive Ayers Rock in Australia. We stopped the car on the side of the road and looked around for any sign of the monolith. It was deathly quiet.

"Do you see a big rock, Heju?" I asked, perplexed, scanning the immediate area.

"No."

"Me either."

We took a few steps along a dirt path toward the agricultural plots, and off to the side, hidden in low brush, we spotted a ridiculously puny and underwhelming pile of small rocks just over a metre tall.

"Is that the monolith?" Heju wondered, puzzled.

"It has to be. There're no other rocks around," I said, adding disparagingly, "It isn't a monolith — it's a little pile of rocks." (Note to the Korea Department of Road Sign Makers Who Alert Passersby to a Monolith: A few small rocks sitting atop each other Do NOT warrant a road sign!)

Just down the hill along the road, we came to a small, shallow reservoir lake called Saam-ji, where we laid out a blanket on the sandy shore under the warm and welcoming sun. It was blissfully quiet; the only sound being tiny waves lapping against the shore. The air was fresh and balmy, and a slight breeze moved across the lake. The view over the water was of the rolling green Charyeong Mountains.

My Canadian mind envisioned rowing a little boat around the shallow lake, or tootling around in a mini sunfish sailboat or even swimming. But, I had rarely seen a watercraft of any kind on any of the reservoir lakes I'd been to in Korea, though there are often a handful of silent and grumpy mid-aged guys sitting on the shore, lines and bobbers in the water, waiting patiently for a fish to bite.

Heju was lying on the blanket so reposed and relaxed that it appeared she might take up permanent residence along the shore. I tried striking up a conversation with her, but she sighed and pleaded: "Can't you stop talking for just a while? I just want to rest my brain, to have some peace and quiet."

"You're like my sister," I observed. "When she goes near the water, she just wants to sit and be at one with nature."

"Men and women are different," Heju said, philosophically. "I just want to have quiet now."

I gave Heju her peace and ate some of the dozen hard-boiled eggs we had bought earlier. I tried to simply sit still on the blanket, but had little success. I fidgeted. I wanted to swim or boat or move. So, I began talking again.

"Would you just sit still for five minutes and not talk," Heju stipulated. "I want peace of mind. That's always what I'm looking for."

After ninety minutes of uncomfortable waiting, I finally asked if we could get going

She was horizontal and blissfully relaxed. "I want to have a longer rest," she insisted.

"Heju, you slept last night. Come on. We need to go," I urged. We had places to go, things to do, people to meet.

She reluctantly acquiesced.

* * *

Chungkang College was basically how I had left it years earlier. The small campus buildings were located on the side of a mountain in a pretty wooded area in the middle of nowhere, about twelve kilometres west of the small but bustling Icheon City. Icheon is situated on a long plain, and the area is well-known for both its rice production and celadon ceramics. Just outside town the road is lined with pottery shops. The tradition of pottery-making in Icheon dates back a thousand years to the Goryeo period.

Below the campus's red-brick buildings, a series of rice paddies sit in a small valley bordered by steep hills. During my tenure at the college, I had stayed at a nearby *mimbak* (family home), just a short walk from the college through these very paddies. On dark spring evenings, I recall being serenaded by croaking frogs as I made my way home. The paddies were full of them. This small valley ends at the Jisan Ski Resort, a popular destination in winter. On the other side of the ridge is the Jisan Golf and Country Club.

Heju and I drove from the campus up the steep incline next to the ski hill. We willed the Scoupe — huffing and puffing like an old dying steam engine — up and over the crest of the hill, the golf club on the other side. We parked the car in the company of dozens of luxury cars. There were shiny Audis, Mercedes, and BMWs, and a few cars from Hyundai's premier lines of Equus and Granger, and from KIA's Opirus. Off to the side sat one dented old Hyundai Sonata. My Scoupe belonged next to it. "That one must belong to the greens keeper," I told Heju.

Inside the grand clubhouse an eager and polite young female clerk informed us that membership required a deposit of $300 million won (255,000 US dollars). Unfortunately, I had left my petty cash in the car, so decided I would join up another day.

In the *JoongAng Daily* I had once read an enlightening opinion piece written by a foreign corporate executive and avid golfer in Seoul named Mathew J. Deakin. He observed that business golf in Korea seemed designed to make everyone feel good about themselves, and apparently missed putts, penalty strokes, and shanked drives tended to be overlooked and not counted. Golfers were also not permitted to carry their golf bags; rather, carts — which seat four and are generously outfitted with drinks, coolers, balls, tees, markers, and first-aid kits — were mandatory to shuttle players around courses. The cost of joining a club in Korea could equal that of buying a house, he wrote, and just one day on the course could cost you up to a thousand US dollars. "The Scottish did not invent the game with the intention it would be only available to the richest people," Deakin wisely concluded.

In the dusk, we surveyed the par-four eighteenth green from outside the clubhouse. I counted nine strokes taken by a man in an approaching foursome before he sank his ball in the cup. This score, I figured, was justifiable punishment from the wrathful Golfing Gods for him having broken the unwritten cardinal rule that bright yellow cardigans are not to be worn on a golf course, anywhere.

Heju and I jumped back in the car and headed slowly back down the road past the ski resort. As we proceeded, Heju suddenly unbuckled her seatbelt.

"What are you doing?" I asked, puzzled.

"I'm getting ready to jump out if the brakes fail," she declared.

A huge and glorious orange-and-red sun was sinking in the west, painting the trees a vivid green as we drove southwest through the narrow green valleys of the Charyeong Mountains. We had the road to ourselves, and I enjoyed the decadence of motoring well below the speed limit, with no impatient drivers on my tail forcing me to speed up. Instead we were able to take in the alluring scenery. This was how Henry Ford intended driving to be, I thought.

"I love this slow driving," I announced contently.

"At least you're not swearing," Heju said, referring to my penchant for fiercely castigating careless and reckless drivers who dared navigate too close to the Scoupe. Only a few years ago there were about 10,000 Korean road fatalities annually. This rate had been reduced to about 6,000. But that's still about sixteen traffic deaths daily. I, for one, am adamantly opposed to being included in this sad list of statistics.

We were heading to Anseong County, to an area called Mirinae, and more specifically to the Mirinae Holy Site. During the four main religious purges of the 1800s, persecuted Catholics sought sanctuary there. It is also the burial spot of Korea's first Catholic priest, St. Andrew Daegon Kim, executed in 1846 at just twenty-four years old. By the time we arrived in the area, however, it was nearly dark, so we decided to get a motel for the night and visit the site next day.

Near Mirinae, in the rustic environs of Gosam, we discovered the secluded and isolated Hite Motel nestled along the far shore of a pretty finger lake, Gosam Reservoir. The motel owner was a kindly elderly gentleman who told us he had moved to the area from Seoul a few years back. There were never more than a few customers staying in the rooms at a time, he told us. Once we were in our room, which faced the water, he brought us complimentary bowls of rice. How's that for service!

Bright sunshine pouring through the gauzy curtains on the large window roused us from sleep at about six in the morning. Heju got up, stood in the middle of the room, and peered around with a puzzled look on her face.

"What direction's the bed facing?" she asked me accusingly.

"I don't know?" I stammered, because Heju seemed poised to deliver a possible censure.

"I didn't sleep well," she said sourly, as if it was my fault.

She took the compass from my waist pack on the bedside table, held it up, and aligned the needle to north.

"This bed's north–south," she concluded loudly and disagreeably. "That's why my body's stiff. I always need to sleep west–east. Tonight I'm going to sleep on the floor facing east–west. I don't want my head to face north again!" A few moments later, she added worriedly, "I feel like I have a blood clot. Too bad the bed isn't west–east."

Obviously, the stress of the trip had been affecting Heju negatively. I hoped she could hold out for another two months. I didn't think she was quite yet ready for a white-padded room. I put on an eye mask to resume my sleep, unencumbered as to whether the bed faced north-south or east-west or even toward purgatory. The direction my bed faced didn't make a difference to me.

In late morning, we departed, and as we drove along Gosam Reservoir, we passed a small shop with six armchairs out front. Each was occupied, and the three elderly men and three elderly women were looking out at the water. The scene reminded me of the 1960s television series *Andy of Mayberry.*

The day was hot and muggy, and the sky was white and hazy as we headed toward the Mirinae Holy Site. Near Misan village, we turned onto a narrow country road, which came to a dead end at a narrow dell. On the far side of the dell stood a most incongruous edifice — a tall angled modern glass and steel building more resembling a pyramid than a church: Trump Tower meets Appalachian Trail. We parked in a lot among scores of other cars and walked across the grass to the church. It was Sunday, and the two o'clock worship service was just beginning.

Inside, the church was wonderfully cool, and it was a relief to be out of the blazing heat. It was about a quarter full, and we took a seat in one of the pews near the front. The interior was spacious, the soaring ceiling lined with chandeliers. The white walls were trimmed with wood, and stained-glass windows adorned the front wall, while high windows lined each side. Large red-brick pillars ran the length of the building. The interior was beautiful.

In the pew behind us, two young boys were fast asleep, heads on their mother's knee. The mom's head was tilted back, eyes closed, mouth agape. I scanned the congregation, and many parishioners were seemingly comatose, eyes closed. We listened to the priest as he gave his sermon, in Korean of course, and at its conclusion, he said to the congregation: "This is a big property," referring to the twelve acres bought by a Catholic organization in 1976. "It takes lots of money for upkeep. The church is poor; it doesn't have enough money. People don't offer much money. Please give generously for the offering."

Row by row, parishioners walked up to the front to deposit money into a wooden box. When it was our row's time to head up, I paused at the box to carefully scrutinize how much my neighbours tithed. The woman sitting on my left dropped in two thousand won. The lady on our right gave four thousand won. No wonder the church suffered from a paucity of funds. Heju inserted three thousand won. I put in one thousand won, though when the cost of the pen I inadvertently pilfered from the pew was subtracted — God have mercy on my soul — my offering was probably closer to fifty cents.

After the service, Heju gave me the gist of the priest's sermon. "He said, 'I was poor as a kid. Look at my face … I didn't get enough vitamins or nutrients, it's not healthy. But look at your faces … they're healthy. Nowadays, people rush and use computers and are busy making money. People ask themselves, "Do I have more money than my neighbour?" But look at Andrew Taegon Kim. He died young. His life was very short, but he was always with God.'"

After the service, Heju and I ascended the stairs to the second level, where there were several exhibits showcasing a collection of torture devices used against Korean Catholics in the 1800s. There was a six-pronged club and a solid oak paddle with which to inflict beatings. A thick "rope saw" would be rapidly pulled back and forth until the flesh ripped. "Scissors" were two wooden poles inserted between knees and twisted until bones broke. Beheading by sword was the ultimate punishment, and there was a plaque in commemoration of three French priests, Bishop Laurent-Marie-Joseph Imbert and Reverends Pierre-Philibert Maubant and Jacques-Honoré Chastan, who had been beheaded at Saenamteo in Seoul on September 21, 1839.

Today there are about forty locations throughout Korea where homage is paid to martyred Catholics. Some sites have a chapel and memorials; others simply a memorial stone, outdoor altar, or simple grave. Masses are celebrated at some shrines, often weekly, and sometimes daily. Mirinae seemed to get a fair number of visitors: we were told two thousand that day, a Sunday, and 1,500 the day before.

Back outside, we strolled to the far end of the grounds to a small memorial chapel where a few people were waiting to be blessed by a Korean priest. When Heju and I came in front of the priest, he had in his hand what looked like a small piece of musical reed. It was said to be part of Andrew Taegon Kim's toe bone. Heju had once attended Saenamteo Catholic Church in Yongsan, close to where Catholics were executed on the Han River. She told me that by the church pulpit were tiny bone fragments on display of the executed French priests. After Father Kim was killed in 1846, the state wouldn't permit his followers to perform a funeral. Several fellow Catholics, including Vincentius Lee Min-sik, clandestinely and bravely carried Kim's body the sixty kilometres from Seoul to Mirinae to bury it.

Interred here also is Kim's mother and the French Bishop Jean Ferreol, who ordained Kim in Shanghai and requested to be buried next to his student. In 1984, Pope John Paul II visited Korea to commemorate two hundred years of Catholicism in the nation, and to canonize 103 Korean martyrs, including Saint Kim. It was the first canonization outside of Rome's St. Peter's Basilica since the Avignon Papacy in the 1300s.

Not being religious, this was not a seminal moment for me. But Heju, who remained quiet, viewed it with a sense of gravitas.

* * *

Somewhere south of Mirinae, in Anseong County's bucolic countryside was our next destination: Hanawon Center, or, officially, The Settlement Support Center for North Korean Refugees.

Hanawon was established by the South Korean intelligence agency, the NIS, in 1999, to help make the transition easier for newly arrived North Korean defectors. When a defector enters South Korea, he or she first undergoes an intensive one-month interrogation by the NIS, meant to weed out possible spies. Then they are required to spend a mandatory three months at the centre undergoing orientation. They receive medical and dental care, fifty hours of counselling, 135 hours of classes schooling them on the ins and outs of their new country, and nearly two hundred hours of vocational training to learn, among other things, baking and computer or automobile repair skills.

I read in an *International Herald Tribune* article that defectors are also taught how to use ATM machines, how not to get conned by online connivers, and how to use flush toilets. The latter is a supposed rare commode … *sorry*, commodity, in the North. During the first decade of operation, 14,247 defectors went through Hanawon. In 2009, 2,929 defectors arrived in South Korea. In 2012, there were 1,509.

Understandably, the South government isn't keen for members of the public to be snooping around the centre; but for a nosy marauding quasi-journalist like me, it was a must-see. Not surprisingly, its address wasn't readily available in the Korean Yellow Pages or on Google. Thus, we were motoring around in the middle of these rural backwoods of God-knows-where, hoping by serendipity, more than anything else, that we were in the right general area.

At one point, we pulled in to a gas station — the only man-made structure for miles around — and asked the attendant if he knew where Hanawon was.

"Just along this road and turn right," he told us.

Serendipity!

We turned onto a lonely country road, and almost immediately came to a tall red-brick wall that ran along the road and up the side of the rather steep and wooded slope. We could make out several red-brick buildings inside the large grounds.

We stopped by the front gate, got out of the car, and approached the guard office. Heju explained to the guard on duty that I was writing a travel book on Korea and would like to include Hanawon Center in it. "Is there anyone we can talk to?" she inquired politely.

The guard got on his phone, spoke to someone briefly, then hung up. About ten minutes later, a man approached us from the compound.

"Can I help you?" he asked in English. He was looking around and over his shoulder, and eyed me suspiciously. He seemed fidgety and tense, like he had just downed ten cups of coffee.

I explained the reason for our visit.

"Well, I really appreciate you visiting and your interest," he continued in English, "but I can't tell you much. We're under Blue House and National Security rules. We don't want to cause problems between North and South Korea. North spies can find these people. It would be dangerous for their relatives back home."

What he meant was that North spies in the South attempt to identify defectors here, then send the information back to the North, where a defector's relatives have been punished and sent to gulags. Of forty-nine North spies uncovered between 2003 and 2013 in the South, twenty-one had arrived under the guise of defector.

"I understand," I acknowledged politely. "But would it be okay if I asked you a few questions?"

He hesitated, but agreed. Suddenly, his gaze narrowed as he looked at the front of my shirt. Underneath it ran a wire from my mini digital recorder in my pant pocket up to the tiny microphone under my top shirt button. I used the recorder to ensure I had a verbal transcription of important dialogue spoken in Korean during the trip. "Are you recording this?" he asked tersely.

"Yes," I admitted. "I tape all conversations for the book."

"You need to turn it off," he ordered. He was obviously a trained professional, the only person I talked to the entire trip so far who had noticed the microphone.

I complied, then extracted a notebook and pen from my waist pack.

"Are you going to write about this?" he inquired, looking worried.

"Yes."

"Don't write my name. Don't write this for a newspaper or magazine."

"Okay," I agreed. My book wasn't a newspaper or a magazine. "How are defectors treated in South Korea?" I continued.

"Lots of people treat them like aliens. But they're just ordinary people."

"Do they adapt well to life in the South?"

"Ninety percent say they're 'worried' about life here. Kids adapt faster than adults."

"What's the hardest part for defectors?" I continued, rapid-fire. I knew he wasn't relishing talking to me.

"For everyone who goes through a new culture, it takes time to adapt. It's the same for North Koreans in the South."

Defectors arrive from a rigidly controlled state where they're not encouraged to think for themselves. After three months of structured daily routine at Hanawon, however, they are let loose, often choosing to live in hectic Seoul, where they are suddenly required to make scores of decisions every day.

As well, the South Korean public does not always view defectors positively. Northerners can be conspicuous in the South. For one, there are linguistic differences. While both sides understand each other, and Korean sentence structure and basic vocabulary have remained the same since separation, speech in the South has long been peppered with "Konglish" — English words altered to fit Korean vernacular, such as *air con*, *eye shopping*, *choco*, and *apart* (for apartment). The North, however, jettisoned from their language all words of foreign origin and created new Korean ones in their place. For example, the English word *doughnut* is commonly heard in the South, while in the North, a Korean word meaning "ring-shaped bread" is used to describe the dessert. *Chandelier* is another word spoken here; but a Korean word equating to "cluster of light bulbs" is used north of the border. Northerners commonly respond using *Ilupsopneda*, meaning "not much," when answering the question "How are you doing?" But the response means "mind your own business" in the South. Here, *Mije* translates to "Made in the U.S.A," but it denotes "American imperialist" up North. Pyongyang opened its first fast-food restaurant in 2009, and instead of using the word *hamburger* on the menu, they list the sandwich as a Korean word meaning "minced beef on bread."

South Koreans find the aggressive tone of their northern brothers to be harsh, even pugilistic, though defectors describe their southern neighbours' intonation as soft and polite, which is saying something. Often when I hear South Koreans conversing, I think they're close to coming to blows; to me, their tone sounds confrontational. Yet, it's just their way of loudly and boldly interacting.

The Hanawon official asked me once again, "You sure you're not going to write about this for a newspaper or write a political piece?"

"I'm sure," I promised.

"Don't write my name."

"I won't."

He then abruptly announced he had no more time, said goodbye, and turned and walked back through the gate and into the facility.

I understood his reticence. The North means business when it comes to punishing the relatives of defectors. There are at least six gulags in which an estimated 150,000-plus political prisoners languish at any one time. According to both defectors and a report by the U.S. State Department on Human Rights, many inmates are held in ghastly, inhumane conditions, often with little chance of ever being released.

A memoir, the first eyewitness account of the concentration camps, was published in 2000. *The Aquariums of Pyongyang: Ten Years in the North Korean Gulag* was written by a defector, Kang Chol-hwan (with French journalist Pierre Rigoulot). Kang was imprisoned in 1977 along with his family at the notorious Yodok Camp in the remote mountains about 120 kilometres northeast of Pyongyang. He was only nine years old at the time. And the family's crime? Kang's grandfather had been accused of being an agent for the Japanese. The entire family was dragged off to the gulag.

Kang watched as his grandmother, mother, and sister died from starvation at the camp. He witnessed hundreds of other deaths as well, from starvation, beatings, neglect, disease, the elements, and execution. Prisoners worked outdoors up to seventeen hours a day. Hunger was a constant, and worms, frogs, salamanders, and rodents caught in fields and forests by inmates were eaten as a matter of survival. The winters were bitterly cold, yet prisoners were only provided with meagre clothing, mere rags really.

Once young inmates reached their teenage years, they were required to attend the execution of prisoners who had attempted to escape.

Seventy-six percent of defectors say they have witnessed executions. The state typically publically executes "criminals." Kang witnessed fifteen executions during his time at Yodok.

In his book, Kang wrote:

> The whole camp walked to a bend in a river and sat in front of a huge boulder. Farther away was a small flatbed truck containing the condemned man. He was screaming, "You Bastards! I'm innocent!" Then there was silence. The guards pulled him from the truck to the big boulder in front of the crowd. He was mere skin and bones, his hair wild, with bruises, crusts of dried blood and bulging eyes, that he resembled an animal. The man's mouth was full of stones: the guards had crammed them in to stop him from yelling. He was tied to a post at eye, chest, and waist levels. From 5-metres; the first volley of shots killed him, cutting the top rope. The second volley sliced the chest rope. The final one cut the lower rope. The corpse fell forward into the pre-dug pit.

Kang was released from Yodok in 1987, at the age of nineteen. Four years later, still in the North, he re-established contact with a friend, Yong-mo, whom he had met at the camp, but whose family had been released in 1983. "In the spring of 1991, Yong-mo's father was accused of criticizing Kim Jong-il, and the whole family was sent back to the camp," wrote Kang. The following year, Kang made his escape from North Korea, crossing the Yalu River into China, then on to South Korea. When former U.S. president George W. Bush read *The Aquariums of Pyongyang*, he reportedly asked to speak with Kang. In 2005, Kang met President Bush at the White House. The 2012 Asian edition of *Time* magazine lauded Kang as a hero. Today, he is employed as a journalist in Seoul at the *Chosun Ilbo* (daily), a major newspaper.

* * *

With the sun setting, Heju and I stood in front of Hanawon Center wondering what to do next. We weren't about to give up on our investigation quite so easily. Across the road from the centre, in a narrow crook in the hills, a series of multi-terraced rice paddies stretched far back. We drove along a concrete lane that branched off the main road alongside the paddies. Half a kilometre back, by the tiny hamlet of Samjuk — comprised of several small dwellings — we parked the car. I took out my binoculars and scanned Hanawon. From this distance, I could see the entire layout, including the outer walls that reached up the sides of the hill, the facility, and a camouflaged guard tower in the woods.

Then, suddenly, what looked to be hundreds of North Koreans started streaming out of the buildings. The women were wearing red sweaters with white stripes and black track pants with red stripes. The men had on white shirts and black pants (Koreans love uniforms). It was six thirty p.m. — dinnertime, I surmised.

Heju and I were startled when two village grandmothers quietly walked up behind us. We were on edge, which was to be expected, considering our covert spy mission. It wasn't everyday that two average citizens such as Heju and me embarked on such a dangerous, high-stakes game of international espionage. The women told us that defectors' kids sometimes studied at the Samjuk Elementary School. They had never seen North adults in the village, though.

Our cover blown we had no choice but to terminate the operation, so we quickly retraced our route along the lane to the main road and motored away from Hanawon. I don't know the name of the nondescript little roadside outpost that we stopped in twenty minutes later, and I didn't particularly want to know. We took a room in the motel, and I immediately locked the door behind us and drew the curtains.

"Let's eat in tonight," I said, which we usually did anyway. We were on high-alert. Our dinner consisted of cans of corn and tuna, which I had in the car. We couldn't chance being seen, I vowed; North spies likely had detected us at Hanawon. At this precise moment, they might be planning the entirely unnecessary and sad demise of some in-over-their-heads greenhorns: Heju and me.

# CHAPTER 8

Eumseong should be well-known to most Koreans; it is the hometown of South Korea's second-most internationally renowned citizen (after Psy of "Gangnam Style" fame, of course), Ban Ki-moon, who was named Secretary-General of the United Nations in 2006, the first Korean to hold the lofty position.

Ban Ki-moon was born and spent his early years in Eumseong, in the province of North Chungcheong. When Ban was designated to succeed Kofi Annan in October 2006, there was much joy in his hometown and throughout the province, and about fifty thousand citizens filled a soccer stadium in the neighbouring city of Chungju to celebrate. The Korean media has trumpeted Ban's impressive rise from poor, humble country boy — trundling ten kilometres back and forth from home to school each day — to his current position.

The *International Herald Tribune ran* a feature on Ban's birth place, a tiny village near Eumseong called Haengchi. Some locals insist that Bodeok Mountain, located immediately behind the village, is of such immaculate geomantic symmetry that its feng shui proprieties played no small role in catapulting Ban into the UN secretary general's job. The article said that some days busloads of Koreans from across the country arrive at the base of the mountain to absorb the positive Earth rays in an attempt to receive the same good fortune the eminence bestowed upon the likable Ban.

Haengchi and Eumseong were on our itinerary, and I was envisioning a two-for-one deal: receiving scuttlebutt on Ban Ki-moon from fellow villagers and eternal success and prosperity from Mount Bodeok's providence. In fact, we had already been blessed with welcome karma the night before, and this morning had woken up … alive. North Korean spies hadn't found us, poisoned us, dissolved us in sulfuric acid, or forced us to watch endless video footage of monotonous Kim Jung-un speeches.

We had spent most of the day in the small city of Gwangju north of Yongin, and around Yongin, visiting two places of interest. Now early evening, we headed toward Eumseong. It was April 30, and Heju and I had spent the last three weeks on the road tootling through Gyeonggi Province. We had been through Ganghwa Island, Suwon, Uiwang, Seoul, Panmunjeom, Incheon, Yongin, Icheon, Mirinae, Anseong and Gwangju. I had nothing against Gyeonggi. But eight more unexplored provinces lay ahead. We needed to make haste.

"At this rate, it'll take a year, not four months, to finish the trip," I said, sighing, as we left Yongin. The amount of territory we still needed to cover seemed daunting.

Heju answered, skeptically, "We'll never finish on time."

I could feel her pain.

* * *

As the crow flies, Eumseong is only seventy kilometres southeast of Yongin. But the tentacles of the Charyeong Mountains spread around and below us. There is no such thing as a straight-line route here. We travelled from Gyeonggi Province on multiple zigzagging country roads and finally found ourselves on Highway 37 — a lovely smooth roadway passing through remote hills covered in abundant forests — on the final leg to Eumseong.

I have no idea why this province is referred to as "North." It's essentially east, not north, of its sister province, South Chungcheong. Korean cartographers named them thusly when the province was split into two in 1894. In the decades since, no one in government seemed to have had the desire to rectify the miscalculation. North Chungcheong is the only landlocked province in the country, and has just 1.5 million people, a paltry number when compared to Gyeonggi's 25 million (when you include Seoul and Incheon).

We arrived in Eumseong at nightfall, the town located on a small narrow plain surrounded by mountain ridges belonging to the Charyeong range. In the distance, on the far side of the plain was a high ridge, from where a slim shaft of bright whie light pierced the darkness like a laser beam. When we stopped at a local Nonghyup Mart to load up on our daily ration of bread, sliced ham, processed cheese, fruit, and orange juice, we asked the young woman behind the counter what the light was.

"It's from the Buddha Temple on Gaseop Mountain," she told us, referring to the mountain that rises up over seven hundred metres.

We asked if she could point us in the direction of Haengchi, Ban's birthplace.

She didn't know where it was, and neither did her two fellow employees. I had wrongly assumed that every Eumseong-ite would be familiar with Haengchi. We decided to call it a night, and checked into a motel nearby.

* * *

The following day was absolutely miserable, with rain pouring down in bucketfuls from skies blanketed by low dark, leaden clouds. It wouldn't be fun being outdoors in this lousy weather, so we opted for a languorous off-day, staying indoors, relaxing, and catching up on reading and a little TV. I busied myself sorting through innumerable copies of unread *Korea Times*, *Korea Herald*, and *IHT* newspapers, scouring for articles on some unusual place or thing that I may have missed and was worth visiting on the trip, though after an hour or so I felt daunted by the prospect of actually clipping them all and gave up. For lunch, Heju and I dined on donkkaseu (fried pork cutlet) and strawberries.

Later in the afternoon, with the rain easing up, Heju went out for a stroll. I stayed in the room and resumed clipping articles. It was a slow day.

* * *

Late the next morning, we drove into town along a street lined with weathered shops. The rain had stopped, though it was still grey. Eumseong seemed a dowdy and sleepy place, small enough that one could drive from one end of town to the other in less than ten minutes, yet large enough that the other citizen wouldn't know your personal business. Even its drivers seemed to navigate with uncharacteristic circumspection. On the edge of town, next to a small park where scores of old-timers were playing a sort of lawn bowling game on dirt, we stopped at an outdoor market. I love outdoor markets — their prices are lower than regular retailers, and the stalls and booths are vibrant and visually interesting.

The first vendor we came to had three dozen bird cages spread out along the sidewalk, with all kinds of colourful birds. The air was filled with a pleasant cacophony of chirps and cheeps.

"The Birdman of Eumseong," I joked to Heju. She didn't get the reference.

Birdman told us this market was held in Eumseong every fifth day — the 2nd, 7th, 12th, 17th, 22nd, and 27th day of each month. We were lucky to be there on May 2. He then told us he travelled to a different location every day. The next day the market would be in Wonju, a moderate-size city about sixty kilometres northeast; the day after, in Jochiwon, sixty kilometres southwest; and the following day in Geumwang, a town just north of Eumseong. It was like being in a travelling circus, I thought.

In 1902, the future British bishop of Korea, Mark Trollope, described Ganghwa town's open public market, its days coincidently falling on the same days as the present-day Eumseong Market: Ganghwa Market "draws country folk by the thousand from every corner of Ganghwa itself, as well as from neighbouring islands and mainland." The Eumseong Market has been ongoing for about six hundred years. In days long past, the peddlers would convey their goods by trekking from town to town with *jigae*, wooden A-frames, on their backs.

"Do you sell many birds?" we asked.

"Some days good, some days bad," he replied tersely. (Today was probably a bad day).

Farther along the sidewalk and in a sort of alleyway were the market's stalls and peddlers. At one, an ajumma was selling husky-type dogs out of a large cardboard box. We talked with her, and wondered if the dogs were given the opportunity to exercise. Sitting on a stool, she replied in a surly tone, "Of course they do! All my dogs exercise with me every morning." Judging from her stout physique, though, I doubted she had done much physical activity since high school. Then she rebuked me. "Don't ask so many questions!"

Nearby were more cages: two containing a total of six husky-type dogs. Sixteen small dogs were confined to a three-by-two-foot cage. Barely able to move, they lay atop each other and slept. Twelve shivering rabbits were scrunched in a two-by-one-and-a half-foot cage.

"Why are they shivering?" we asked the owner. It was a sweltering thirty degrees outside.

"They're scared," she said.

I didn't like this aspect of the market at all.

In a big cardboard box were scores of chirping ducks, chickens, roosters, and geese, and the pungent stench of their feces and urine pierced the hot, humid air. We strolled along the alley past stalls offering plants, dried fish, clothing, spices, cookware, and ginseng for sale.

We chatted for a while to a loquacious man who was selling a variety of hats. Mr. Eum Doo-hyun was upbeat and spoke English. During his mandatory two-year ROK military service as a young man, he was assigned to KATUSA (Korean Augmentation to the United States Army), in which Korean soldiers are stationed at U.S. bases in the country to assist American soldiers (the ratio is about one KATUSA to every ten Americans). Mr. Eum sang the praises of the U.S. military's presence in South Korea since 1945. "If the U.S hadn't helped Korea, we wouldn't have gotten our independence from the North," he insisted. "Older Koreans who went through the Korean War, they thank America. But the younger generation didn't experience the war. They don't know about it," he said, referring to the fact that the U.S. presence in Korea is sometimes viewed resentfully by the young.

Mr. Eum said he had been working at this market for thirty years. Prior to that he had painted wooden marquees at movie theatres. "In the

1970s, though, cinemas switched from painted signs to posters, and I lost my job," he told us.

His surname, Eum, was a rare one in Korea, and I had not heard it before. While there are about ten million Kims, four million Parks, and seven million Lees in Korea, there are still 286 different surnames. Hence, Koreans often identify themselves by the birthplace of their forefathers. Ban Ki-moon, for example, is an Eumseong Ban. Heju is a Gyeongju-Kim. There are said to be 4,170 places of origin in Korea.

"I guess my name originated about six or seven hundred years ago, about the time the Eumseong Market did," Mr. Eum told us, adding, "Maybe my name came from the 'Eum' in Eumseong?"

Sadly, outdoor market numbers are in decline. In 2005, there were 1,660 across the peninsula. By 2010, just 1,517 remained. The decrease seems to correlate with the surfeit of mega discount supermarket and department store chains that began popping up across the country in the 1990s and are today hugely popular with shoppers. When new subdivisions of apartment complexes are developed in Seoul and other towns and cities around the country, a location for outdoor markets are usually not included in the plans.

"Business isn't so good," lamented Mr. Eum. "Politicians don't want outdoor markets anymore."

Well, I loved them. In Myeongil-dong, in Seoul, I was a regular at the market, and also at the nearby Godeok Market, where I'd load up on chicken, fish, beef, and kilograms of fruits and vegetables in season.

As we conversed with Mr. Eum, a frail, severely hunchbacked woman resolutely pushed a rickety old pushcart full of cardboard past us. It wasn't unusual to see elderly women such as her in these rural areas, the curvature of their spines a result of decades of backbreaking labour spent bent over crops.

Mr. Eum watched the woman pass, and remarked with a sigh, "We're the eleventh-richest country in the world, but compared to the U.S., we're so far behind."

We bid goodbye to Mr. Eum and drove off to try to find Haengchi. As we passed the Eumseong Post Office building in the middle of town, we noticed a handful of post office employees in the rear parking lot kneeling and bowing on a mat with bowls of food that had been placed next to what appeared to us to be a new postal delivery truck.

"What are they doing?" I asked Heju, puzzled.

"They're blessing the truck so it'll be safe to drive. It's an old custom in Korea," she explained.

"Wouldn't it be safer to just drive slowly instead of praying?" I replied skeptically, shaking my head.

A few kilometres southwest of town, we stopped at a gas station to ask for directions to Haengchi. The fellow pointed us in the right direction and soon, in a corridor of agricultural land dotted with hills, we pulled into a bumpy concrete lane that ran parallel to the road, a high green ridge rising steeply beside it. There were a small number of country dwellings and farm sheds along the lane.

A solitary woman sauntered slowly along the lane. "Excuse me!" Heju called through our open window. "Is this the way to Ban Ki-moon's house?"

The woman turned, her expression severe, and muttered, "Up ahead."

We were in Haengchi! I inquired of the woman, *"San, aisa feng shui joahamanida?"* (Do you get good feng shui from the mountain?).

She stared back at me as if I was demented, and commanded darkly, "Just follow the road," before striding off.

A short distance along, the lane came to a dead end at a house and a couple of farm sheds that stood next to dusty plots of earth where red peppers, tobacco, and rice were growing. Haengchi seemed to have seen better days. It was very quiet and still, and there was not a soul around. We stared up at the steep, imposing ridge directly behind the little hamlet. The ridge line was strikingly even and symmetrical. "It's the shape of a bird spreading its wings," Heju said admiringly of Mount Bodeok, the feng shui–fortuitous mountain described in the *IHT* article.

"But where are the visitors and buses?" I wondered aloud, a bit crestfallen. "The article said lots of visitors came here." I had been expecting to see an army of Bohemian-type Earth people, arms reaching toward the mountain to absorb the intangible rays of prosperity that had catapulted Ban Ki-moon from country lad to the UN's top gun.

Suddenly, a man appeared from behind one of the sheds near us. We tried conversing with him, but he uttered only one or two words at a time and mostly stared silently and intently at us. Shortly after, a group of about a dozen men came walking toward us along the lane. We exchanged salutations and asked if any of them knew if anyone in the village belonged to Ban Ki-moon's family. This made the fellows chuckle. Grinning, one announced brightly, "We're Ki-moon's family! We're his second cousins!"

*Well, hallelujah! The mountain's feng shui really did work!*

One of the men, whose name was Ban Ki-jong, said, "My father's the twin brother of Ban Ki-moon's father."

The men lived in Eumseong, but were in Haengchi for a family meeting. Only twenty residents lived in Haengchi now, they said, down from fifty when Ban Ki-moon was a boy here; and yes, it was true that the village's residents were bothered by all the visitors who showed up here to experience "Banmania." The Ban men were very engaging, well-spoken, and intelligent. Real gentlemen. It wasn't difficult to deduct Ban Ki-moon was of the same solid pedigree. They told us that the man we had met a few minutes earlier was also a Ban, though he had been struck with polio as a child, and it had affected his mind.

Korean newspapers are fond of mentioning how Ban walked ten kilometres back and forth to school every day as a kid. I politely asked if that statement was accurate. The men grinned, and one confessed, "Well, maybe closer to three or four kilometres."

One of the Ban men provided us with a brief history of their famous cousin. Ban Ki-moon was born in 1944 in Haengchi, the eldest of six children. When the Korean War broke out in 1950, his family fled to the nearby hills, then later resettled in Eumseong, and then Chungju, thirty kilometres east, when he was about nine. The family was poor, but highly intelligent. His father had been a top student. His grandmother was a herbal doctor. One uncle attended nearby Cheongju University (at a time when few Koreans had the opportunity to ascend past secondary school); another was a town vice-mayor. Ban was a diligent, ambitious student. To assist him in learning English, his mother took him to a local American fertilizer company so he could converse with native English speakers. At eighteen, he won an English-language speech contest sponsored by the American Red Cross. His prize was a meeting with John F. Kennedy at the White House, where he informed the president he wanted to be a diplomat.

Ban attended prestigious Seoul National University, then went on to Harvard, where he earned a master's degree. Back in Seoul, he entered the diplomatic corps in the 1970s and moved quickly up the ladder, with postings in India, Austria, and the United States. In the 1990s, he was named assistant foreign minister, and in 2004 he was appointed South Korea's foreign minister. A Korean journalist who covered the Ministry of Foreign Affairs in the 1980s remembered Ban well. Politicians then tended to bask in their celebrity and accomplishments, she wrote, but Ban kept a low profile, had a mild manner, and spoke softly. However, Ban has said that people should not misconstrue his Asian modesty for a lack of grit and toughness.

The men remembered that after their cousin was given the position of Secretary General, he visited Haengchi accompanied by his assistants, staff, and members of the press. "We met him in Haengchi. But he only had time to shake our hands and say hello," said Ban Ki-jong. "He had lots of people with him."

Even Ban's mother, who lives in Chungju, wasn't exempt from her son's celebrity, they added. She moved to her daughter's house, then to a temple, in an attempt to evade Ban's fans. "Lots of people wanted to touch her hands, to receive good luck and energy from her," one of the men explained, adding that Haengchi's few residents were bothered by the curious visitors, receiving upwards of three hundred daily during holidays.

Yes, Mount Bodeok, in their opinion, did emit positive energy, but that wasn't the reason for Ban's ascension. "Only every one hundred years does someone like Ban Ki-moon come along," one stated. They were immensely proud of their cousin.

And what was Ban Ki-moon like, we wondered. Well, a regular fellow: he enjoyed spending time with his family and having a few drinks with his pals.

The men departed to attend their meeting, and we strolled to the base of Mount Bodeok, where landscaped grounds contained a series of low burial mounds, each with a low marble platform. As we walked among the graves, we counted seventeen rows of mounds. There were 131 graves in all. On one gravestone was the name of the first Ban buried here, back in 1643. The first had arrived in Korea from China around the 1600s, the men had told us. Ban Ki-moon was an eleventh-generation Ban, they added. There are only about four thousand Bans in Korea today.

Despite standing directly on Mount Bodeok — a feng shui Holy Grail — we couldn't feel any discernible manifestations, tangible or intangible. I for one was not yet convinced that life-changing energy could be derived from mountains.

* * *

We departed Haengchi and headed southwest toward the next city over, Jincheon. As we drove, a beautiful sunset was just beginning — the large orange sun burnishing the landscape of hills and a haphazard array of farm dwellings in a soft yellow glow. We passed a lovely little hillside hamlet, where a small creek crossed a rolling meadow, a scene right out of a Homer Winslow painting. Yet, the landscape wasn't perfect, and was blighted sometimes by concrete telephone poles and by white plastic hot houses, where vegetables and fruits are grown in the cold season. These hothouses can sometimes be found massed in great numbers in low-lying areas.

We took our time on the empty road, enjoying the vistas. In the passenger seat, Heju had open on her lap a large calendar that featured colour photographs of ancient bridges located in various areas of Korea. One photo showed a millennium-old granite-block footbridge called Jincheon Nong-gyo (*gyo* means bridge) that crossed a river in an area called Gugok, just east of Jincheon. I wanted to find the bridge.

East of Gukok, we came upon Hwasan Reservoir, more of a deep serpentine-like river actually, the calm water a dark green-black, bordered by a hilly area of thick woods. We turned onto a dirt road that ran alongside the lake, the earthen track so rutted and rough with potholes and craters that the Scoupe had to crawl along at a snail's pace. Finally, after nearly an hour, we emerged onto a paved road in Gugok.

We stopped at a small roadside barn to ask for directions to the bridge. A woman pouring milk from aluminum cow pails pointed to a nearby country lane. We drove along it just a short distance before it ducked under No. 35, the Jungbu Expressway — a major highway connecting east Seoul to Tongyeong on the southeast coast. As we exited the underpass, the lane dead-ended at a shallow river with gently sloping and muddy banks. A stone bridge spanned the water, leading to the woods that lined the far bank. We were the only ones there. We parked and Heju held up the photo while we looked out at the bridge. They matched! A plaque nearby confirmed that it was indeed Jincheon Nong-gyo. (We had managed to track it down with only the calendar photo). The sign said the bridge spanned a distance of ninety-three metres and had been constructed about one thousand years ago, during the Goryeo Dynasty, under the direction of a general named Im Yeon.

In near darkness, Heju and I ambled out onto the bridge, constructed of ancient granite blocks spaced about a metre apart with large flat stones placed on top. About halfway across the river, we were suddenly attacked by a couple of tiny, ravenous insects, which obviously hadn't eaten in weeks. They sunk their sharp fangs into our soft flesh, removing large chunks. If you've experienced the notorious sharp nip of the tiny black fly, the incision from this insect was painfully similar.

"They're getting me!" Heju cried.

"Me, too!" I shouted.

We stood on the bridge, momentarily dumbfounded, frozen to the spot with indecision. With the bugs signalling for their comrades to join them for a feast, we were suddenly set upon en masse, in danger of being eaten alive. If we stayed on the bridge much longer, the newspaper headlines in the morning would trumpet "Duo Unrecognizable After Horrific Attack; Found Dead on Bridge."

We sprinted back toward the car, appearing, I'm sure, much like Tippi Hedren as she scampered along the coast road to evade the crazed gulls in *The Birds*. We were swatting wildly at the blood-thirsty, frenzied insurgents as we flung open the car doors and dove in. As quickly as we could, we slammed the doors shut behind us, but many of the bugs managed to follow us in. Thousands more massed outside, clamouring to join their brothers. I couldn't blame them — they had tasted the sweet and succulent nectar of our haemoglobin and were now in a near state of hysteria, lusting for seconds.

Heju and I spent a few panicked minutes trying to smite them dead with rolled-up newspapers in the front and back seats. After we had exterminated those inside and could relax a bit, I took out the magnifying glass from my waist pack, put it up to my side window, and peered through it at the insects crawling around on the outside of the pane. "My God, they're aliens!" I exclaimed, enthralled by the creatures that were magnified about thirty times. Clearly visible were their massive, fierce, pincer-like mandibles opening and closing rapidly. No wonder the bites were so piercing. I had never seen such jaws, like killer zombie insects you might see in a B Hollywood horror movie.

"Let's get out of here," I declared

I drove back along the lane and onto the country road, headlight beams cutting through the grey-black night. I sped up once we hit the pavement, but the insects on my window hung on with plucky resolve. They were definitely Korean.

"I'm going to speed up to get rid of them," I said with some alarm, accelerating to eighty. But they wouldn't budge, as if their little feet were coated with some sort of super glue. "How am I going to get rid of them?" I yelped.

Heju remained calm and advised me nonchalantly, "Just open your window and they'll fall off."

She was a mad-hatter!

"If I open it, they'll get in and get us again!" I said, baffled at the absurdity of her idea.

She sighed, and told me to just open it.

So, I did as I was commanded, and pressed the button. As the window slowly descended, lo and behold, the bugs tumbled right off. We were saved! Heju just shook her head.

We puttered west into what we thought was the town of Jincheon. I say "thought" because, according to the road atlas, it *was* Jincheon, but there wasn't a single road sign indicating that this was true. We drove into the small downtown area and found the short main street's shops awash in a multitude of bright neon. When I spotted a police station, I pulled into the parking lot. "I'm going to ask them why there're no signs in town," I said, feeling somewhat disgruntled.

We entered the old building and found a few officers standing behind the front desk. We exchanged salutations, and without further preamble, I asked in a matter-of-fact tone, because I was slightly peeved: "Is this Jincheon?"

"Yes," said one officer.

"Well, there are no signs anywhere saying this is Jincheon," I replied officiously. "It might be a good idea to put up a sign or two to let people know this *is* Jincheon. And when we leave Jincheon, we'll be heading to Cheonan [the next city west] but we haven't seen any road signs in town telling us which road leads to Cheonan."

The kindly officers were very apologetic, and told us which road was the correct one to take. Then one announced magnanimously in English, "We'll give you an accord."

"Sorry … a what?" I asked, puzzled.

"An accord."

I certainly could use an upgrade to my lowly Scoupe. "If they want to give us a Honda, that's fine with me," I said facetiously to Heju.

"He means an escort," she explained, in a tone reserved for communicating with those whose brains don't function on all cylinders. "He's volunteering to give us a police escort out of town."

*Ohhhhh!* You had to love these guys (though I would have preferred the Accord). We thanked him for the offer, but politely declined.

Being close to eight o'clock, it was dinnertime, so we returned to the main street and stopped at a Lotteria, Korea's domestic fast-food burger chain, where we ordered a couple of *bulgogi* (beef) burgers, which taste nothing like any burger you'd get in the West. The thin patties had a sharp, tangy flavour, as it was topped with steak sauce of some sort. The place was empty.

After dinner we strolled over and went into the small independent "Donut Shop." The owner was a twenty-something Korean fellow who spoke fluent English. He complained to us that Dunkin' Donuts wouldn't permit him to open a franchise in Jincheon, because the town didn't have the requisite minimum of a hundred thousand residents.

"That's okay, though," he concluded somewhat spitefully, "because in my shop I can put doughnuts out on the shelf anytime I want. But at Dunkin' Donuts, they stop putting new doughnuts on the shelf in the evening."

The things you learn!

# CHAPTER 9

Heju and I were having a dickens of a time finding the Yu Gwan-sun Memorial Hall. We were west of Jincheon, where we had stayed the previous night, and east of Cheonan, in South Chungcheong Province. Now late morning, we moved west through the low Charyeong Mountains, through fingers of plains that ran between the hills, then entered into a wider area of agricultural land with small farm dwellings dotting the landscape. Under a hazy white sky, the day was a scorching thirty degrees. The area we were driving through seemed as a dry as a bone. Then suddenly, off to the side of a country road in Byeongcheon County, near Yong-du village, we spotted a low, formal-looking white building at the end of a long driveway. We pulled in and parked in the nearly empty lot. There seemed to be no one around. But it was the memorial hall we were seeking.

We walked past a solitary shop that sold, among other things, incongruous black-and-white masks depicting Edvard Munch's famous painting *The Scream*. Inside the hall, which opened on April 1, 2003, we took seats in a small screening room and viewed rare film footage of what is referred to as the Independent Movement protests, which began on March 1, 1919.

At some point, a handful of retirement-aged Koreans wandered in and took seats. After several minutes, one of the men stood up, announced dejectedly, "I can't take it anymore. It makes me too sad," and walked out of the room.

Years earlier, in 1910, Korea had signed, under duress, the Japan-Korea Annexation Treaty, which permitted Japan to rule Korea, and gave it power over almost every aspect and detail of Korean society, from running schools, prisons, banks, and businesses to control of the courts, media, and government. The Japanese held command over Korea ruthlessly, with their strict brand of law and order including summary executions. Finally, in 1919, the Koreans rebelled against their oppressors, and on March 1 launched a series of protests, involving millions of citizens, across the country. Many of these protests were brutally suppressed and thousands of Koreans were killed by the Japanese.

One of these protestors had been Yu Gwan-sun, at the time a sixteen-year-old student at Ewha Womans School in Seoul. The Japanese had closed many schools while they dealt with the uprising, so Yu returned to her hometown of Yongdu. She and her father organized a protest for April 1 that drew about three thousand locals, who marched to the local Aunae Marketplace to demand independence from Japan. Japanese military police reinforcements were called in and opened fire on the protestors, killing nineteen and seriously injuring thirty others. Yu's parents both died during the uprising and their family home was burned to the ground by police.

Yu was arrested and sent to the Cheonan Japanese military police unit. Imprisoned by a district court in Gongju, a Japanese judge sentenced her to three years at the federal Seodaemun Prison in Seoul. At Seodaemun, Yu was inmate No 371. About eighteen months later, on September 28, 1920, Yu died in prison. She was just seventeen.

It is often written that Yu succumbed to torture at the hands of her Japanese jailers. Her body was retrieved by officials from Ehwa Womans School. One of the teachers, Jeannette Walter, prepared the body for burial, and Yu was interred at a public cemetery in Itaewon, Seoul. Yu's remains were later lost. On March 1, 1962, Yu was posthumously awarded the Order of Merit for National Foundation, and today she is recognized by all Koreans as a symbol of the brave national resistance to the colonizers.

Heju and I entered an administration office next to the hall to ask a few questions. An English-speaking employee, Ms. Lee, told us that no documents existed to prove exactly how Yu died. Though the Japanese were prolific record-keepers, when they were forced to surrender on August 15, 1945, at the end of the Second World War, they destroyed as many records as they could before fleeing. "We can't really say if Yu was tortured," said Lee. "She had a kidney problem that wasn't treated in prison. She probably died from that. That's according to witnessess."

About six weeks earlier, when Heju and I were in Seoul, we had taken a guided tour of the prison where Yu had spent the last year and a half of her life. The March morning had been chilly and overcast as we strolled through the grounds that lay behind a red-brick wall about a mile west of Gyeongbok Palace. Walking paths on the well-appointed grounds connect a series of formidable red-brick buildings that include cell blocks, watchtowers, torture cells, and an execution room. I had seen pictures of the prison before the Japanese began construction in 1908, when the site had consisted of just a few thatched huts built to hold small-time convicts.

The Japanese established a pan-Korea network of prisons, constructing twenty-nine of them during colonization, and undertaking a major upgrade of Seodaemun Prison. Only Seodaemun remains today.

There are no surviving records to show how many Korean prisoners the Japanese interned at Seodaemun Prison from 1908 to 1945. It is almost certainly true that the Japanese destroyed these files before they fled the country at the end of the war. But the Korean government estimates the total number of Korean prisoners held there during more than three decades was around forty thousand. Korean political prisoners and independence fighters who opposed the Japanese were locked up alongside regular criminals. Sometimes, political inmates were held for years without being formally charged. Some were tortured; others were executed by hanging, often having been led to the on-site execution chamber without prior notice.

Our tour guide at Seodaemun had been Bae Jeong-hee, a serious woman with an assiduous nature who chose her English words slowly and carefully like a surgeon making a delicate incision. Heju and I were the only ones on the tour. In the first building, the History Hall, it aggrieved me that all the written information about what was in the glass display cabinets was written in Korea's native alphabet, Hangul, despite the fact that this was a prominent tourist site, patronized by visitors from all over the world. On display was a thick, pyramid-shaped straw mask, which prisoners — being escorted to Seodaemun by Japanese guards — were forced to wear as a form of public humiliation. The mask reached down to the shoulders and had only two small slits for the eyes. There was also a horse whip on display that Japanese guards had used to punish prisoners. Hundreds of new laws were promulgated by the Japanese during colonization, including the 1912 "whipping decree," Ms. Bae told us.

A black-and-white photo showed three Korean men tied to stakes in a field, in the process of being executed by a Japanese firing squad. Ms. Bae told us that when Korean guerillas were arrested, they were killed on-site, without a trial.

Another photo showed a Korean man missing his ears and an arm, said to have been severed by a Japanese soldier's sword. A drawing showed a girl with no hands. "Two Japanese policemen cut off her hands because she carried the Korean flag," said Ms. Bae.

I was peppering Ms. Bae with questions, but my queries flustered her. "If you keep asking so many questions, we'll never finish the tour on time," she scolded.

We slipped into an adjacent room and were met by the type of eerie music usually played during a horror movie. Standing upright against the wall were three small coffin-like wooden closets, which prisoners would be wedged into for up to three days, unable to move a muscle. When the poor wretches were released, they were sometimes permanently physically and psychologically crippled.

"They'd sometimes come out crazy," said Ms. Bae.

The glorified broom closets measured just five feet ten inches high, eighteen inches wide, and six inches deep.

"Try standing in it," Heju suggested to me brightly.

The very thought filled me with dread. I admit that a fear of heights and of tight, closed spaces ranks around the top of my list of phobias.

At six foot two and 110 kilos, there was no way I could squeeze myself into the tight space. Heju, though, was just five foot four and fifty kilos, and apparently not claustrophobic, because she voluntarily stepped inside and closed the door.

"You okay in there?" I called.

"Yah," came the muffled response.

She came out a minute later. "How was it?" I asked.

"I liked it," she said enthusiastically.

"You liked it?" I said incredulously

"Yeah."

"Wasn't it too small?"

"No, I did a little dance," she said.

"A dance?"

"Yah, I turned around and danced."

"How about if you had to spend three days in there?" I said ominously.

Heju's expression turned dark. "I'd go crazy."

"Yeah, just like Ms. Bae said."

Heju then wandered across the room and ducked into a low, dark cubicle. A few moments later from within it emanated a petrified scream. I hustled over and peeked in. In the corner, facing Heju, was a lifelike male mannequin sitting on the floor dressed in traditional Korean garb.

We then walked down into a shadowy, stone dungeon known as the Temporary Detention Room or Torture Room. On each side of the stone corridor ran a row of cells, and in each, lifelike mannequins of uniformed Japanese guards were torturing Korean prisoners. Loudspeakers broadcast a loop of the anguished cries of howling inmates and the harshly barked orders of the Japanese guards. It was over the top, but made its point.

In one cell, a Korean figure hung upside down, feet shackled to the ceiling, a guard pouring pepper-laced water down his nose. In another, a victim's head was being submerged in a tub. There was a woman sitting on a chair — hands handcuffed on top of the table — a Japanese officer sitting opposite her, thrusting a long needle in and out under her fingernails. Seodaemun management had done a good job in milking the situation, and had presented the Japanese in a very negative light. I asked Ms. Bae what Japanese tourists visiting the prison thought of it.

"Some young Japanese say, 'I think this was made up by the Korean government.' Others say, 'Ah, now I know what real history is. We didn't learn this kind of history at school.' They had read in their textbooks that the Japanese helped Koreans. Older Japanese say, 'We feel very sorry about this.'"

We then moved on to the next building, a long red-brick prison block that once housed male inmates. A spacious stone corridor ran down the centre of the block, and there were cells lining either side, each behind a thick wooden door. Prison regulations stated that prisoners were forbidden to speak to one another or to the Japanese guards. If an inmate wanted to get the attention of a guard, he had to push a lever in the cell, triggering a signal. Overcrowding was likely a problem, with many prisoners crammed into each cell, a situation that may have required the inmates to sleep in shifts.

We entered one of the cells and noticed some graffiti had been scrawled on one of the walls: "Kill the Japanese" and "Japanese should die." I wondered why the management hadn't removed it.

Back outside, we strolled past another prison block, which had once held inmates afflicted with leprosy and other disease that were thought to be contagious. Though the sick were quarantined, they were not usually given treatment or medication. "Many died there," Ms. Bae told us.

We continued past a watchtower to the far corner of the grounds, where our guide stopped in front of an innocuous-looking building. This, she told us, was the execution chamber, constructed in 1923. In front of it stood an old poplar tree, referred to as the "Wailing Tree." Because the Japanese didn't announce executions until the last moment, the condemned person would not know why he or she was being led outside. "Suddenly, realizing he [the prisoner] would die, he'd hold onto this tree, and cry and cry, so it was called the Wailing Tree," Ms. Bae lamented dramatically.

We went inside the execution room, which was also staged with mannequins: uniformed Japanese sat on one side, while on the other the condemned prisoner — a noose around his neck — was secured to a chair placed on top of a trap door. In order to covertly dispose of these bodies, the Japanese dug a two-hundred-metre tunnel that ran from directly under the chamber to the grounds of a nearby cemetery. This tunnel was not discovered until 1994, when the prison was being converted to a tourist site.

The Korean government took over the prison in 1945, and ironically continued to execute convicts there until 1984, when a new penitentiary was constructed in Gyeonggi Province. Ms. Bae led us back to the front hall, past the meagre remnants of the women's prison block, where Yu Gwan-sun had been interned. The tour over, I asked several of the guides in the front office if any of the Koreans interned at Seodaemun all those decades ago were still alive. The ladies made some calls and discovered that indeed one former inmate, an eighty-nine-year-old Korean woman by the name of Lee Bong-hui, still resided in Seoul.

A few days later, Heju and I found ourselves at Ms. Lee's apartment in south Seoul. She was a wisp of a woman who looked unusually young for her age. She was remarkably sharp and alert, with dark, probing eyes and a strong presence. She sat in a wicker chair and recounted her time spent in the prison more than seven decades earlier.

Ms. Lee said she was arrested and sent to prison in 1935 when she was only sixteen. She would not see freedom again until she was twenty. Her "crime" had been to organize an anti-Japanese protest while employed at a Japanese-run garment factory in central Seoul. Originally from Daegu, Ms. Lee's family had moved to Seoul when she was young. Her family members were anti-Japanese activists. She told us her father had placed a bomb in a Japanese bank in Daegu and was jailed, and that her brother, cousin, and a niece also spent time behind bars.

"I grew up hating the Japanese, too, and learned that we had to fight against them," she said, her eyes sharp.

She explained that, because Japanese law dictated that a prisoner must be seventeen years old before being incarcerated at federal Seodaemun Prison, and since she was only sixteen at the time of her arrest, she spent the first few months being shuttled between local jails, including Seodaemun, Dongdaemun, and Namdaemun, in Seoul. The maximum time an underage prisoner could be jailed for was twenty-one days, but the Japanese had a way of circumventing this. "I'd be released after twenty-one days, then rearrested the next day and sent back to jail for twenty-one days, then released and arrested and be sent back again," she said. "I tried to escape once, but the guard caught me. I just gave up. I thought I'd die in prison."

Ms. Lee became most familiar with Dongdaemun Police Prison,

located in Seoul's central east end. There were about ten cells, with about ten prisoners in each, the women separated from the men. The first thing the Japanese jailers did when a female inmate arrived was to cut the tie-ribbons off their hanbok clothing, so they couldn't hang themselves with it. There was no heat in the cells during the winter and the prisoners slept on the floor with just a single blanket for warmth. Several women gave birth in jail; mothers were permitted to keep their infants for six months, but were then forced to give them up for adoption. The daily diet was comprised of barley and kimchi (spiced cabbage), but no protein (beef, chicken, or fish). Prisoners were not allowed to talk, and communicated amongst themselves with facial expressions and hand signals.

The Japanese, in an attempt to glean the whereabouts of the ringleaders of the Korean guerillas involved in the underground campaign to gain back the country's independence, tortured inmates such as Ms. Lee. Regular criminals were sometimes tortured, too, but not to the same extent, she said. "The most terrifying time came when the key turned in my cell door and my name was called. Each time I went into shock. When I was being tortured, I wanted to die. I'd tell them, 'Kill me. Kill me.'"

She listed various punishments. The "airplane," for example, was when a detainee's hands were tied behind them and secured to their feet. They were then suspended by a rope from the ceiling until they passed out. "I was tortured in this way about thirty times at Dongdaemun Prison," Ms. Lee said. "They put a cloth in our mouths so we couldn't scream." It was so painful, she told us, that each time she passed out after about thirty minutes.

Other depravities included hot pepper being mixed into water and poured into a victim's nasal cavity, and a cloth drenched in hot water was placed over the face until the prisoner passed out. "Chicken Feet" meant fingers and toes hooked to electric wires, the current switched on, appendages curling up like chicken feet. Ms. Lee experienced this, too. Heads were submerged in tubs of water. Rods were twisted through the legs of a sitting prisoner. If someone sustained an injury during the punishment, no medicine was provided. "There were no kind acts in the police stations. None," Ms. Lee stated emphatically.

Having read Iris Chang's masterpiece, *The Rape of Nanking*, which detailed the Japanese Army's execution and killing of up to 300,000 Chinese citizens and soldiers in Nanking in 1937 and 1938 — in this context — it did not surprise me to hear about the torture Ms. Lee was describing. What was startling, though, was that the men who administered the punishment were Korean. "Japanese officers watched as the Koreans tortured us," she said. "I hated them. They worked for money. They were traitors. The Japanese would say, 'I'm sorry, this is my duty, an order from my government. If you give us the information we need, we won't torture you.' But the Korean torturers said nothing. They were cold-hearted. They didn't care about their own people." Ms. Lee hated but admired the Japanese. She said they would fight to the death if they thought they were right. "Koreans would fight, but were opportunistic, and changed sides if it benefitted them."

When she turned seventeen — still not charged with any crime or told how long she would be incarcerated for — she was led from Dongdaemun Police Station, on foot, and then by streetcar, wearing the dreaded straw head covering, to Seodaemun Prison. She said she felt like an animal. An animal on its way to the slaughterhouse.

By now Heju and I had been listening to Ms. Lee for about ninety minutes. Ms. Lee talked slowly, and with Heju translating everything, it took time, so I suggested we take a break. We offered her orange juice from a bottle we had brought, but Ms. Lee said that since she never got much to drink in prison, she couldn't drink much now. She told us she wanted to keep going.

At Seodaemun, she continued, she was disrobed to have her orifices checked by a Japanese female guard. She was then handed a blue prison uniform with the number 1009 on it, and placed in the women's wing, in a small cell with eight other non-violent prisoners. Thin boards covered a cement floor. The only window was high up on the wall. Ms. Lee said she would jump onto the wall and hang from the bars to gaze out, the view being of Inwang Mountain's bare granite face just a kilometre away. During the winter, it was bitterly cold, the cell floors sometimes icy. "Some prisoners died from cold and frostbite," she said.

During the winter, inmates were only provided with a bucket of cold water with which to wash themselves. Food rations — beans, barley, rice, and water — were meagre and sometimes accompanied by grain worms and bugs. Prisoners weren't permitted to stand in the cells and were only allowed out into the grounds once a month. A trumpet sounding marked the five o'clock wake-up call. Ms. Lee often spent her days meditating or knitting.

Female guards were both Japanese and Korean. "One Korean guard went to school with me. She told me, 'I'm sorry, you fight for your country, but I work for the Japanese government. But my mother's sick and I need money to care for her and for my family.'"

Ms. Lee sometimes heard shrieking when prisoners were taken from their cells to the torture chamber. One woman in her wing had been convicted of conspiring with her boyfriend, the family servant, to kill her husband with whom she had six kids. The boyfriend and she had run off, but were later apprehended. A Japanese judge ordered her to be hanged. When it was time to go to the execution room, Ms. Lee said the guards put a hat over the woman's face and tied her hands behind her. She was screaming.

In 1939, now twenty, Ms. Lee finally went to trial, and she and about twenty inmates were brought before a Japanese judge, who rattled off their sentences: "Prisoner number 17: three-years. You: six-years. You: three-years. You: one-year."

"It was a kangaroo court. We threw stuff at the judge. He had to leave the room. There was no justice. The Japanese had lawyers, but there were no lawyers for us."

Ms. Lee was found guilty under Japan's National Security Law, handed a one-year sentence and three years' probation. Since she had already served four years, she was free to go at midnight. She walked home and, not surprisingly, her muscles and joints were stiff and arthritic from lack of use. She found her home empty. Her father, wanted by the Japanese, had fled to China. Her mother, she discovered, had died from starvation and cold in the house.

"The Japanese were guarding the house. They stood by and watched my mother die. They did nothing to help her," she said.

Ms. Lee fled to Beijing, where she said the Japanese again jailed her for six months. In 1942, she finally returned to Korea, and has remained here ever since. She was married briefly.

I wondered aloud if Ms. Lee would have taken a Japanese life for her cause. "If someone had asked me to assassinate a Japanese general when I was young, I would have done it, definitely," she said.

I suggested that if all Koreans had fought the Japanese as she had, Korean history might have played out differently. Ms. Lee just shook her head and replied skeptically, that no, Koreans couldn't work together; too many were simply out for themselves.

"Even some Japanese cared about Koreans. But if Koreans had the opportunity to become rich, they betrayed you. It's the same today."

Heju and I spent two days, a total of seven hours, at Ms. Lee's apartment; though it was barely time to scratch the surface of her difficult life. Her social worker sat in with us for part of the time, and explained that Korean journalists sometimes visited Ms. Lee for interviews, but only asked a couple of questions before leaving. "You've stayed so many hours," she added admiringly.

"Because Ms. Lee's life is fascinating," I replied. To be the last remaining survivor, the sole window and vital link to a particularly seminal and historic sliver of Korean history should be permanently recorded. I wondered, though, why a Korean journalist hadn't written a book about Ms. Lee's life and her time at Seodaemun Prison.

Sadly, four years later Ms. Lee passed away at the age of ninety-three.

* * *

From the Yu Gwan-sun Memorial Hall, Heju and I drove west to the city of Cheonan, where we planned to visit the Independence Hall of Korea, which opened to the public on August 15, 1987 — the forty-second anniversary of Korean Independence. I had heard the hall was impressive, and we were not to be disappointed.

As we approached the site, we drove up a long boulevard lined with cherry trees, and we were lucky enough to arrive during the time of the year when the trees were displaying their white and pink spring blossoms.

"They're beautiful," said Heju.

We parked and walked along a stone path that led to a series of large squares. In the centre of the first square stands the Monument to the Nation, looking like two slender arrowheads soaring up fifteen storeys. As we continued on, we passed the waters of the beautiful White Lotus Pond, stocked with large orange and white koi, which ran along both sides of the avenue. We then walked though another square — the Grand Plaza — at the end of which stood the magnificent Grand Hall of the Nation.

The Grand Hall looms over visitors like a majestic monument to an Egyptian pharaoh. The front of the hall is open, and its sixteen great columns support a massive roof constructed of greenish-blue shale tiles. I circled around one of the columns and estimated its circumference at about twelve metres. It is twenty-nine metres in height and said to be the largest tiled-roof structure in Asia. On the grounds behind the Grand Hall are seven exhibition halls. The long ridge of Mount Heukseong provides the backdrop, its long green slopes blanketed by woods.

Against the back wall of the Grand Hall, an enormous white granite sculpture stands five storeys high. *The Statue of Indomitable Koreans* depicts eight men and one woman — each representing a Korean province — arms pointing forward and resolutely charging ahead. To give you a sense of the scale, the sculpture comprises 274 individual granite blocks, each weighing between three and four tons.

We were curious about how exactly it had been constructed, so we asked at the information office. We were told that the sculptor had initially placed 274 wooden blocks together and had carved the entire statue out of the that medium. Then, one by one, he had each wooden block removed and transported to his workshop, where he sculpted a matching granite block. That block was then returned and placed back into the statue and the next block removed and copied in stone. This continued until all the wooden blocks had been replaced with granite ones. When we examined the statue more closely, we could see the outline of the individual blocks.

We then wandered through the adjacent Hall of National Heritage, where many historical and cultural artifacts from prehistoric times up to the Joseon period are housed. We spent close to two hours exploring the hall, leaving a little before closing time and returning to the information office to ask a few more questions.

You see, a few pieces of information we had read in the exhibit were presented as empirical and absolute fact; I did not consider them to be such.

For example, in one case, information was provided that stated that humans first wandered from mainland Asia down into what is today Korea between 350,000 and 700,000 years ago. But this is just an educated guess on the part of some Korean anthropologists. To date, the oldest scientifically proven artifacts unearthed on the peninsula are stone implements that were discovered in 1964 along the Geum River in Gongju. These date to about 31,000 years ago. While humans certainly could have been in today's Korea 350,000 years ago, there is not yet empirical evidence to back up the theory.

Information in the hall also stated that a five-hundred-year-old wooden pulley device used to lift rocks, referred to in Korean as *geojunggi*, was invented by a Korean by the name of Jeong Yak-yong. Three weeks earlier, in Suwon, during our tour of the summer palace, Peter Bartholomew said the device had been invented in Europe. To add to the confusion, the employee we spoke to in the office told us it was first designed in China. It's quite possible that the tool was, in fact, invented in Korea, but what I'm saying is that there seemed to be some uncertainty as to its exact origin.

There were also lines written about how, during the Joseon period, "People were able to enter the political world and govern under kings." True ... if one was born the son of yangban, the hereditary "noble" class that comprised perhaps 15 percent of the total population. For the majority of peasants, farmers, and commoners, though, they stood about as much chance of governing as I did of being elected president of Korea. We noticed several other inconsistencies, as well.

I was miffed because I believe that a museum, of all places, ought to be completely objective.

* * *

The next morning I took a stroll across the street and purchased two warm cinnamon buns from a bakery. Back at the motel, I knocked on the locked door of our room, but to my surprise a woman who was decidedly not Heju answered.

*"Sillyehamnida,"* ("Excuse me,") I stammered. I checked my key: Room 205. I looked at the door: Room 505. *Whoops!* I was forever doing things like this, almost always in the mornings, when the battery power in my night-owl brain was lower than usual. I took my leave and delivered the cinnamon bun to its rightful owner.

Heju and I returned to Independence Hall later that morning, and while walking through the parking lot, we encountered three girls who looked to be about thirteen years old. As we passed, two of them nonchalantly dropped their empty soda cans onto the pavement, even though there was a garbage can not far away.

*"Sseuregitong,"* ("Garbage can,") I announced charitably but loudly.

The girls stared at me with all the defiance their little hearts could muster; as if it was the first time in their young lives they had received a direct order. They remained glued to the spot, no doubt trying to decide whether to pick up the cans and deposit them in the garbage bin or make a run for it. They wisely chose the former, but let me know, in no uncertain terms, with grimaces and by slowly picking up the cans as if they were doggie doo and reluctantly depositing them into the garbage can, where I could put my edict.

*"Kamsahamnida,"* ("Thank you,") I declared pleasantly, smiling at them. They ignored me and walked away.

Heju and I strolled slowly through the large exhibition halls. But there was so much interesting information, photos, and exhibits available that it would take days here to get a deeper understanding of this particular period of history in which the Japanese colonized Korea.

The idea to rule Korea was first given serious consideration when the Meiji government came to fruition in Japan in the early 1870s. What then transpired was an assiduous and relentless drive over the next three decades that culminated with the signing of the Japan-Korea Annexation Treaty of 1910. The five Korean politicians who signed the document are still considered by Koreans to be traitors.

On display was a series of poignant black-and-white photos taken during this period. One, from 1910, showed an elderly Korean lying on the street in front of Gyeongbok Palace, sobbing at the sight of the huge raised Japanese flag. Another image was of Ahn Jung-guen, a Korean man who, on October 26, 1909, at the Harbin Train Station in Manchuria, shot and killed sixty-eight-year-old Itō Hirobumi, the Japanese governor-general (1905–09) in Korea. Ahn was ordered hanged by a Japanese court in Manchuria, and was executed on March 26, 1910.

In the mid afternoon, Heju and I sought out a few moments of respite in a little parkette. We sat down on a bench in the bright, warm sunshine. Across from us sat a couple I guessed was in their seventies. I'm fascinated by the dichotomy I observe in Korea between that of formal education and general knowledge. Statistics show that about 85 percent of Korean students graduate university. Korean parents' quest to provide supplementary and after-school education to their children is legendary. But perhaps all this formal and intensive scholarship doesn't leave much time to enjoy the simple pleasures, such as reading novels or newspapers. While Koreans excel in global testing in sciences and math, I find that when I talk with them, there is often a lack of awareness of of global current events or even about their own country's history.

We introduced ourselves to this couple, who told us they were from Pyeongtaek, a town about sixty kilometres southwest of Seoul. Like us, they were taking a breather from walking through the many halls.

"Would you happen to know how Queen Min died?" we asked, because in one of the halls we had read a bit about the queen.

The Pyeongtaek pair did not know how she had been assassinated (stabbed to death in 1905 by Japanese agents in Gyeongbok Palace), and the wife defiantly half-shouted at us, "I don't know about her … I didn't read the explanations in the halls!"

Empress Myeongseong, or Queen Min, is well-known, even outside the country. The Korean-produced musical T*he Last Empress*, inspired by her life, was performed at the New York State Theater, in London's West End, and in both Los Angeles and Toronto. There have also been numerous Korean television dramas made about the queen.

Married at sixteen to King Gojeong (just fifteen years old himself at the time) in 1866, Queen Min was a formidable individual, most certainly not a reticent Confucian girl. She was highly intelligent, studied politics, and was not one to participate in parties, dwell on fashion, or attend afternoon tea sessions with aristocratic court ladies. She involved herself intensely in the political arena, and was not shy about throwing her weight around in it.

The queen's personal physician, American Lillias Underwood, lauded her, writing she was incongruous in this "half-civilized" nation. Underwood described the queen as "slightly pale and quite thin, with somewhat sharp features and brilliant, piercing eyes. She did not strike me at first sight as being beautiful, but no one could help reading force, intellect and strength of character in that face."

British travel writer Isabella Bird, who met the queen in Seoul, wrote, "She had sharp eyes, full of wisdom. When conversation began, her face shined with intelligence."

When I asked the couple about King Gojong, the man replied, "He was a king, but I don't know about him. Why don't you read the explanations in the hall?"

His wife concurred, insisting, "If you don't read the explanations, you won't know!"

Thoroughly censured, I slunk away in abject ignominy.

After our break, we walked through the remaining areas, finishing our tour at the Circle Vision Theatre, where visitors stand in the centre of a hall to view a documentary that is projected onto a 360-degree screen. The view shown was from a fighter jet, which swooped fast and low over famous Korean landmarks. It was all very exciting, fast and visceral, and when we dive-bombed from high above a mountain peak, it was so realistic that I felt nauseated.

It was late afternoon when we departed Independence Hall. We had spent the better part of two days there, and though I had been expecting something more modest and humble, everything about Independence Hall is illuminating.

# CHAPTER 10

We spent the following hot and hazy afternoon out on the tidal flats in Wolpo, north of the city of Gunsan in North Jeolla Province. The tidal flats along Gunsan originate in part from the Geum River, the third longest confluence in the country, which deposits enormous amounts of sediment, creating the mile-wide Geum River Estuary.

These mud flats support innumerable sea worms, mollusks, and crustaceans, which in turn attract migratory birds, which stop for up to six weeks here in the spring, during their northbound flight from Australia and New Zealand to breeding areas in Siberia and Alaska. In the autumn, they sometimes return on the trip back Down Under. Heju and I observed a flock of about a thousand birds, including Grey Plovers, Bar-tailed Godwits, and Great Knots, searching for food out on the flats.

Gunsan lies within one of Korea's largest breadbasket regions, the vast flat Honam Plain (*nam* means "south"), an unbroken swath of fertile soil. As we drove through this plain east of Gunsan, what seemed like a million neat rectangular agricultural fields spread to the horizon like a great verdant prairie. I loved the expansiveness. There was room to breathe.

After our day of birdwatching on the coast, Heju and I stayed the night at a modern motel in Vegas-like Naun-dong, the entertainment district of Gunsan, an area of tightly packed motels, night clubs, and bars. Though gaudy and bedecked in bright neon lights, the streets were almost completely bereft of humans. In such districts, nightlife can be very hush-hush, with bar and club patrons parking their cars in underground lots and entering the establishments from below street level. From the street you can still hear the music pulsating from inside the clubs.

* * *

In the morning we headed to "Japantown."

Gunsan was once a small fishing village, but in 1899, the Japanese forced upon it the role of port city, after they decided it would be a convenient place from which to ship rice and timber, among other commodities, to Japan. Japanese merchants and officials established Japantown, which was separate from the Korean area. After 1945, Japantown was preserved and remains to this day. It is located in Sinheung-dong, on the western edge of the city, where the Yellow Sea meets the Geum River estuary next to the old port, which was once overseen by the Japanese authorities.

Located off the main drag, in an area with just a few small streets, Gunsan's Japantown makes the dwellings in the surrounding neighbourhood seem shabby in comparison. The Japanese-built homes are handsome and stately, and great attention has been paid to the smallest details. Most of the homes have gardens that are surrounded by stone walls and landscaped with grass and Juniper trees, their delicate branches growing sideways like gentle waves. The two- and three-storey homes have triangular roofs (Korean roofs are almost always flat). We could hear birds chirping from the trees. It was very quiet and peaceful.

One of the homes we saw was of white clay bordered with wood panelling, and it had large windows trimmed with artisan woodwork and rafters of brass. Another had white stucco walls and a red-shale roof. Everything here is neat, tidy, and organized — a well-planned neighbourhood that would be considered upper middle class by Western standards.

We were standing alone on a quiet, narrow street admiring one of the houses when a Korean gentleman emerged from behind the gate. We chatted, and he told us his name was Mr. Yu and that he owned the home and wanted to sell it, but was unable to because the government had designated Japantown a cultural heritage site in 1989. Apparently, one stipulation of this designation was that the current owners were not permitted to sell their properties. "The government offers no financial assistance for upkeep," Mr. Yu complained.

He said he could give us a tour of his house for ten thousand won. I was incredulous. Seeking compensation in exchange for hospitality was absolutely un-Korean. Hike a mountain trail, wander along a beach, or stroll through a park, and it was not uncommon for a family or group of Koreans sitting on a mat enjoying a picnic to insist you join them for a taste of the kimchi or perhaps a shot of soju.

We politely declined his offer, and he quickly apologized. "I'm sorry to ask for money, but maintenance is expensive," he confessed.

Mr. Yu told us about his former career. In the 1960s and '70s, he had worked for the Peace Salvage Company out of Busan, doing a very unusual job. Under contract to the government, he and his fellow shipmates had searched the waters off Korea's south coast for Japanese ships and submarines sunk by the Allies during the Second World War. When the salvage company detected a vessel, it would detonate any unexploded ordinances that were found aboard.

"We found so many Japanese ships we lost count," he explained.

After exploring Japantown, Heju and I walked across the main street, Haemang Road, which ran alongside the quiet port area, and took a stroll. We passed what looked like the bombed-out shell of a large building that was obviously once handsome, but had been long-abandoned. A plaque out front said it was the former Chosun Bank, which had been built in 1917 by the Japanese. (After our visit, I discovered, the building was restored and is now the Modern Architecture Exhibition Hall.)

A bit farther along we came to a most aesthetically pleasing piece of architecture: a small, handsome red-brick building that was the former Gunsan Customs Building. It had been constructed in 1899 by the Japanese, and the plaque outside read: DESIGNED BY GERMANS. BELGIUM-IMPORTED BRICK; INNER WALLS, WOOD; ROOF, SLATE, COPPER. THIS BUILDING IS A SYMBOL OF JAPANESE IMPERIALISM TO PLUNDER RICE IN HONAM REGION (SOUTHWEST KOREA), A RICH AGRICULTURAL PLAIN.

Gunsan's inner harbour had also been built by the Japanese. We crossed a short steel foot-bridge that doubled as a mini lock, with chains to raise and lower a steel door to allow the water level to be altered. The sea was a flat, steely grey, and dark clouds hovered low overhead. A collection of traditional wooden fishing boats were moored along the docks, but there was little boat traffic in the harbour.

We walked out on one of the docks and happened upon a small party that was in full swing, a celebration in honour of the christening of a new fishing vessel. On board were a handful of middle-aged fishermen and their spouses, everyone seemingly enjoying themselves, partaking in plates of sushi and drinks. In the bow was a tray with a boiled pig's head on it. In its mouth, a white envelope contained a traditional gift of money.

"Come aboard!" one of the fellows called to us, Korean hospitality was unparalleled. So we sat in the bow, leaning back against the railing.

Sitting at the head of the bow was the vessel's luminary, a short, loquacious man who introduced himself to us as Mr. Kim. He had an engaging face, though he had dark circles under his eyes, no top front teeth, and his face was flushed, likely the result of imbibing soju from the bottle that sat next to him. He could speak some English, he told us, but continued in Korean. "As a kid, I learned English from U.S. soldiers who hung out in Gunsan's bars and night clubs during the Korean War," he announced with gusto. "I met so many U.S. soldiers from the U.S. Air Force and Navy and Army. They gave us chocolates and cigarettes. To this day, I still smoke Marlboros."

Mr. Kim loved to talk, particularly about the Vietnam War. He said he had spent sixteen months there between 1969 and 1971 with an ROK "Tiger" division. The U.S. had sent more than 300,000 troops to South Korea to fight during the Korean War, and South Korea wanted to return the favour to America, and did so by dispatching a total of 320,000 troops to Vietnam between 1965 and 1973. While the conflict was a disaster for Vietnam and America, it earned the cash-strapped nation of Korea hundreds of millions of US dollars in war construction and supply contracts.

More than 23,000 South Koreans, including 15,000 technicians, were employed in Vietnam, mainly on U.S. military construction projects. In 1966, South Korea's gross revenue from Vietnam accounted for 10 percent of foreign exchange earnings, and this increased to 20 percent in 1967. In total, the country earned more than $660 million during the war. Korea's president at the time, Park Chung-hee, even campaigned to extend the conflict.

The South Korean military had a fearsome reputation. "We chased the Viet Cong until we caught them. We never gave up," boasted Mr. Kim.

On search and destroy missions, the Korean troops would seal off a small area and tighten the cordon until each resident had been searched three or four times. Korean Special Forces plugged the holes in the perimeter. Civilians were separated, interrogated, and offered rewards for cooperation. A U.S. general once remarked that Koreans were the best at cordon and search operations.

Mr. Kim said the Vietnamese loved Koreans, and the soldiers would even receive bows. The first Korean troops arriving in Vietnam in 1965 were free to marry, but the second wave — on orders of President Park — were not. "These days, Korean men in the Jeolla provinces marry Vietnamese women, but it's not good — Vietnamese women are very lazy," he lamented.

He was in his element, talking non-stop, holding court over his guests. His mates good-naturedly ribbed him about his extended soliloquies. "We've heard all these stories about Vietnam before. You'll be talking for three days and four nights. We don't want to hear them anymore," one quipped.

But Mr. Kim was stubborn, and replied pugnaciously, "I don't care, I'm going to talk about it," and he was true to his word. He said the Viet Cong hid in holes in the ground at night to try to ambush the enemy. To demonstrate his one-on-one fighting prowess, he suddenly stood and pretended to engage an imaginary Viet Cong soldier, and in quick succession he thrust out his leg to trip his adversary, and threw punches and jabbed his fingers into his enemy's eyes. With his nemesis down and subdued, our hero stood smiling and triumphant. He was a consummate showman. His friends all laughed.

After an hour and a half, with early evening upon us and the light fading, Heju and I bid adieu to our new acquaintances and walked back to Japantown to retrieve the car.

* * *

After renting a room in the modest Hangdojang Yeogwan nearby, I went off alone to a local PC room, and while catching up on my emails, received some disappointing news: the Australian teacher I had sublet my flat to at the start of April was prematurely vacating it. I would need to find another tenant. When I arrived back at the yeogwan, I got even worse news.

"I'm going to quit the trip," Heju announced dejectedly.

I was stunned. "You're kidding, right?"

Heju's mood was glum and despondent. "No. I don't want to do the trip any more. I need to take a break."

She had previously teased me about how tough the trip was, and how she was going to quit, but I hadn't taken her seriously. This time was different, though. I could tell from the finality of her tone.

*"But why?"* I asked, though I knew. She wasn't having much fun. At the end of the long days, we were both physically and mentally fatigued. However, Heju bore the brunt of the mental work, having to translate whenever and wherever we talked to Koreans, which was pretty much all the time. And I admit I was not being the best trip-mate, either, with all my energy focused on getting the story, on writing down what I saw and heard, all the while trying to stay on schedule.

"I want to go home tomorrow," she said adamantly.

"What will you do?" I asked, because I knew her teaching job in Daejeon did not resume until the first of July, still seven weeks off.

"I'll go to the Philippines or Thailand," she said.

"But it's summer there. It'll be boiling," I responded with surprise.

But she had made up her mind. And once Heju decided something — like most Koreans — Zeus himself couldn't sway her. And so, after three weeks exploring Seoul and five weeks on the road, this was the end of the road for Heju. It was May 6.

I couldn't continue the trip without a translator, and I still had the southwest, the entire south and east coasts, and the northern belt to cover. I would need to return to Seoul to find both a tenant and a new translator.

"Let's leave tomorrow. I'll drop you off in Daejeon, then head up to Seoul," I said with obvious disappointment.

# CHAPTER 11

When I was back in Seoul, I placed an ad online to find a new tenant to sublet my flat. It didn't take long before I had a response from a young American, who agreed to rent it for the next two months. Finding a Korean who spoke English to accompany me as a translator was a bit more complicated. I put an ad on a Korean website and received about twenty-five inquiries, mostly from retired men, though there were a few from single women. I was reticent about travelling with an older fellow, because it was my experience that this age group tended to retain the Joseon sense of noble yangban and stolid pride, and I thought that casual (okay, any) conversation might not be a priority with them.

As I waited to secure a translator, I busied myself with taking day trips into Seoul. One included a visit to the tomb of King Yeonsan, a bad boy and tyrannical Joseon monarch who, when he died in 1506, was held in such low esteem by the court that they refused to bury him in the customary area reserved for kings outside Seoul's walls. (His remains were permitted to be moved to Seoul not long after his death on the condition that they would be buried on private, not public, land.)

Another day, I took a tour of the National Assembly building in Yoido in west Seoul. I was holding out hope that I'd witness a donnybrook between the two political factions, which break out about once a year. Alas, on this day the parties were not sitting in the hall.

After about ten days I received an email from a thirty-six-year-old single fellow who not only spoke fluent English, but was raring to go. I was more than happy to connect with someone in this age range. "Min-jun" (not his real name) was incredulous that I would be chauffeuring him around the country for free.

"Really? You'll pay for meals, motels, and gas?" he inquired in his email.

"Yes," I responded. *Unless, of course, he wanted to pay.*

Min-jun and I met by Cheonggye Stream near Gyeongbok Palace the next day. He had a boyish face and a youthful way about him. He could have passed for twenty-six in appearance and manner. He told me he was an aspiring movie script writer.

"Travelling around the country will give me ideas for new scripts," he said enthusiastically.

We arranged to depart after the coming weekend.

The evening before Min-jun and I were to start out, he phoned me. "I've packed ten T-shirts, ten pairs of underwear, and ten pairs of socks," he said with some angst. "Do you think that's enough?"

Min-jun obviously had not travelled a lot, or if he had, I suspected his mother had packed for him. I rolled my eyes, shook my head, and answered patiently, "I think ten pairs of everything may be a little much. Five pairs would be fine."

That Monday morning, I drove to west Seoul to pick up Min-jun. The first thing I noticed was that his belongings were in a suitcase on wheels, the type flight cabin crews tote around airports. *This does not bode well,* I thought. The moment he got in the car, he said excitedly, "Hurry, let's go!"

I had thought it prudent to be straight with Min-jun, to caution him that the trip would be tiring, we would be on a tight schedule, and that we would have little time to waste. This was just his way of announcing that he was ready to rock 'n' roll.

"It's okay, Min-jun, take it easy, we're not in *that much* of a hurry," I replied calmly.

* * *

Our itinerary for the first two days had a military theme. On the first day, we headed south into Gyeonggi Province to the ROK-administered Suwon Air Base, then to the U.S.-administered Osan Air Base, and finally to the U.S. Army garrison Camp Humphreys. At the Osan base we watched F-16 Falcons and A-10 Thunderbolt 11s swoop in for landings after their training runs. Through a fence at Camp Humphreys, we watched scores of attack helicopters belonging to the 2nd Combat Aviation Brigade, 2nd Infantry Division, conducting training missions — in preparation, just in case Kim Jung Un, up there in the North, ever did something foolish.

That evening, we travelled the short distance from Pyeongtaek west to the coast, then crossed Asan Bay over the modern, six-kilometre-long Seohae Bridge. Once over the bridge, we stopped at Sapgyo Hamsang Park — a modern amusement park with a few rides, two old warships, and only a small number of visitors that evening.

There were several hotels located on the grounds, but they were all too expensive for my taste, so we departed and found a room a few kilometres away that was more in keeping with my budget.The following day we spent back on Sapgyo Park grounds. In the morning we strolled around the amusement area packed with families and kids, pop music piping from the public speakers. It was May 24, a national holiday celebrating Buddha's birthday. His 2,570th, or somewhere in that neighbourhood, if you're counting.

Min-Jun and I spent the entire afternoon on tours through two decommissioned war ships docked nearby. The pervasive feeling I got as we explored the ships' interiors was of confinement. The claustrophobic grey steel passageways, low overhead, and sleeping berths with cots designed for very small people made me quite glad I hadn't signed up to join the navy.

When we left the ships in late afternoon, a cold, hard rain was falling. I drove to the nearby Sapgyo Seawall, which blocked the seawater to the north from entering Sapgyo Lake. To ensure the respective sides were indeed salt and fresh water, I strode through soaking wet weeds and grass, then clambered up and over and down the dike's huge boulders on either side in the driving rain to taste it for myself. Satisfied, I returned to the car, my pants soaked. Min-jun thought me nutty.

A few kilometres west of the dike we found ourselves in the township of Shinpyeong, at a featureless little roadside village. With the rain still pelting down, we parked the car outside a restaurant and sprinted through the darkness to get inside. We sat on the floor at a long, low table and ordered from the young server. Min-jun requested *danjanjikai* — soup with tofu, vegetables, and hot peppers — while I asked for three bowls of rice (the bowls are small) and soup. Fifteen minutes later, our server returned carrying a tray that held a large, steaming pot of soup. "I ordered one bowl!" Min-jun barked at the girl unkindly. "You brought me a big pot for two people by mistake. The big pot costs ten thousand won, and the small one's five thousand won. I'm not paying for two! I want to exchange it."

The timid server was unsure what to do, so she suggested he wait for the owner, who would be back in about ten minutes.

When the owner hadn't returned in the allotted time, Min-jun told me curtly before digging in, "Fuck it, I'm too hungry to wait. I'd be patient if I wasn't starving."

In our two days together thus far, I had noticed that Min-jun had eaten a grand total of one hotdog, a little rice, one slice of bread, and two bananas. I had offered him baguettes, cheese, ham, and fruit in the car, but he said he did not want them. His temperamental eruption over a minor incident like this caused me some concern.

After dinner we checked into the simple Shinpyeongjang Yeogwan, rooms a pleasing 25,000 won. We were given the option of either sleeping in one room on mats, or in another with one modest-sized double bed. We chose the latter, with Min-jun kindly volunteering to sleep on the floor. We asked at the front desk for a blanket for him, but were met with stubborn resistance.

"Why should I give you extra blankets?" the ajumma protested. "Just sleep together in the bed."

This was not going to happen, and Min-jun explained to her that the bed was not only too small for the two of us, but that we preferred to sleep separately.

"So take the room with no bed then!" she ordered.

"But my friend likes the bed," Min-jun said.

The woman repeated her suggestion that we sleep together in one bed. We were going in circles. Min-jun was beginning to come to a slow boil. "Why aren't you willing to give us a blanket?" he asked, his face drawing taut.

"There wouldn't be a problem if you got the room with no bed; then I wouldn't need to get you a blanket," she insisted.

After more than five minutes of back and forth, Min-jun had reached his threshold, and with his face turning red, he shouted at the woman, "Why don't you give good service?" He then turned to me: "I don't want to stay here anymore!"

I understood his frustration, but I did not particularly want to have to search around for another yeogwan in the cold, lashing rain and darkness. But then I had an idea. Koreans were business people, right? So, I solemnly asked her to return our money and told her that we would depart. My plan worked. She reluctantly walked down the hall, returning a few moments later carrying two blankets, which she handed to us without a word.

We returned to our room, Min-jun still cursing the woman under his breath: "What a bitch. She's so lazy!"

* * *

I had been snoozing for what seemed like only a few minutes when I was awakened by what sounded like squeaking mice. I opened my eyes to find Min-jun sitting on a chair leaning against the door, watching TV, the volume turned way down and barely audible.

"What time is it?" I asked, eyes half-closed, mind numb.

"Six," Min-jun said quite perkily.

"How long you been sitting there?"

"Since five thirty. I can't sleep."

I tried to go back to sleep, but didn't have much luck. Feeling guilty, I got up for good at seven thirty and said resignedly, "Let's go." I racked my brain trying to think of the last time I was up so early: I believe it was 1966, when, as an eight-year-old in Toronto, I roused myself at four thirty on a freezing February morning in order to make it to a six o'clock hockey game.

Just outside the nearby town of Dangjin, we stopped at a Hyundai auto shop so that a mechanic could repair the Scoupe's odometer, which had stopped clicking off the kilometres the day before. Then we headed south along the west coast, through the Pyeongtaek coastal plain. We were treated to quite a sight as we meandered along the country road through this area of flat plain. The landscape was an oasis of millions of rice paddies, now all flooded for the planting season with knee-deep water and looking like shallow lakes. It reminded me of being in the Netherlands. Farmers were out in the paddies, most using what looked like a push lawnmower that automatically placed bunches of green rice shoots into the muddy water.

Farther down the coast, by the town of Hongseong, we turned west and headed toward Seosan and Cheonsu Bay. We drove out onto the approximately eleven-kilometre-long dike that was completed in 1984 in order to reclaim land from the sea. South of the dike was the salty Cheonsu Bay; north of it two freshwater lakes and tens of thousands of rice paddies. The area belongs to Seosan Farm, the largest single-farm rice producer in the country.

Now afternoon, we then headed inland toward the ancient city of Gongju, once the capital of Baekje. We rolled across the Pyeongtaek coastal plain and then wound our way slowly through a wide swath of the Charyeong Mountains. These were not tall but very green and steep, with abundant trees. As we neared Gongju, the setting sun highlighting the walls of green, the road for a short while ran along beside the wide and meandering Geum River, which starts its journey near Jiri Mountain, in the southern reaches of the country, flows north to Daejeon, and makes a wide turn to the west before heading south from Gongju, emptying into the sea near Gunsan. The river has carved out a narrow valley of beautiful steep green hills, which made for a lovely drive into the city.

We entered the Gongju area from the west along the Geum's north shore. The scenery on the north side was not terribly conducive with the natural local habitat: a short stretch of the road was lined with a few shops, motels, gas stations, and modern white apartment buildings. Several bridges crossed over the river to the south bank, to the old city of Gongju, which remained hidden behind a low green hill that ran along the water. We did, however, catch a glimpse of the stone remnants of a fortress wall constructed in the fourth century on the hill.

We stopped on the north bank by the old single-lane Geum River Bridge, which was built by the Japanese in 1933, and looked out and over the water. A local who was walking by told us that prior to 1980, when the seventy-two-metre high Daecheong Dam was built upriver, the summer monsoon rains would raise water levels as high as the top of the high concrete embankment on which we were standing, which I would estimate at around eight metres high.

Waterways in Korea can become awesomely swollen and dangerous during monsoon season. Monsoon rains are like no other rains I have ever experienced. The water falls in large, heavy dollops. Annual precipitation in South Korea averages about 1.2 metres, though Seoul gets a little more. What packs a wallop, though, is that 70 percent of the rain falls between June and September. In 1940, the worst year on record, Seoul received more than two metres of rainfall.

After these torrential downpours, rivers quickly rise and swell to metres above their normal level. In narrow mountains passes, campers who have pitched tents on the banks of rivers have been swept away. I have seen the Han River in Seoul rise at least five metres, flooding the expressway beside it.

Min-jun and I wandered down the embankment and across the dry, exposed silt flats along the riverbank next to the old Japanese bridge. We noticed rows of small rocks piled up in the river with sticks protruding out of them. They were exposed at set intervals in the shallow water, and reached all the way to the far shore. *Perhaps 1,500 years ago, during Baekje, people had placed the rocks there to form as stepping bridge?*

We asked several passersby if they knew the purpose of the rocks.

"They flowed along and built up naturally over time," explained one ajumma confidently.

Well, no, two other ajummas announced a few minutes later. "They were put there to protect the bridge. When big things float down the river, the rocks and poles catch them. Without the rocks, big things could knock down the bridge. It's not very strong."

Min-jun shook his head and replied in disbelief: "Those little rocks can stop big things?"

The ladies looked rather indignant, and declared, with total conviction, "Of course!"

Now here's the thing: Koreans could sell a cardboard box to a cardboard box salesman. They will proclaim things as fact with such absolute certainty and sincerity that if they were to give you advice on which horse to wager money on at the racetrack, you'd be so convinced that you'd bet your entire life savings on it, despite the fact that the horse would probably go on to finish dead last.

I was surprised after we crossed the bridge into old Gongju. I had been expecting a quiet country town, a kind of Main Street, U.S.A., with perhaps a library, grocery, and hardware store, a Korean Mayberry of sorts. But instead, this section of Gongju turned out to be a teeming mini version of Seoul, a concentrated and chaotic hubbub of human activity. The main road was lined with an assortment of mini-marts, mobile phone shops, restaurants, clothing stores, and small office buildings. And it was as if every one of Gongju's 115,000 citizens was out and about, either jostling for room on the sidewalks or clogging the roads with their vehicles.

After grabbing a bit of dinner, we stole across the street and checked into the Gongju Bosak Sauna. I had mentioned to Min-jun that we would need to stay not only at motels but at saunas, also known as *jimjilbangs.* A jimjilbang, to me, was a YMCA/health club/spa/holiday retreat/refugee centre rolled into one. I have seen nothing like them in North America or Europe. For about ten dollars per person, you get access to locker rooms, showers, hot tubs, sauna, snack shop, TV room, and a large sleeping area where customers place a thin mat on a floor among the other guests. Patrons typically wear orange shorts and T-shirts, which are provided by the jimjilbang. These are always inevitably too small for my frame.

Men's and women's amenities are available, and at the facilities are almost always efficiently run, well-organized, and are kept spic and span. They can also be very confusingly laid out. The few times I have stayed at a jimjilbang, I have found myself totally lost, either entering some room or descending some stairway where I was not permitted. Once, I walked down a flight of stairs and heard a shriek as I mistakenly entered the women's change room.

Min-jun, I immediately noted, took to the place like a pig to shit. First, we both took long showers. It is amazing how much sweat and grime accumulates in one day from simply sitting behind the wheel of a car. We then luxuriated in the hot tub and sauna, before, pink as piglets, making our way to the sleeping floor, where we threw down our mats in front of a big-screen TV and stretched out. When the nine o'clock national news came on, Min-jun kindly translated for me.

After the news, Min-jun mysteriously disappeared, rematerializing about thirty minutes later.

"Where did you go?" I asked.

"I had a shower."

"But you had one before the news," I said, puzzled.

"I know, but I sweated watching the news," he said with a straight face.

Koreans are, without doubt, the cleanest, shiniest people in the world. Whenever I'm at my local fitness club, the fellows in the showers lather up until they are a thick, frothy white, and then systematically scrub every pore on their bodies for maybe twenty minutes. Fathers will wash their young sons in a longstanding tradition, using a coarse cloth to buff the lads to a red sheen as if sandpapering a coat of shellac off an old piece of furniture. The kids seem to enjoy this as much as getting a root canal.

* * *

In the morning, I was out in the car in the parking lot at eight thirty waiting for Min-jun, when my cellphone rang.

"Where are you?" Min-jun asked, puzzled.

"In the car," I said.

There was a few moments' silence, then, in an incredulous tone, he said, "You're leaving without a shower?"

"I had one last night," I replied nonchalantly. In the ensuing twelve hours, I had not rolled in cow dung, so I figured I was still relatively clean. "Where are you?"

"I'm in the sauna. I just had a shower."

If you're counting, and I was, this was his third in less than twelve hours. When he finally appeared at the car — a shade lighter and brighter than when he entered the sauna last night — we headed toward the Gongju National Museum, located in the bucolic area of Ungjin-dong, just west of town. This is a large and modern facility that was built in 2004. Our car was the only one in the sprawling parking lot. Not surprising to me, considering most sane people were where they ought to be at this time of the morning: home sleeping.

We went up to the booth and purchased our tickets from a woman sitting behind the window with her nose buried in a book. I naively assumed she would happily answer a few questions about the kingdom of Baekje, in existence from about the time of Christ to AD 660. But when I put my first query to her, she raised her head, fixed me with an expression of irritation, and replied, "I can't answer questions — I'm reading." Her gaze quickly returned to the page.

I may be in the minority, but I believe employees on the public payroll at publically funded institutions have a responsibility to assist mere proletarians like myself who contribute to her paycheque via our taxes. Not that I pay much in taxes in Korea, but you know what I mean. So I tried again with a different question. This time she looked up from her book with an expression of enmity, and hissed, "If you want to learn about Baekje, visit a bookstore and buy a book on it." Again, she resumed her reading.

I uttered a third query, just to antagonize her, and, to get rid of me, she reluctantly mumbled a few words about Baekje, which didn't explain anything, and then went back to her book.

The ancient Baekje region encompassed the four modern-day provinces of South and North Jeolla and North and South Chungcheong. In the year 660, Silla, the kingdom to the east of Baekje (which included today's North and South Gyeongsang) led an attack and usurped Baekje, resulting in its demise. Some citizens in the Jeolla provinces have apparently not forgiven those in the Gyeongsang provinces for the invasion that took place nearly 1,400 years ago. This is coupled with the fact that, beginning in the 1960s, a line of presidents hailing from the Gyeongsang provinces awarded the lion's share of industry to the east, leaving the Jeollas to rely on farming. When presidential elections are held, the long-time rivalry is unmistakable: about 95 percent of Jeollanites vote liberal, and about 95 percent of Gyeongsangites vote conservative. Sort of like how Texas goes Republican and California is staunchly Democratic.

In 1971, when the seventh tomb in a series of Baekje-era hillside tombs — the first six tombs uncovered between 1927 and 1933 — was discovered, the Korean archaeological community was exalted. A stone tablet confirmed that the tomb belonged to Baekje's twenty-sixth king, Muryeong, and his queen, and had remained undisturbed since AD 529. More than 2,900 artifacts were recovered, including a gold crown, silver accessories, and lacquered wooden pillows. Many of the late king's belongings are on display in the museum. The ancient items were alluring, with many exquisitely designed bronze, silver, and gold earrings, bracelets, necklaces, bowls, spoons, and swords. Baekje culture was renowned for its artisans, and sea trade between the kingdom and China and Japan flourished.

Next, we drove the short distance to the Songsan-ri Burial Mounds, the location of seven royal tombs. I was looking forward to entering the 1,500-year-old tomb of King Muryeong, but when we arrived, we were disappointed to learn that the tomb was no longer open to the public. Apparently the body heat of visitors and the heat from the artificial lights had caused condensation that had accumulated on the walls and caused some damage to the tomb and artifacts. "We don't have the technology to protect it," one of the guides told us.

The grounds were busy, with many families out for the day. We walked up the path to the earthen burial mounds, which were each about three metres high.

Had we had access to Muryeong's tomb, it would have been through a short tunnel that leads into a large stone inner chamber lined in dark-coloured brick, with the other chambers lined with decorative brick. It is adorned with murals, now faded, depicting a blue dragon, white tiger, red phoenix, and a tortoise.

The modest museum at the base of the hill, however, features an exceptionally well-done recreation of the interior of the tomb, highlighting the intricately detailed brickwork, most with lotus motifs.

That afternoon, we began to cruise eastward so we would be on time for our reservation at the Jakwang Buddhist Temple, located an hour away on the western outskirts of Daejeon. The temple was part of the Temple Stay Korea network, established in 2002 by the Jogye Order of Korean Buddhism, so visitors could "sample ordained lifestyle and experience the mental training and cultural experience of Korea's ancient Buddhist tradition." The first year, fourteen temples were in the program. By 2005, about fifty temples were participating, and at last check, ninety-seven were involved.

I had learned about the program from a pamphlet I picked up at a tourist information centre in Seoul, and had reserved two spots at Jakwang Temple. The pamphlet stated that no payment was required, though "donations were accepted." I had called the temple directly to inquire about that policy. A pleasant-sounding fellow named Cedric, sporting a definite New Zealand accent, answered. "Everyone asks me about donations," he said, chuckling. "There'll be an envelope on the floor of your room, and if you want, you can leave a donation in it without writing your name on the envelope."

This pleased me.

The road we took paralleled the Geum River for a while before cutting up through an area of rolling countryside in Yuseong district, where we located the temple on a quiet country lane lush with vegetation. We parked in the sun-drenched lot in front of the three-storey wood temple.

We met Cedric, an intelligent, easy-going New Zealander who had been living and studying Buddhism at the temple for the past four-and-a-half months. We were then introduced to the other weekend guests, who included twelve earthy young women and four men in their twenties, some wearing bohemian attire, none of them Korean. Cedric gave us a tour of the temple, then we congregated (all of us except Min-jun, who had gone off alone somewhere) on the upper floor, the large sliding wood doors open to the bright sunshine and the elements. A dog barked in the distance. Nearby, the tree limbs rustled in the slight breeze. It was very peaceful and quiet.

Cedric introduced us to a few stories from the Buddhist Sutra (or canonical scriptures) and they seemed very simple to me. We were then each given a small mat and Cedric led us in a few chants. Then we were taught the traditional Buddhist bows. These are not your simple bend-from-the-waist-kind of bows that you would present to Queen Elizabeth. Rather, these are body-breaking, Marine Corps training bows. From a standing position, you sink to your knees and bend forward from the waist until your stomach and forehead touch the floor, arms stretched forward. You then reverse the process and stand up. And that counted as just one bloody bow!

I do not recall how many we did, because I soon lost count, due to being in supreme physical agony. For about fifteen minutes we practised the bows — about fifteen minutes longer than I had hoped. Monks in Korea perform 108 bows every day, which I am told takes about twenty minutes. On special occasions, they will do 1,080 without pausing, which takes about three hours. That, to me, sounds terribly unreasonable.

In the booklet *Everyday Korean Buddha Practices*, Zen Master Ilta explains that bows jettison negative karma and achieve enlightenment. "The ideal method for laypeople to eliminate the 108 mental sufferings is to do 108 prostrations in the morning and chant at nights." Doing so will mean less difficulties and more peace and joy in your life, he added.

I guessed we had done about thirty bows already. Zen Master Ilta was wrong, though: bowing only brought hardship and suffering to my life.

Afterward, we were forced to sit cross-legged for about thirty minutes. It took me another half-hour to loosen up my mummified legs and get the blood circulating again.

That evening, we ate dinner together at a long table in the basement. There was a kitchen in the corner, and perhaps twenty-five of us in total. Considering Buddhists do not eat meat, and there was none in the meal — vegetables and probably lentils — it was surprisingly tasty. The meal was a rather convivial affair, sort of like a casual Thanksgiving dinner with your relatives. Sitting to my right was a young woman who I had met earlier in the afternoon. Judging from her accent, she hailed from South Africa. I gathered she was also teaching English in Korea.

I am not sure how she got onto the topic, but she suddenly began a rather pedantic riff about the evils of money, and how it meant little in her life. She complained that many young ladies in Korea, however, were slaves to money and shopped excessively.

"In Singapore, that's all they do, too, is shop," she added, not with a spiteful ethos, but with a bit of an edge. "Money controls you," she continued, producing a short screed on the bane of the almighty dollar.

I wanted to respond that perhaps in her private Shangri-La utopia, money may not be necessary, though I sincerely doubted it. In the innocence of youth and beyond, I had also harboured a similar sentiment, believing money was a foolish pursuit. But I later came to realize — after subsisting on noodles and peanut butter sandwiches — that money can be rather useful. Money in itself was not evil, I wanted to tell her. But I held my tongue.

After dinner, we all headed upstairs to watch a film in which the narrator explained the Buddhist philosophy. There was a clip of English crowds cheering British soldiers during a parade, having returned home from the "victorious" Falklands War of 1982 in which 649 Argentinean soldiers were killed. The narrator asked if this was not a bit depraved — celebrating the death of others. Well, yes, I concurred silently, it was.

When the film ended, Cedric sat at the front of the room and answered questions. One person asked if monks could marry. Cedric replied they could, but like money, they did not get attached to it or their partner. "If you lose something tomorrow, you won't get upset if you're not attached to it," he said. "If your wife died, you'd be upset but not depressed."

I have never married. But if I loved my wife, which I assume would be the reason I married her, and she died, I am sure I would be plenty depressed. I posed a query of my own: "Monks spend a lot of time doing solitary things, like meditating, chanting, and praying, which doesn't seem to leave much time to help others."

Cedric remained silent, looked at me for a few moments, then smiled and said, "I knew you were going to ask that." (How, I had no idea). He agreed that monks spend a lot of time alone, but added they have time for other things. "At Jakwang Temple, monks give free English lessons to kids," he told us.

It was about ten o'clock by the time we wrapped up and I returned to the somewhat mouldy-smelling basement room I was sharing with Min-jun. I decided to go out for a late-night jog along the adjacent country lane, which was quiet and desolate at this hour. The night was beautiful and warm, and the bright moon illuminated the black starry sky. When I returned, I sat alone in the temple courtyard for a long spell. It felt good to be under the stars, and alone as I attempted to contemplate the meaning of life.

I raised my head from my mat at about ten in the morning. Temple Stay brochures explain that guests can rise at three in the morning to begin doing chants and prayers. I expect this was the case at Jakwang, too, but I had conveniently overlooked this option and instead enjoyed a lovely long sleep. I strolled into the silent, empty courtyard, shielding my eyes from the sun's bright glare reflecting off the sandy earth.

I spotted Cedric and we chatted for a while. He recounted an incident that illustrated the zeal that many Korean parents have for their children's education.

"A mother dropped off her elementary school-aged son at the temple, and said she wanted him to stay alone for a week," said Cedric. "I asked, 'Why a week?' She said, 'I want him to reflect on life.'" Cedric shook his head in disbelief. "Reflect on life? He was only nine years old!" he told me.

At about noon, Min-jun and I headed to the car, preparing to depart. I stuck the key in the ignition and turned it. Not a peep from the engine. I tried several more times, but to no avail. The battery was dead. A Korean monk — surprisingly one of the few we had seen at the temple — appeared in the courtyard, and, observing our plight, offered his assistance. He was no ordinary monk; rather, he appeared to me as the reincarnation of martial arts legend Bruce Lee.

Our man looked about the same age as Lee had been when he passed away, with Koreawood heart-throb good looks to boot, a chiseled jaw, and the top half of his semi-open Buddhist garb revealing a sculpted chest. He seemed very fit. He also had long black hair, though I was unclear why he did not have to shave his head like other Buddhists. Anyways, Bruce jumped into the driver's seat and waited for Min-jun and me to push the vehicle so he could try to jump-start it. We got behind the Scoupe and began heaving it slowly through the courtyard, Bruce turning the key to try to ignite the engine. Nothing.

Min-jun and I took a breather, while Bruce — the strong, silent type — stayed behind the steering wheel, waiting for us to resume our labours. We pushed again, and after several more fruitless minutes, it became obvious the car was not going to start this way.

"Jump-starting it isn't possible with a dead battery," I informed Bruce, who did not seem to be in a hurry to vacate the front seat. Bruce silently contemplated this, then got out of the car and walked away. So much for our hero.

We phoned a local garage and soon a kind young mechanic arrived and jumped the battery, charging us just 10,000 won. What service!

I'm terribly embarrassed to admit it, but I did not leave a cash donation in the envelope in our room. I should have, of course. I felt mighty guilty I had not, and promised myself that if I sold more than a few books I would donate some of the proceeds to Jakwang Temple. I phoned Cedric from the car to thank him for the stay and to wish him success. I am certain he had already checked my room, and, finding the envelope free of any bills, had rightly concluded that I was a Dutch-Scottish parsimonious spendthrift.

Min-jun and I headed toward the Seokjangri Paleolithic Settlement Site, more commonly referred to as Seokjangri Museum, which is located along the north bank of the Geum River a few kilometres upstream from Gongju. There is an interesting story about this Seokjangri area.

In 1964, a major discovery of Stone Age tools dating back 31,000 years was made here. Two young American students from the University of Wisconsin — visiting research students at Yonsei University in Seoul at the time — are credited with the initial find. Albert D. Mohr and L. Laetetia Sample were on their honeymoon in Korea and had reason to believe, it seemed, that this area along the Geum River was a potential site for Stone Age artifacts. Strolling along the recently flooded banks of the river — likely keeping their eyes to the ground — they had spotted what looked like an ancient stone tool.

Lee Yung-jo, now Professor Emeritus at Chungbuk National University in Cheongju in North Chungcheong, met Mohr and Sample in 1964. Lee was a student then at Yonsei University in Seoul, and he recalled the pair bringing samples of the tools to Seoul, which were then tested at the Korean Atomic Energy Institute, Lee said, where it was determined that they were 30,690 years old. The discovery was monumental, archaeologically, for South Korea — the first Stone Age artifacts ever uncovered. Up to this point, the oldest implements found only dated back to the Neolithic period, about 4000–5000 BC.

A Yonsei University team headed to Gongju that November to begin excavating the newly christened Seokjangri Prehistoric Site. Over the next ten years, from 1964 to 1974, about ten thousand separate stone items, including pottery, bowls, grinders, knives, and axes were unearthed. Professor Lee spent every spring over the next decade here assisting with the dig.

The Seokjangri Museum was housed in a low, modern building. Inside was, save for several guides at the front desk, devoid of visitors. Our guide was Jeong Seung-ae, a serious woman who recited a rehearsed spiel to us in Korean. Via Min-jun, I posed numerous questions about the artifacts as we slowly made our way past glass exhibits containing thousands of examples of Stone Age tools discovered in Korea as well as Europe. I knew next to nothing about Korean anthropology and archaeology, and was curious to learn. *When was the Stone Age? Were these the oldest stone tools found in Korea? Was there a difference between Stone Age tools found in Europe and Korea? When did humans first wander from the Asian continent to the Korean peninsula? Had Peking Man — unearthed near Beijing and delineated as being as old as 770,000 years — traipsed the relatively short distance east to Korea? Would I have made an exemplary caveman?* It became quite obvious Ms. Jeong took umbrage at having her memorized speech interrupted, and she began to throw up her hands in frustration.

Min-jun, exasperated too, whispered to me at one point, "She's not answering my questions." Though I couldn't understand their dialogue, their terse tones told the story. By the time we had seen the entire collection and were back at the front desk, all three of us were suffering from frayed nerves.

In the parking lot after, Min-jun confided to me, "I told Ms. Jeong: 'I don't mean to give you offence, but the information we were asking you is very important. You really should know it.'"

I had to hand it to Min-jun; he spoke his mind.

# CHAPTER 12

During a 1964 visit to Germany, South Korean president Park Chung-hee was so impressed with the Autobahn and how it served as a lifeline to German industry that he determined South Korea must have an expressway, too, to connect Seoul to Busan, and ensure that industrialization and modernization would proceed quickly.

But the South Korean national legislature had little money, and it balked at the project's enormous price tag. In 1964, South Korea's GNP was just US$142. The country was a financial aid recipient, receiving about $4 billion in U.S. aid between 1954 and 1970. In the 1960s, Japan provided South Korea with $1 billion in grants and loans and economic assistance over a ten-year period. The World Bank, in a detailed study of the proposed project, warned the Korean government against it, saying it was economically and technologically unfeasible. The Korean legislature agreed.

The country certainly could use an expressway, despite the fact that there were only 109,000 vehicles in 1969 — an average of one private passenger car per 1,400 people — and about half of those vehicles were in Seoul, and half still of those were taxis. There were only two thousand kilometres of paved roads at that time, again mainly around Seoul, although a total of thirty-five thousand kilometres of narrow, earthen foot paths and gravel tracks existed across the country. Graded paths had not been created because horse-drawn carriages and four-wheeled wagons were never adopted. About one third of the roads during those years were maintained by locals who laboured with picks and shovels in a sort of corvée system (unpaid labour). At the time the expressway was proposed, some roads and bridges that had suffered heavy damage during the Korean War had still not been repaired.

"By Western standards, most roads were unfit for passenger vehicles and justly notorious," wrote author Patricia Bartz. From a topographical viewpoint, it was easy to understand that the construction of an expressway would require a Herculean effort. In the proposed expressway's path reared up the "young granite" of the Charyeong, Sobaek, and Taebaek mountain ranges, which sit atop a bedrock layer of predominantly granite-gneiss that dates back about 900 million years. Very hard stuff indeed. Although the surface has been undergoing erosion for millions of years (the reason most ranges are under a thousand metres in height), the topography is very dissected, with ridge after ridge in close array.

President Park, a former schoolteacher and Major General in the ROK army, who led a military coup to come to power in 1961, after President Rhee had ruled from 1948 to 1960, did not seem concerned about the rugged topography. Trained as an officer under the Japanese, even adopting a Japanese name (Tagaki Masao), Park did not give a hoot what the "experts" thought. He had an iron will and a disdain for the democratic process, and often used strong-armed tactics to get what he wanted.

Bernard Krisher, a reporter for the *New York World-Telegram and Sun*, interviewed Park at Columbia University in 1961 after the coup, and referred to him as "an unlikely looking coup leader. He was short, barely audible and uncomfortable in a Western setting."

Richard M. Steers, author of *Made in Korea: Chung Ju Yung and the Rise of Hyundai*, wrote about how the president mandated that construction go ahead. Groundbreaking for Gyeongbu Expressway (*Gyeong* means Seoul; *bu* is short for Busan) began in February 1968. Park enlisted the assistance of Hyundai's young chairman, Chung Ju Yung, to oversee the project, though Hyundai's international experience in road construction was limited to building a ninety-three-kilometre highway in 1964, one which linked the southern areas of Pattani and Narathiwat in Thailand. And that project did not go well: Hyundai's shoddy equipment constantly broke down, pavement laid in monsoon season buckled, and Thai workers — paid less than their Korean counterparts — staged violent strikes, noted Steers.

But the Korean government and *chaebol* — family-run conglomerates — worked hand-in-hand, with businesses granted low-interest, government-backed loans and credit for any reasonable export project during the Park administration.

Korean engineers favoured a straight-line expressway between Seoul and Busan that would require tunnelling through myriad mountains. But Chung desired a longer route, essentially following the existing Geongbu Rail Line: Seoul to Daejeon, then southeast 138 kilometres through the Sobaek Range and Chupungnyeong Pass to Daegu, and finally south to Busan. This would require less tunnelling. Chung won out, of course. Hyundai led a consortium of seventeen construction firms, and was allotted more than two hundred kilometres of the most difficult terrain, including the notorious Daejeon–Daegu swath.

Chung hired multiple work crews to labour round the clock. Workers got only two days off each month. To lead by example, Chung ate and slept at the worksites. But the old machinery frequently broke down on the steep and unforgiving slopes, and construction sometimes ground to a halt. It was a painstaking process, with tons of earth needed to fill in low areas between successive hills and to build up roadbeds. Short of quality equipment, Chung was forced to order 1,900 new units of heavy machinery for the project.

Road building at that time and in this terrain was dangerous work. "Several workers died in landslides and cave-ins. Accidents were frequent. Thirteen serious cave-ins occurred during the drilling of the Tangjae Tunnel [today spelled *Dangjae*] alone," wrote Steers.

President Park constantly flew by helicopter over the route. In Steers's book, an engineer recalled: "Up and down he would go, this time with a team of geologists to figure out what had gone wrong with some mountainside that had crumbled on our tunnel-makers, the next time with a couple of United Nations hydrologists to figure out how our surveyors had got some water table wrong. If he didn't know the answer on Tuesday, Mr. Park was back with it on Thursday."

By Christmas 1969, three sections — Seoul to Daejeon and between Daegu and Busan — had been completed and were open to traffic. Eight months later, on July 7, 1970, the final and most difficult section east of Daejeon was finished. The 416 kilometres of pavement joining Seoul to Busan moved through three different mountain ranges, and required the construction of numerous tunnels and bridges. It was quite an engineering feat.

I have driven Gyeongbu Expressway — also known as Highway One — though I much prefer the train or bus for the Seoul–Busan journey. However, I was curious about Steer's reference to Dangjae Tunnel being the site of thirteen cave-ins during its construction. Someone needed to snoop around, to investigate why the section was so treacherous. It seemed I was the only volunteer.

The morning after our tour of the Seokjangri Museum, Min-jun and I were in east Daejeon. We had passed through the city the night before, and I thought I would never again see so many consecutive blocks of apartment buildings. They seemed to stretch on forever. Standing on a ridge on the outskirts of the city, one can see the entire city, the fifth largest in the country, laid out on the plain before you.

Dangjae Tunnel was about thirty kilometres east of the city, and I opted to take a meandering route along country roads. A great route choice, if I do say so myself, as for a good portion of the drive we traced the impossibly serpentine and seemingly inaccessible Geum River, which flowed through remote razor-thin valleys that lay between steep-walled blankets of green. The view along this route is arrestingly lovely.

After a leisurely, scenic drive, we entered Okcheon County and stopped at the Geum River Resort, a fancy name for what was essentially a rest stop beside the river. A steep wall of trees rose up on the opposite shore and behind us, to the north, was a gentler mountain slope. The "resort" included a parking area, a motel, a few restaurants, and a shallow area along the river where a few people were wading. Just on the other side of the river, behind the "resort," was the Gyeongbu Expressway.

We drove a short ways up the slope from the river to a tiny square in the small village of Joryeong and got out of the car. It was noon and the sun was blistering hot. A resident informed us that there was a memorial nearby that was dedicated to those who died during the construction of the Gyeongbu Expressway, so we drove the short distance along a narrow country lane, stopping at the base of a long, steep row of stone steps. We climbed to the top and emerged onto a small stone clearing. In the centre was a thin, vertical slab of dark marble with rows of engraved names. I counted seventy-seven — the number of men who had perished during the construction of the expressway.

I was astonished. Steers had written about how "several workers died." But seventy-seven was significantly more than several; that was one death every twelve days, on average, during the two and a half years of construction. President Park had demanded the project catapult ahead at breakneck speed, and apparently worker safety had not been paramount.

Safety aside, Park was prescient in his vision that the expressway would play a crucial role in driving South Korea to economic success. The highway enabled industrialization to spread from Seoul, and to connect the capital to Busan and its major port. When I talk with Koreans from Park's era, the ex-president is almost unanimously referred to in glowing and reverential terms. More than any other single figure, Park helped shape the modern Korean political economy. Yet, labour during that time was carried out on the backs of regular Korean citizens, who worked tirelessly for long hours, often for notoriously low wages. The success was theirs.

Despite his popularity among the people of that time, Park's human rights record is dismal. Under the constitution, the president was limited to two terms in office. However, the National Assembly, dominated by Park's Democratic Republican Party, amended the document in 1969 to allow a third term. In the 1971 presidential election, Park's party took 113 of 204 seats, but two-thirds majority was required to pass a constitutional amendment. To get around this, Park dissolved the National Assembly, suspended the constitution, and enacted martial law. Universities were closed. The press was censored. The right to free speech was no longer. In 1972, Park unilaterally revised the constitution to allow himself to assume and retain power without any checks and balances. He called the new era Yushin, meaning "rejuvenation." Essentially, he became a dictator, and would remain so until he was assassinated in 1979 by the director of the Korean Central Intelligence Agency.

The most notorious case of that era involved seven Korean men who were expeditiously hanged in 1975 on Park's secret order, accused of plotting to overthrow his government. In 2005, the seven were exonerated by the Korean Supreme Court. In 2013, Park's daughter, Geun-hye, was elected on the conservative ticket as the eleventh, and first female, president of the Republic of Korea.

Back in Joryeong, we were given the number for a resident by the name of Mr. Park, who, as a boy, had witnessed the plowing and grading of the expressway through the area. We called and spoke with him, and he offered to take us to Dangjae Tunnel the next day.

With time to spare, Min-jun and I headed east to look for another tunnel I had read about, one in which, during the Korean War, a large group of local refugees had been massacred by U.S. troops. The incident came to international prominence in 1999, when several Associated Press reporters published a series of articles proving that from July 26 to 29, 1950, U.S. soldiers at No Gun Ri bridge had machine-gunned and dropped bombs on villagers, killing between three hundred and four hundred (the exact figure is still unknown). The three reporters, Choe Sang-hun, Charles J. Hanley, and Martha Mendoza, published a book about the incident entitled *The Bridge at No Gun Ri: A Hidden Nightmare from the Korean War*, which won the 2000 Pulitzer Prize for Investigative Reporting.

We found an on-ramp to Gyeongbu Expressway and headed east about twenty-five kilometres through a series of six tunnels, exiting near Nogeun village (No Gun Ri). After turning off, we then proceeded to get lost for an hour in the desolate and rough countryside looking for the bridge, and spent another hour chatting with an elderly resident in a pretty little hamlet about the time he spent as a soldier during the Korean War. Since it was then too late in the day to visit the bridge, we found a motel room nearby.

Despite the fact that No Gun Ri bridge is just south of the expressway, it is hidden in such a secluded area, up against a long wooded ridge in a narrow pass between hills, that without detailed directions and a lot of luck, we would never have found it. There was not a dwelling or person around when we arrived at the bridge at eight thirty the next morning for our nine o'clock appointment with a local resident — the father of a university student who had translated for me in Seoul — who had promised to show us around. Even at this early hour, it was already a scorcher of a day, the air hot and still.

Min-jun and I wandered under the concrete trestle over which a dual rail line ran. There were actually two arched tunnels, side by side, both tall and narrow. A country lane passed through one and a small creek through the other. At 8:46, a speeding eastbound passenger train flew over the trestle, disappearing a kilometre or so farther on behind a low mountain. At 8:53, a slow-moving westbound freight train rolled by. This rail line ran between Daegu and Daejeon.

The concrete walls inside the tunnel were pockmarked with bullet holes, some circled in blue, evidence of the U.S. machine gun fire from July 1950.

When Mr. Nam Jeong-hyeon arrived, we followed him in our car for several kilometres along a local road that passed through a narrow area of dry farmland with a few scattered dwellings, the ever-present hills rising up around us. We soon came to the nondescript Jugok village, little more than a dusty clearing with a few agricultural plots and a couple of little farmsteads. We turned onto a small laneway and drove until it dead-ended by a small farm compound. This was Imgye village.

Mr. Nam introduced us to the owner of the farm, Yang Hyae-chan, a handsome, lean man with a quiet, dignified, no-nonsense air and intelligent sad eyes. "I'm busy now doing chores, so I can only talk for a few minutes," said Mr. Yang in a matter-of-fact tone. He told us that in July 1950, when he was only nine years old, he had spent four days in the No Gun Ri tunnel under fire.

The four of us stood under a canopied shed where feed and fertilizer were stored, to get out of the sun. I sat on a yellow plastic milk crate and listened as Mr. Yang — who had been interviewed for the book by the AP reporters — recounted his story.

"I was in third grade then, attending Hwagok Elementary School. Our class teacher informed us not to come to school anymore."

This was early July 1950, and Seoul was being overrun by North troops, who had entered the city on June 25, sparking all-out war. An exodus of refugees from Seoul was streaming east through Jugok — their belongings strapped to their backs — heading to Busan. Jugok at the time was along the main west–east route that connected Daejeon and Daegu. The dirt road was narrow and potholed, and the only vehicles that were using it were the odd jeep, which went bouncing along every few days or so.

With North soldiers approaching the area from the west, U.S. troops gave evacuation orders to the locals. Mr. Yang estimated that about six or seven hundred displaced persons had massed at Jugok. That first night, they slept outside. Village elders had announced that the U.S. soldiers were friendly. Late the second night, the soldiers told the villagers they had two hours to get ready to depart.

"We moved out onto the road around midnight," recalled Mr. Yang. "We had clothes, food, and blankets on our backs." The mass of humanity began trundling east. Yang's mother, father, grandmother, two aunts, two brothers, and his sister were in the back of the group.

Mr. Yang had been talking to us for about twenty minutes when he suddenly got agitated. It was planting season, he told us, and he had lots of work to do We were imposing on his time, so we agreed to meet again that night at the bridge to hear the rest of his tragic story.

Since we had the whole day, and it was still only mid-morning, Min-jun and I headed west along a country road back toward Okcheon to meet Mr. Park for our afternoon rendezvous at Dangjae Tunnel. The countryside is rustic and pretty here. Along the side of the road we stopped in Yeongdong County at the Château Mani Winery, and we were lucky enough to get a tour of the premises and a free lunch.

The château is in a former school — a long, low building refurbished to look like a European chalet. The manager, Jeong Dong-hwan, led us through the far wing, containing large metal vats for fermenting the grapes, and into the basement, where the wine was stored in great oak casks. He then took us outside into the vineyards. The winery opened in 1997 and was the first in the country. "Korean consumers are changing to wine," Mr. Jeong told us, adding that the switch coincided with the country's rising GNP. In the past few years, a series of small private wineries have sprouted up.

* * *

Back in Joryeong village, Mr. Park had us follow him in our car up onto a closed expressway ramp nearby. Skirting around the barrier at the top, we drove onto the permanently shuttered section of the old Gyeongbu Expressway, which is located just north of the current roadway. The closed section was only about three kilometres long, but along it, far below, the Geum River changed directions, requiring a tight 90 degree turn in the road. The old section of expressway ended at the notorious and now-sealed Dangjae Tunnel, where about a dozen men lost their lives.

We stopped the cars by the tunnel. "There used to be a lot of car accidents along this stretch," Mr. Park said as we stood next to the cars, "trucks, too. And in 1981 or '82 a bus went over the cliff. The road was too winding and too steep at the side."

The decision was finally made that the section was too dangerous, and a new section was built. Constructing the new strip of expressway entailed excavating three new tunnels through the mountains just east of the old one. The old section of highway was permanently closed to traffic in 2003. As you drive through these tunnels, Okcheon 1, 2, and 3, you can appreciate the enormity of the task faced by the construction workers who were given the task of bulldozing their way through this unforgiving terrain.

As for Dangjae Tunnel, well, it now has a rather ignominous vocation: Mr. Park told us it is now used as a cool storage area by a kimchi factory, which stores big ceramic pots full of the pickled dish here to ferment. Had something very sweet, such as maple syrup or chocolate, been housed there, I would have already been drilling through the sealed door to get at it. Korea's national dish is far too sour for my taste. As we left, and the tunnel faded from view, I didn't give the kimchi a second thought.

* * *

By seven o'clock, Min-jun and I were back at the No Gun Ri bridge, sitting at a picnic table and listening intently to Mr. Yang as he continued his story.

The villagers, he told us, had slept outside on the ground that night in the area near his family's small farm. At daybreak, the U.S. soldiers were nowhere to be seen, so the village leaders decided to trundle east. But the soldiers soon appeared along the road and blocked it with trucks, about three hundred metres from No Gun Ri bridge. About thirty soldiers led the villagers onto the train tracks, surrounding them and then searching each person.

"I was wearing my school uniform," Mr. Yang said — long, black Japanese-style pants, a white shirt, and rubber shoes. It was a hot day, he remembered. "Soldiers gave orders in Japanese, because they had been stationed in Japan, and some Koreans who spent time under the Japanese spoke it."

The troops then disappeared, but a short while later, a small American plane flew low overhead. Suddenly, more U.S. planes appeared, dropping bombs directly onto the refugees.

"People were running everywhere. Some just dropped on the spot, too scared to run. I don't know how long it lasted. I was too scared to know. I think my grandmother was struck directly by a bomb, and died instantly. My two brothers were killed, too. My father ran into the hills." Mr. Yang's thirteen-year-old sister, Hae-sook, lost an eye. In the book written by the AP writers is a 1955 photo showing her with an artificial left eye.

The Americans later showed up to check the bodies on the tracks, prodding them with bayonets. Survivors, estimated to number about four hundred, were herded into the No Gun Ri tunnel. It measured just twelve metres high by twenty-three metres long and seven-metres wide.

As darkness fell upon us, I found the diffused faint light from the yellow street lamp nearby was not enough illumination by which to write. I withdrew a small flashlight from my waist pack and continued jotting in my notepad. The chirping of crickets permeated the evening air as Mr. Yang continued.

The Americans with their machine guns took up positions at the four corners of the tunnel's exit and entrance. That night, occasional shots rang out. In the morning, he saw a heap of dead bodies — those who had tried to leave the tunnel. "They were piled up. Some people were hiding behind the bodies; others had dug themselves into the ground." He and his mother and sister lay together, motionless, not daring to utter a word or even whisper, for fear of receiving a bullet. "One move got you killed. It was horror. I didn't even go to the bathroom, I was so scared. Maybe I fell asleep, but I have no memory of sleeping. I never even saw the soldiers." He did, though, hear the *clack-clack-clack* of gunfire and the whirr of bullets if someone moved or tried to escape.

After three days, with North Korean troops nearby, the U.S. troops positioned at the tunnel suddenly departed. That night, North soldiers poked their heads into the tunnel. "Hey, comrades, the area has been liberated. You're free!" they hollered. In an ironic twist, the "enemy" were rescuing villagers from death at the hands of the "allies," the Americans.

In the morning, Mr. Yang's father appeared from the hills and carried his mother home. Survivors returned to the tracks and tunnel looking for missing relatives. Many corpses were strewn about, decomposing in the hot sun. Some found their family members, others didn't. The bodies of Mr. Yang's brothers and grandmother were never found. He also lost two aunts, two cousins, and an uncle.

The reason given for the attack was that U.S. officers suspected North spies to be among the villagers. North soldiers and snipers were known to impersonate village residents, donning civilian garb. But Mr. Yang shook his head at the mention of spies being among his group. "It was impossible. We all knew each other," he said.

One machine-gunner, Edward Daily, positioned ninety metres from the tunnel — could not bring himself to shoot at the huddled masses. "He shot above us. There's a row of bullet marks on the wall where he aimed," said Mr. Yang.

Mr. Yang looked haggard, his eyes sad, his spirit listless. He said he was dejected growing up without his brothers. He had played a lot with them prior to the killings and he missed them dearly. I felt an enormous pang of empathy for him; when his brothers, grandmother, and other relatives were killed, I am certain a part of his childhood, and many of his dreams were lost, too.

# CHAPTER 13

I was very much looking forward to our next destination, the South Chungcheong Forest and Environmental Research Center, where I hoped that the director, Mr. Kwon Young-ho, could shed some light on how the peninsula was altered from, well, to be blunt, a virtually treeless and barren landscape to today's canopy of green, which covered almost every hill, protuberance, and mountain across the country. Several days earlier, when Min-jun and I were tootling around Gongju, we had spotted a large road sign providing directions to the environmental centre. We had gone in, but Mr. Kwon had not been there, so we had booked an appointment to meet with him today.

The three of us sat at a table by an outdoor snack shop near the entrance to the grounds. Steep green hills rose up behind the modern Forestry Museum building. In my mind, I had envisioned Mr. Kwon as a typical park ranger type — khaki-clad, brawny, and bearded — but instead he looked to me like the Korean reincarnation of the Great Gatsby — slight, polished, and looking quite dapper in a white formal blazer, dress shirt, blue slacks, and shiny black loafers. He seemed more suited to hosting genteel embassy garden parties than trudging through thick brush over logs and into insect-laden woods. But Mr. Kwon was indeed a true forest man, and really knew his stuff, having majored at university in tropical wood and forest research.

He walked with a slight limp and used a cane. Later, his young assistant told us that Mr. Kwon had been injured in a car accident a couple of months previous. Mr. Kwon explained that the centre had been established in 1997, and that its mandate was to manage the South Chungcheong forest region — three quarters of which was woods — and to study new species of flora and fauna and investigate harmful effects of insect-borne disease on trees.

The successful reforestation of the peninsula, he explained, was traceable to President Park, who decreed in early 1970 that 150 species of trees would receive protection from being felled. For centuries, wood had been critical to survival in Korea: to build homes, to stoke fireplaces to heat floors during the winter, and to heat stoves for cooking. In many areas, lower mountain slopes had been cleared to create more agricultural land for the growing of barley, potatoes, rice, and other staples. The Japanese had cut timber and shipped it home, as well, and later, many thousands of acres of woodland were destroyed during the Korean War, another casualty of the bombings and their resultant fires. All these factors combined so that by the 1950s and '60s, much of the Korean peninsula's forests had been severely depleted.

It was in the large province of Gangwon, east of Seoul, where the woods had the best chance to be replenished, not coincidently because most of the forests there were protected by the national government. But the remaining forests across the country, about three-quarters, were privately owned, controlled, and managed by individual villages. The federal government owned less than a fifth of the total forested areas, and the provincial governments oversaw only about 8 percent. Under the new law, private owners were now required to get government permission to cut down trees.

"There were cases of farmers being fined under the new law," said Mr. Kwon, the penalty for cutting illegally ranging from fines to as many as two years in jail. "But jail time was seen as a last resort. Officials worried that once the culprit finished serving his jail term, he might seek revenge and chop more trees."

The government introduced various tree species. Pitch pine (*Pinus rigida*) is a hardy, small- to medium-sized species that prospers in inhospitable conditions, the trunks sometimes becoming twisty and gnarled, and usually not suitable for timber. They are commonly found in the eastern United States. Korea planted seedlings in large numbers on the peninsula. Also planted were native white and red pines, resilient against forest fires, and larches, cedars, and cypress. In low areas and along streams, poplars were seeded.

Helping the cause was that after the Korean War, wood as fuel was largely being replaced by coal. More than 80 percent of domestic coal production was earmarked to produce briquettes, used to heat homes and for cooking. Then, by the late 1960s, oil began replacing coal.

After more than five decades of sustained and scrupulous adherence to the preservation and planting of forests, about 63,000 square kilometres of South Korea's total area (100,000 kilometres) are now treed. Nearly every knoll, hill, and mountain, whether in the cities or along the broad sweeping Sobaeks or the steep, rugged Taebaeks — everywhere that is not a plain, river valley, or flat land — is treed. Pines comprise about a third of all mountainous woods. An expert in South Korean forestation, Victor Teplyakov, a former professor at the Department of Forest Sciences at Seoul National University, estimated that 11 billion trees have been planted since the 1960s.

Mr. Kwon said there are now 6,800 species of flora and fauna, and that the nation's reforestation program has been heralded as a model by other nations looking to develop and maintain woodlands. In 2007, China signed an agreement with South Korea for the latter to assist it in reforesting a vast tract of treeless terrain adjacent to the Gobi Desert.

But Mr. Kwon conceded that not all was rosy: areas of woodland in South Korea have not been faring well due to disease. Pine forests in the northeast have been infected by parasites, which he believes originated from on an illegal shipment of monkeys arriving in Busan from Japan in the 1990s. "The parasites slowly made their way up to the northern forests. They block tree veins. Millions of trees have been dying over the years. It's a slow process. There's no cure. It's a state of emergency now."

After our talk with Mr. Kwon, Min-jun and I spent some time rambling through the Forestry Museum. For me it was an exercise in vexation, because all the signage, information, and exhibits were written in Hangul. I was not able to learn anything new about the country's flora and fauna.

* * *

Min-jun and I stayed the night at the jimjilbang in Gongju and the following afternoon made our way to Gyeryong Mountain National Park. The park is located southeast of Gongju on the way to Daejeon, and although not huge, covering just sixty-five square kilometres, it is the most popular hiking spot in the province, with twenty-one "young" granite peaks, a spur of outliers from the Charyeong range, the tallest rising up 845 metres.

The park is also home to the Donghak Buddhist Temple for female monks, and this was the main reason I was heading there. The women would have stories to tell, I was certain.

The final section of Donghak Temple Road into the park was straight and tree-lined, flanked with a number of restaurants, cafés, souvenir shops, a convenience store, and a minbak or two. On weekends and holidays, especially when the cherry blossoms are in bloom, Gyeryong and other mountain parks can resemble fairgrounds, with upwards of ten thousand visitors arriving each day. But because we had ventured here on a weekday at the end of May, there was only a smattering of cars and a few hikers. The sign posted at the ticket hut at the entrance informed us that it was a 1.6-kilometre hike to the Donghak Temple.

The wide path rose gradually through the trees, whose high, bountiful branches formed a solid canopy that virtually blocked out the hot sun. Under this green umbrella, the temperature was a perfect 18 degrees. Not a twig rustled. Only the shrill tweets of a songbird and the gurgling of a mountain brook could be heard. We were passed by only a couple of hikers who were on their way down. It was a lovely walk.

The grounds of Donghak Temple, like other Buddhist temples I had visited, were of compacted dry earth on which sat the main temple hall, a three-storey stone pagoda, and several other structures. I paid the structures no heed. I wasn't there for aesthetics, but to get the lowdown from the women. Inside the small office by the gate, several nuns were working away. One, who looked to be in her sixties, with bushy eyebrows and a gold front tooth, greeted us warmly. I handed her my business card and Min-jun explained that I was writing a travel book about Korea, and would like to include in it a bit about the nuns of Donghak Temple.

She sternly surveyed the card, nodded, and then slowly read my name out loud: "Dake … Mark, Dake … Mark."

I politely corrected her: "Mark Dake."

She laughed merrily.

Now was not the time to talk to the nuns, she told us. "We're having a meeting soon. Go up the mountain and come back, then we can talk."

"Good idea … I need the exercise," I joked, and she laughed heartily again.

We had not planned on hiking, as we figured it would take several hours to get up and back down the trail. But why not? It would do us good to stretch our legs; plus, the view from the top would likely be impressive. It was already four-thirty in the afternoon, and we had agreed to meet the nun at the temple at about eight. That gave us more than three hours to make the climb.

The trail map showed three separate trails leading to the various peaks, and we opted to trek the one that summited at Jwanueumbong (*bong* means "peak"). We had the trail to ourselves, and Min-jun, who was quicker and nimbler than me, went on ahead. At first the path was soft and gradual, but soon became steeper and generously strewn with an annoying, uneven layer of small uneven rocks. Each step I took felt like I was walking with bare feet on a shallow, rocky stream. I cursed the park management.

When I emerged from the gloomy shadows, Min-jun was waiting for me by a wooden gazebo beside a wide ridge of exposed, jagged granite. It was six thirty. A posted sign read 816 METRES, GYERYONGSAN, JWANUEMBONG. We made it! We were only about eight thousand metres shy of the summit of Mount Everest; nonetheless, it was a small matter of pride to be at the top.

As expected, the view from the top was captivating in the grey-blue twilit sky. To the north and west we had an expansive view of the low rocky ridges of the Charyeongs. To the southwest was the Geum River plain, divided into tens of thousands of small rectangular yellow-brown rice paddies, and far beyond that the start of the great Honam Plain. The flat plain seemed to stretch forever. We could also make the fringes of the city of Daejeon and its innumerable blocks of white apartment buildings. Directly below us, in a V in the wooded mountain, sat Donghak Temple. It was much farther away than I expected.

With dusk fast approaching, we started off back down the trail, the jagged pieces of rock underfoot making the trek about as enjoyable as getting a root canal.

We were a bit late getting back, and when we went into the temple office we were told by one of the nuns that no one could talk to us because the lights had to be out by nine o'clock.

"Come back tomorrow," we were told.

Disappointed but not undaunted, I decided we'd do just that. Min-jun and I headed down to the park entrance, where we ran into one of the park rangers. Park No-san was a thoroughly decent and loquacious chap who had been with the Korean National Park Service for more than three decades. The three of us sat on a bench and chatted for quite some time. Mr. Park told us that the biggest change he had observed over his thirty years was the visitors' attitudes with respect to the environment.

"People used to throw garbage on the trail," he told us. "They'd be drunk. We'd ask them to pick up their garbage and they'd tell us 'you're park officials … it's your job to pick up garbage. That's what you get paid for.' It's taken a lot of time to change. It's been a very gradual process."

He told us about a hiker who died from a heart attack while walking the trails, women who had attempted to ascend the mountain while wearing high-heeled shoes, only to be forced to remove them and trek in barefoot. And as for that annoying bed of sharp rocks along the trail that Min-jun and I had just traversed, he told us that other hikers had also complained, and that the park was considering jettisoning them.

It was approaching ten o'clock by the time the three of us strolled onto Donghak Temple Road and past the still-open and brightly-lit but empty restaurants. Mr. Park asked us to join him for dinner, but Min-jun and I were both sweaty and grubby, so we thanked him but told him we really needed to get going.

"Come and visit my room then," he said, motioning to a little unit next to one of the restaurants.

But the evening air in the mountains was nippy, and my shirt was sweaty and damp. "Thanks, but we need to take showers," I told him.

"You can take shower in my room!" Mr. Park invited brightly.

I suddenly had an alarming vision of sharing a shower stall with a happy and buck-naked park ranger offering to scrub my back under a jet of hot water. I thanked him again, but we declined and were on our way. Later, I regretted that we had not accompanied Mr. Park to dinner. He was a very friendly man, and perhaps a tad lonely stationed by himself at the park. He simply wanted a little company. I vowed that when I returned to Gyeryong, I would buy good ol' Mr. Park a hearty dinner and we'd drink soju into the wee hours of the late evening together and get rip-roaring tipsy.

Min-jun and I drove a few hundred metres to the Gyeryong Minbak, where we rented a room. I had a welcome shower, long and hot and under which I stomped my sweaty garments to clean them. Min-jun did likewise. Afterward, we threw our wet clothes over a line on the front porch. Back in the room, we unrolled mats on the floor and I fell asleep almost instantly. There must have been something in the mountain air.

* * *

It was June 1, and the Scoupe had been along for the ride for eight weeks — minus the interlude in Seoul. The car had covered over four thousand kilometres of blacktop in that time, equivalent to driving the length of the country ten times. Hopefully, she'd keep motoring for the next four thousand clicks.

The cool grey morning was heavy with dampness as Min-jun and I made our way back up to Donghak Temple. Across from the temple, atop a small knoll, we saw several nuns dressed in grey smocks labouring in a modest vegetable garden. Two appeared to be in their early thirties, and wore oversized straw hats while they squatted on their haunches, silently hoeing between the plants. The third was much older, and obviously in a position of power because when we walked up and introduced ourselves, only she responded.

Her name was Ryo Myoung, but I nicknamed her "Attila the Nun" for her hefty girth and touchy disposition. Attila, whose head was shaved, as custom dictates, though she was wearing a wide-brimmed straw hat, told us that she had been a monk for fifty-two years and been at the temple for five decades. "But I'm not the oldest resident," she added." One is ninety-five years old."

I asked how old she was, and she said, "Why do you want to know my age? Is age important to you?"

"No, I was just curious," I said.

"Sixty-nine," she proudly asserted.

She informed us that prospective nuns could stay on at the temple on a two-year trial basis. If the women decided they were ready to commit the rest of their lives to the nunhood, they could choose to reside there permanently. There were currently about 150 full-time nuns at Donghak and they welcomed about fifteen new arrivals each year. I asked Ryo Myoung about the Buddhist regimen of early-to-bed and early-to-rise.

She quickly rebuked me: "You're asking a stupid question! Life's always a repetition. Today exists because there's yesterday. Tomorrow exists because there's today."

Well, I already knew that. I recalled that the night before the soles of my feet had felt like hammers were pounding them, and that the next day I'd be in the car driving, because that is what I had been doing almost daily for the past two months, and what I would likely continue to do for another two months. Not particularly wanting to be chastised as dimwitted again, I opted for a softer approach. "Do you miss the outside world?"

"Another stupid question!" I began to doubt whether she had voluntarily joined the nunhood. "Those who practice aesthetics don't think about the outside world!" she added.

Realizing that any of my inquiries would see me labelled a blockhead, I attempted to appeal to her latent emotional side, and explained to her that I knew very little about Buddhism, and that if she could help demystify it for me a bit, I would be very appreciative.

"Ah, ask me more questions!" she said brightly.

"But how do I know what's a good and what's a bad question?" I squeaked.

"There are no bad ones!" she declared.

Well, of course not.

I asked what the most important element of being a Buddhist was. She said it was recognizing the truth, to be like Buddha, that all animals had the ability to live and survive, but only humans could do better than animals and could attain a higher plane. "Humans must be enlightened in the circle of life." She believed in reincarnation and revealed that she was probably a nun in her former life.

I suggested that living at Gyeryong Mountain was spiritually rewarding. She agreed. It permitted her to be close to Buddha, to enjoy the clean mountain air. The only negative was that it was a little cold during winter, she admitted. She pointed down to the path, where a man was taking a photo in front of the temple. "I don't like that. Before Gyeryong became a national park in 1968, visitors rarely came here."

"But visitors are more environmentally friendly now," I said, recalling what Mr. Park had told us the night before.

"No, they're not — they still leave garbage."

Attila opened her lunch bag, extricated rice cake, melon slices, and a small thermos of orange juice, then sat on a stool and began to eat and drink. Despite her outwardly gruff manner, school-girl innocence shone through.

"Why don't you become a monk?" she asked me.

Oh, my goodness, another Venerable Jae-un, who at Jogye Temple in Seoul almost kidnapped me into the monkhood. The thought of being at bed at nine o'clock, waking at three a.m., living a fettered, regimented, and orderly life was totally counterproductive to my somewhat undisciplined and occasionally whimsical existence. Left to my own nocturnal rhythms, I'd be putting a good book on the bedside table and heading to bed at three or four a.m., the same time nuns woke to begin each day! There was no way I could meditate either. I explained this and told her I would miss playing sports, too.

"The 108 bows monks do every day is a good substitute for exercise," she interjected.

"But I need to swim and cycle and to play tennis," I countered.

I couldn't help thinking that the daily bowing had done little to help Attila in that regard.

She then pointed to my stomach, which I tried, unsuccessfully, to suck in, and said "If you do the 108 bows every day, that'll reduce its size!" (I then knew she was, without a doubt, related to the Venerable Jae-un in Seoul.)

When we finally took our leave, we thanked her and I said "bye bye."

"Mark ... not 'bye,'" she corrected, then demonstrated the proper protocol, Buddhist-style, for bidding adieu, by forming one's hands in front, as if in prayer. I followed her lead, and when she was satisfied, we had her divine permission to depart.

Min-jun and I walked back down the path to our minbak. Our washing on the line was still damp, but we threw it in the car anyway. It was then that we noticed a small, mangy dog was tied up outside the minbak on a two-foot chain. Its water bowl was empty, so we filled it from our water bottle and fed it a handful of strawberies we had in the car. We asked two elderly women sitting on the veranda if the dog was theirs.

Yes, they replied. We then asked politely if they always kept the dog chained. Yes again, they said.

"Do you think you could let it off the chain sometimes to get some exercise?" we added hopefully.

"No. If we do, it tries to bite people," one of the women told us.

We tried again, explaining that it was bad for the dog's health if it didn't get any exercise, but the women were not swayed. "We don't have to let it off the chain... It's not sick."

I briefly harboured an evil but thoroughly satisfying thought of tying the ladies to the side of the house with two-foot ropes. But what could we do?

We sighed, got in the car, and departed for Gwangju, the largest city in the southwest, about 170 kilometres away. We had an appointment to meet a young woman by the name of Miki, who would be arriving on the high-speed KTX train from Seoul at nine o'clock that evening.

I had met Miki three weeks previous in Seoul after she answered my online ad seeking a translator for the trip. She was employed as a tour guide for Koreans visiting Japan and she spoke fluent Japanese, Korean, and English. When I mentioned to her that I would be visiting Sorok Island off the south coast, she had expressed enthusiasm to join us there and see it, too.

Min-jun and I headed south out along backcountry roads that parallel the western edge of the Sobaek Mountains and then continued into the short Noryeong range that runs from north of Gwangju to the west coast. The route is remote and mountainous much of the way.

Fifty kilometres northeast of Gwangju, we stopped at a tiny village, a mere blip on the map that is hemmed in by steep wooded mountains. I pulled into a gas station and asked the woman behind the counter if I could use the facilities. She pointed out back, behind the shop.

"It's dirty," she warned.

Well, that was an understatement. It was, in fact, filthy. Constructed of concrete and tile, the small unit stood next to the main building. As I entered, the stench hit my nose like a freight train. The urinals appeared not to have been cleaned since about 1867. I dashed outside, took a deep breath, held it, darted back inside. Thirty seconds later, my face turning red from lack of oxygen, I sprinted back outside and sucked in deep gulps of fresh air.

"Was that a washroom?" I asked Min-jun, incredulously.

He gave a knowing smile: "That's how country washrooms used to be before Korea started the movement for cleaner ones." He then explained that many public toilets in the country were in a state similar to this one until the government began a campaign to improve their cleanliness back in the 1990s. These days, when you enter a public facility at, say, the foot of a mountain trail or at a highway rest stop, you might find an official plaque on the wall reading: "Best Toilet 2009," or "Best Toilet 2011." This one, I guarantee you, had never been a contender.

In March, when Heju and I hiked Mount Acha in Seoul, a sign hanging outside the facilities at the base stated SEOUL BEST TOILET — AUGUST, 2002 — 1ST PRIZE FROM MAYOR OF SEOUL. We each went inside our respective washroom to see for ourselves what an award-winning one looked like, and I must say we were impressed with the heated seats and overhead lighting on motion sensors — as I sat on the throne, the light overhead would blink off every thirty seconds or so, but with just a simple movement of my head, it would flick back on.

That's progress, for you!

* * *

It was dark by the time Min-jun and I finally arrived in Gwangju, and it was obvious that all of the city's 1.8 million people had come out in their vehicles to welcome us. We were immediately ensnarled in traffic on one of the main streets, which was teeming with cars, taxis, Bongo trucks, SUVs, and buses. It took us more than an hour to reach the Gwangju Train Station, where we met Miki.

We'd have a third along for our next leg of the tour!

# CHAPTER 14

The morning after Miki joined us was cool and overcast, with grey clouds hovering low in the sky. The three of us drove southeast from Gwangju, along quiet, winding roads that led toward the coast. The landscape here was decidedly different from the mountainous interior Min-jun and I had travelled through the day before. There were areas of coastal plains, and I enjoyed the feeling of openness and space. The mountains, though, were never far away.

In several places we noticed that farmers had set small fires in the fields to burn off the remnants of the winter crops, readying the ground for summer planting. Tall, narrow plumes of white smoke snaked high into the air, meeting the clouds, while below, the earth was scorched to black stubble.

We stopped briefly in the rural town of Boseong, ten kilometres from the coast. Boseong was renowned for its long history of growing tea leaves on the lower mountain slopes in neatly terraced rows. When I asked my travel companions if they would like to stop and see the tea fields, they declined. Which surprised me a bit, since it wasn't everyday one got to Boseong.

So we continued on into the formidable county of Goheung, a peninsula that hangs prominently off the south coast, its form irregular, its coastline jagged with coves, inlets, and offshore islands. When the tide is out, vast areas of mud flats are exposed. A long string of low mountains tightly hug the shoreline at this, the southern end of the Korean peninsula, their slopes often sweeping steeply into the sea. This topography continues throughout Goheung, though the peninsula also includes swaths of agricultural plains.

We drove south along Goheung's smooth, modern main highway to the old harbour town of Doyang, off Goheung's southwestern tip. Doyang is a busy hub of activity, its old dwellings and shops concentrated around the small harbour. Across the narrow channel were the lush green mountains of Sorok Island. Farther south, out across the greenish-blue sea, was the much larger and mountainous Geogeum Island.

Fishing trawlers were moored along the wharf in Doyang. There was a fish market, with vendors standing behind large plastic buckets containing fresh seafood, including eels, clams, crabs, octopus, sea worms, oysters, and anything else that was remotely edible and could be harvested from the sea. It was really quite amazing — from a Western perspective — to observe the bewildering variety of sea things that Koreans voluntarily ingest.

Before us, in the buckets of water, were live mini octopus caught on the mudflats, sometimes swallowed by Koreans whole and live or sliced up — tentacles squirming — on restaurant plates. Fat pink sea worms were in abundance, as were oysters, which are eaten raw. At one stall a woman was nimbly and skillfully gutting live fish.

We took the small pedestrian ferry across the channel to Sorok Island. Once there, we walked under a canopy of lovely old trees to a small white building, the Sorok Island National Hospital, which sat on a small bay. We went in and asked if there was anyone who could explain a bit about the island's history. We were told to return Monday morning, when a guide would show us around. It was only Saturday.

We caught the last ferry back to Doyang at six o'clock, then strolled west along the harbour, past the fish stalls and a row of old shops, and on the edge of the harbour climbed up a grassy knoll to get a better view. What we couldn't miss was the steel and concrete bulk of the newly built

Sorok Bridge, which spans the water between Doyang and Sorok. This massive construction project, so incongruous here, had put an end to Sorok Island's pedestrian-only status in 2009.

On top of the knoll was a plaque honouring two fallen Korean naval heroes: Lee Dae-won, killed by Japanese pirates in 1587, and Jeong-un, who died at the hands of the Japanese in a naval battle during the 1592–98 Imjin War. Japanese pirates — their base on Tsushima Island, fifty kilometres south of Busan — had once plundered Korea's coasts.

Out of the blue, Miki suddenly blurted out, "Sorok's boring … I want to see Boseong."

Min-jun nodded his agreement.

I was taken aback. First, we hadn't even explored Sorok yet. Second, we had stopped in Boseong about four hours previous, so I explained to Miki now that I was not going to retrace our route at this point.

"Well, then, let's go to Yeosu," she declared glibly.

I gritted my teeth. While Yeosu was the next peninsula east, to reach it required driving all the way back out of Goheung, east across the mainland, and then thirty kilometres south. But in the past twenty-four hours, I had already driven several hundred kilometres. I have large reserves of energy, but I have my limit. Miki had told me in Seoul that she wanted to see Sorok Island, and I reminded her of this. The two did not argue with me, though I could tell they wanted to.

We walked back to town, and on the other side of the harbour, near the waterfront, found a well-used yeogwan, where we took a large, spacious room with a yellow linoleum floor and no beds, plunked our stuff down, unrolled our mats and bedding, and relaxed for a while. A little later, Min-jun and Miki went out together for dinner. I stayed in and had a nap.

* * *

Sunday was perfect: twenty-seven degrees, low humidity, fresh sea breeze, hazy blue sky, and bright sunshine. I drove Min-jun and Miki all around Goheung. We toured its indented south coast, and looked down from high atop coastal hills out over the lovely views of the green sea and scores of small offshore islands. We puttered along the scenic and mountainous eastern shoreline, a ten-kilometre-wide bay separating us from the steep green slopes of Yeosu. Goheung's coastline is primarily made up of shallow mud flats, though there are some sections of rocks and the odd little sandy beach. And I can't even begin to explain how many bays and coves there are here. The year before, Heju and I had attempted to explore them all, and after seven days and six hundred kilometres, we thought we had seen nearly every remote cove and bay in the county.

In the late afternoon, Min-jun, Miki, and I relaxed at the secluded Balpo Beach, accessible only by foot. (Heju and I had discovered it during that same backroads trip the previous year.) Inland from the beach was a little grassy meadow, where several cows were grazing. There was not another soul on the beach that day, and Min-jun and I took a dip in the twenty-two-degree water. I believe my companions would agree that it was an extremely pleasurable day.

We returned to Doyang in time for dinner, and I dropped Min-jun at the yeogwan. Miki wanted to head back up-island to Goheung City to hit some golf balls. She was a beginner, taking lessons in Seoul, she said. No matter what city you're in, there is always a driving range not far off in golf-mad Korea.

Just outside Goheung City — a small collection of flat-roofed dwellings concentrated in a narrow space between steep low hills — was the driving range, where Miki and I spent an hour hitting golf balls under the floodlights. The young instructor kindly gave me some free pointers, and I concentrated on his every word. I had played a fair bit of golf during my middle school years with my classmates in Toronto, but none of us had ever had a lesson. Our swings were rough and homemade. But when we did connect with the ball just right, and sent it sailing in a glorious arc whistling high above the fairway, there was no better feeling. Being out on a foursome on a warm spring or summer day with regulars Richard Earl, Mike Day, Cliff Flint, Shane Bury, Stuart Nicol, Dennis Hisey, Rick Thorsteinson, Mark Richardson, and Bruce McCann is among my fondest boyhood memories.

At the practice range, Miki was swinging her club as if she were embalmed, the balls consistently dribbling off her club face and skidding unceremoniously along the ground, landing just a few dozen metres away. "Maybe loosen up and relax a bit when you swing," I congenially suggested.

"No," she insisted, as if she was in a playoff at the finals of the U.S Women's Open, "my golf instructor told me that proper technique was the most important thing. He said not to worry about where the ball goes." She resolutely kept up the same technique, and her balls continued to decimate the driving range's entire population of worms with ruthless efficiency.

Back in Doyang, Miki and I stopped at a little fried chicken restaurant along a back lane and shared a plate of chicken at a small booth in the dim interior. Miki, who was single and in her early thirties, explained to me her rather inflexible dating philosophy.

"My mommy wants me to join a dating agency," she said.

"How does it work?" I asked.

"You pay two million, four million, or eight million won."

"What does two million get you?"

"A lower class of man," she said.

"Four million?"

"Middle class."

"Eight?"

"Top class."

"What do you mean by *class*?" I asked.

A lower-class man costs two million won, she explained, this segment apparently including office workers with a bachelor's degree. A four million won fellow had a BA, too, but a higher-paying job. A doctor or lawyer cost eight million. Men without a university degree were not permitted to join the agency. The men had to show a certificate proving what their job was, and how much money they earned, she said.

"But what if you met a taxi driver who didn't have a degree but who you loved?"

"I wouldn't love him. I couldn't. A taxi driver doesn't think and most have bad character," she said quite mercilessly.

I had driven taxi for six months after high school in Toronto, and depending on whom you talked to, my character was not that bad. "What if the taxi driver had a bachelor degree?" I said, probing to find a chink in Miki's armour.

"Then he wouldn't be a taxi driver… He'd work at a different job," she said with amazingly skewered logic.

"But what if a banker lost his job and became a taxi driver?" I continued. In 1997, in Korea, during the Asian financial crisis, hundreds of bank branches were permanently shuttered, and thousands of bankers, through no fault of their own, had lost their jobs.

Miki remained unmoved. "No one would lose his job at a bank unless he was a failure. I wouldn't want him."

When I asked what would happen if she did marry a taxi driver, she said that her friends and family would not talk to her anymore.

"Well, then they aren't real friends … they're phonies," I said.

"No," Miki answered in a matter-of-fact tone, "it's how the Korean system works. We have to marry the same class."

What Miki was conveniently failing to acknowledge, of course, was that if she held herself to her own rigid standards, then doctors, lawyers, industrialists, Samsung executive scions, and sugar daddies would all be out of her league. She was, after all, a tour guide. But I didn't tell her this.

Early Monday morning, I drove Miki from the yeogwan to the nearby Doyang bus station. She had decided to bus it back to Seoul after she told me she did not want to go back to tour Sorok Island with us. I do not think that Miki really enjoyed her two days in Goheung. She seemed to have a preference for high-end travel.

I returned to the yeogwan to pick up Min-jun. The weather again was gorgeous, bright and fresh, the sea green and glassy smooth, a blue haze enveloping Geogeum Island in the distance. We boarded the ferry for Sorok Island to be on time for our nine o'clock appointment.

Mr. Kim Gwang-mun, an official with the Doyang Ministry of Health and Welfare, greeted us in front of the hospital. He would be giving us our tour. Mr. Kim led us behind the hospital to a large, shaded park, and pointed out a handful of small, handsome red-brick units nearby that he informed us were constructed in 1916.

More than six hundred, mostly elderly, patients afflicted with leprosy live on Sorok Island in their own little community near the hospital. Most were brought here as young children by their families, and the island is the only home many of them have known. None came here voluntarily, and fearful parents and family often never set foot on the island again.

"About two hundred of the brick units were built. The Japanese forced the lepers to construct them. If they resisted, they were sometimes punished by being given prison terms," said Mr. Kim.

The Japanese had rounded up lepers from across the country and conveyed them to Sorok, sequestering them away from society. Lepers at the time were considered social outcasts, forced to beg on the streets. Japanese motives, though, were far from altruistic, and life on the island for the lepers could be harsher than experienced on the streets. Here, they were forced to perform hard manual labour, were often malnourished, and were sometimes imprisoned for minor infractions. After death, some bodies were surgically experimented on, on the island. After the Japanese departed in 1945, the Korean government took control of Sorok. Lepers, however, continued to be involuntarily sent here by their families.

We entered one of the small red-brick units, which our guide tells us was the former "Building No. 1," or the autopsy room. The bodies of the dead lepers were sometimes dissected for body parts, explained Mr. Kim. The shelves that lined the walls were now empty, but up until 1996, they had held jars of formaldehyde preserving the organs of former patients.

In an effort to locate the families of the deceased to repatriate organs, Korean authorities tried to contact next of kin. But since the Japanese destroyed most of the records, no one knew how many autopsies had been performed or who the families of the patients were. Fast forward to 1996, when public announcements were made to try to locate the families; many came to Sorok to claim body parts, but Mr. Kim said it had been very difficult to match organs to next of kin.

Next door, behind a low brick wall, sat the tiny prison, and opposite the prison was a five-room schoolhouse that had been built in 1918. There was also what remained of a baseball field with patchy grass and crumbling stone bleachers. A room contained memorabilia, including a photograph of one of the four Japanese governors who once ruled Sorok. Another image showed hundreds of lepers labouring on the island.

Our guide led us back up into the park, which he told us had been a formidable hill until the Japanese forced the lepers to excavate it down to a lower level. The rigorous work took four years. In the park, we passed several elderly patients, one with a disfigured face, another with no legs who was navigating a motorized wheelchair. Lepers often need to have limbs amputated due to infection.

A plaque commemorated Pope John Paul II's May 4, 1984, visit to the island. Another honoured a Japanese military doctor, Hanai Jenkichi, who was employed at the island hospital from 1921 to 1929 and was apparently compassionate and caring toward the lepers.

After a couple of hours with Mr. Kim, we thanked him, and Min-jun and I returned to the hospital. Inside was quiet, with no sign of staff, doctors, or patients.

On the fourth floor, we met an English-speaking nurse, Park Seong-hui, who asked that we call her Elizabeth. She had been attending to lepers on Sorok for twenty-seven years. She was calm and down to earth, with a tired and wizened visage, as if she had seen everything life had to offer, which she probably had. She was not one to sugarcoat things, preferring reality. Of the 640 patients currently on the island, she told us, only thirty-two received any sort of visitation from their family or relatives. Many families had purposely cut ties with their afflicted family members. "Sometimes, the family moved to another town and left no notice. Sometimes, they reported to the local government that their family member with the disease had died," she explained.

An irrational fear that the disease was contagious was one of the main reasons why families gave up their kin on Sorok, even though there were government facilities for lepers on the mainland. For more than five decades, the medical community had known that leprosy was not contagious, said Elizabeth, but the shame of having a family member with the disease was often a factor.

At the time of our visit, the oldest patient on Sorok was 103, the youngest just thirty-five, having been sent there by his family in 1997. "They send him things, but have never visited," Elizabeth old us. "His family is ashamed of him."

Most patients were religious. There were marriages between lepers, though the concept of marriage was not in the traditional sense; rather, if one was blind and the other deaf, they could be the other's eyes and ears.

Three saintly Austrian nuns: Marianne Stöger, Margreth Pissarek, and Maria Dittrich, who arrived on Sorok in 1964, were instrumental in raising money for patients on the island during a period when Korea had scant funds to spare. Proceeds were used to construct a tuberculosis ward and a dormitory for the blind, among other things.

The nuns departed Sorok for Austria after forty years, in 2004. Elizabeth, the nurse, told us she had travelled to Austria to visit her friends. "They left Sorok because they were old, and because they felt Korea was developed enough so that they didn't need to serve here anymore … and they didn't want the bridge coming over," she said.

When Min-jun and I emerged from the hospital after more than two hours, the afternoon was oppressively hot. We strolled up through the deserted but shaded park and encountered a man wearing a cowboy hat and holding a Polaroid camera. "Would you like your photo taken?" he asked us.

"Thanks, not at the moment," I replied.

He seemed disappointed. "Business isn't good these days. Everyone has a digital camera," he lamented.

He introduced himself as Choi Yong-gap. He looked to be in his sixties, was enthusiastic and outgoing, and seemed to have boundless energy. I wasn't sure if he was a patient, because, except for an area of his face that had a slightly plastic appearance, he seemed not to have a notable impediment. We shook hands, and when I felt his gnarled, stiff fingers, I realized he did indeed have leprosy; yet, had I encountered him in my neighbourhood in Seoul, I would not have given him a second glance.

We sat down on a bench and talked. Mr. Choi had been born in 1943 in Mokpo, on the southwest coast. When he was six, he was afflicted with leprosy. His mother brought him to Sorok. Since then, she has visited him only once, in 1956, when he was thirteen. "My father and three brothers and sister have never visited," he told us.

At the age of twenty-four, he travelled to Mokpo to see his family. When he tried to touch his nieces' and nephews' hands, they had walked away. People did not want to sit next to him on the bus or eat at the same table. He was not invited to family birthdays. Six months later, he returned to the island. Then, at the age of thirty, in 1973, he tried again to live in Mokpo. Again he was rejected. He has not been back to Mokpo since. "I kept telling my family that I was safe, that they wouldn't get leprosy from me. It did no good. Even now, they won't accept me; they won't give me their phone number. I've given up ever seeing them again."

Then, as I was prone to do, I spoke before thinking, and absent-mindedly asked, "How does it feel to be abandoned?" I immediately wished a big hole would open up before me to crawl into.

Mr. Choi remained silent a few moments, and then suddenly burst into anguished, gut-wrenching sobs. "Even if I conquered the world, it would mean nothing to me," he wailed. "I just want to see my family once!"

I felt like a louse. A few moments later, he regained his composure.

"Min-jun and I will be heading to Mokpo tomorrow. We could try to contact your family for you there," I offered brightly, trying to make up for my insensitivity.

He shook his head and said it was impossible. His family had moved. Plus, they didn't want him to visit. "I tried to find them with a friend's help, but it didn't work," he added.

I persevered: "The police might be able to track them down. I could contact the Mokpo police for you."

"No, I gave up a long time ago," he said resignedly.

His optimistic nature was quickly rejuvenated, however, and he suggested a tour of the park. He led us down the path, noting there used to be factory here that produced red bricks. The bricks to construct Seoul's Seodaemun Prison had been made there, he added. Mr. Choi told us about one of the island's Japanese governors, who had a statue of himself made. From 1933 to 1942, Suho was the vainglorious fourth Japanese governor of Sorok, and he was collectively despised by the lepers.

"Suho paid for this statue to be built by stealing money from lepers," Mr. Choi told us. When the lepers passed him, he forced them to bow to him. Suho met his untimely death when a leper named Lee Chun-sang stabbed him to death. A month later, Lee was executed by hanging at Seodaemun Prison. The statue was torn down by the Japanese in 1943 and melted down to make ammunition for the war effort.

When a group of nine women wandered up, Mr. Choi immediately began educating them about Mr. Suho and Sorok history. Min-jun and I waved and called goodbye to him, but Mr. Choi did not hear us, so engrossed he was in tutoring his new charges.

It was now four o'clock, and we had been on the island for seven hours. We were tired, hot, and quickly wilting, so we headed in the direction of the ferry dock, though on the way we stopped for a respite at a lovely little sandy beach on the east shore with a view of Geogeum Island. On the path back to the ferry, we passed a Shinto Shrine, the Japanese homage to the Sun God erected by Suho in 1935.

Back in Doyang, just outside town, we checked into the modern and large four-floor Pada Spaland jimjilbang. In its empty gymnasium-like second-floor sleeping area, the windows were shut, the air inside stifling. I threw open a window, and a welcome breeze wafted in.

Min-jun and I were the only customers. In one corner, I spotted several large padded armchairs provided automatic massage for a small fee of 1,000 won. My leg muscles ached from standing all day, so I parked myself in a chair and deposited my money. Immediately, the hidden coils and hammers hummed to life and began thumping me up and down, sideways and crossways. My shoulders, back, spine, thighs, and calves were kneaded, ground, beaten, and pummelled in a glorious twelve-minute assault. When the chair finally fell silent — my body tingling with relief and delight — I immediately deposited another 1,000 won. It was marvellous. I would have stayed ensconced in the chair for months, were I a millionaire. When I ascend to Heaven, I would appreciate it if such a chair was there waiting for me.

Afterward, I caught up on some much-needed sleep, taking a siesta on one of the mats. Min-jun headed off to the showers to scrape off more skin.

Later that evening, lying on our mats (we still had the entire floor to ourselves), we turned on the big screen TV and watched *Great Police Chases*. It is astonishing how thoroughly American television has infiltrated the world airwaves, even on remote little Sorok Island. Mr. Choi had told us his favourite program was American wrestling.

As we were preparing to sleep, seven ajummas wearing sauna uniforms — orange shorts and T-shirts — suddenly appeared on the floor, and silently and assiduously placed their sleeping mats side by side in a neat and straight row and immediately went to sleep. They reminded me of the seven dwarfs in *Snow White*.

When I awoke at seven thirty the next morning, the mats, and the dwarfs, were gone.

# CHAPTER 15

Entering Mokpo was not the scenic experience I had imagined. We approached from the east, having just driven west from Goheung across the mixed bag of coastal plains, with an infinite number of orderly agricultural fields interspersed with pockets of low mountains. Mokpo was located at the mouth of the mile-wide estuary of the Yeongsan River. Concrete lined both banks.

We entered the city along the main road, and it seemed the part of the city north of the river was mostly residential, with a densely packed core. I was amazed at the sheer number of apartment blocks that stretched unabated for kilometres along the thoroughfare. There was a lot of traffic, too. Mokpo seemed a rather energized and modern city. To the south, across the river, the shore was lined with warehouses and factories.

Mokpo was once one of the more populated and important cities in the entire country, its port large and bustling. During Japanese colonization, it had been a major commercial hub, with natural resources such as minerals, rice, and lumber transported to the port from across the country, then loaded up and shipped to Japan. But with industrialization in the 1960s and '70s, many young people from outside of Seoul flocked to the capital to secure jobs in the factories, and Mokpo lost a number of its residents and some of it significance.

A few kilometres inland of the Yellow Sea, Yeongsan Dike and its six-lane road cross the Yeongsan River and connect the north and south parts of Mokpo. Water east of the embankment is fresh; to the west saltwater. West of this dike is the National Maritime Museum, where we were headed.

Korea has a renowned seafarer, a merchant and quasi-naval commander named Jang Bo-go, who sailed to Japan and China in the 900s. But there are no records that I'm aware of that list a single Korean maritimer who tested the limits, other than the local seas. Particularly with the onset of the last, highly conservative Joseon Dynasty in 1392, an anti-foreigner, stay-at-home mentality prevailed, and with it any thought of taking to the high seas. The government even placed limits on how far from land fishing boats could travel. To exceed that limit could mean being fined.

The museum is housed in a large, modern white building. We parked and strolled out onto the large square in front, where the sun reflected so harshly off the stone that I was forced to shield my eyes. Moored in the water at the side of the square was the strangest-looking vessel I had ever seen. Min-jun and I walked over for a closer look. Its name in Korean was *meongteongguribae* ("fool's boat"), though I thought it should have been called Noah's Ark. It was an example of a type of vessel that was common along the southwest coast for close to five hundred years until they were suddenly phased out in the mid-1990s. It was constructed from wooden planks, and was so large and boxy that I half-expected that pairs of donkeys, goats, and giraffes would start wandering out of its hold in an orderly fashion.

It is forty-seven feet long, an impossibly unwieldy twenty feet wide, and weighs thirteen tons. Fool's boats had no locomotion — no engines, no sails, no oars. To get from shore to sea, they had to be towed out by another vessel. Once out among the hundreds of small offshore islands clustered off the southwest coast, the boat would be anchored, and from its ungainly sixty-foot wooden arms, which reach out from its the port and starboard sides, giant nets would be lowered into the water to ensnare shrimp being swept along in the powerful current. Shrimp season here is April to June and September to November.

Off Mokpo's coast are 320 islands, 258 of them inhabited, part of an approximately 130-kilometre-long archipelago. Many are close to the mainland, but a handful of them are located more than forty kilometres from the coast. The farthest out is Gageo Island, part of an undersea ridge thought to extend all the way to mainland China and separating the Yellow Sea from the South China Sea. When British captain Basil Hall sailed south along Korea's west coast in 1816, he entered this tangle of islands, and wrote that hundreds lay in immense clusters spreading in all directions. He thought about counting and charting them all, but decided there were simply too many. He was right: a total of about 1,700 islands are situated off South Jeolla's coast.

"They vary in size, from a few hundred yards in length to five or six miles, and are of all shapes," Hall penned. "From the mast-head, other groups were perceived lying one behind the other to the east and south as far as the eye could reach. Frequently about a hundred islands were in sight from deck at one moment."

Fool's boats were designed specifically for the shallow and fast waters off the southwest coast, and were anchored between the islands. These were "factory" ships, staying put for six months or so, with the crew living onboard. Smaller vessels regularly sailed out to replenish the crew's supply of food and water and relieve the hold of its catch. Unfortunately, fool's boats suffered their share of maritime disasters. During bad weather, not only could they not move on their own, but smaller craft could not sail out to assist them.

The year 1994 was a particularly horrendous one for the boats. Summer is typhoon season in East Asia, the genesis for many being the western part of the North Pacific Ocean. A major storm, Typhoon Thelma, was spotted by weather forecasters in the sea south of Korea, but was not predicted to make landfall. Fool's boats were anchored along the coastline, their nets in the water, when Thelma's course unexpectedly shifted north. During the storm, the immense weight of the nets toppled a number of the vessels. Sixty men drowned.

I have read that, after the disaster, then-president Kim Young-sam ordered all fool's boats destroyed to prevent similar future events. Of 107 *meongteongguribae* in existence at the time, most were destroyed over the next year. Today, shrimp fishermen along the west coast catch their quarry from motorized craft.

Min-jun and I took a look at the fool's boat's giant wooden anchor, which sat in the square. The sign stated it weighed an astounding three tons, and its main vertical beam was eight metres long and its crossbeam nearly six metres across. The immense weight was needed to keep the boat securely anchored in the swift, turbulent currents around the islands.

We gratefully escaped the heat of the day in the air-conditioned museum, and were relieved to discover that the displays were in both Korean and English. Hallelujah! Min-jun sighed happily, temporarily off the hook from translating.

In 1967, Korea salvaged its first ship in the muddy waters south of Mokpo, and before us now was the result: a sleek, 200-ton, three-masted fourteenth-century Chinese Yuan sailing ship, which, amazingly, looked almost new. Its cargo had been 28,000 tons of ceramic pieces and eight million copper coins (then a major Chinese export to Japan).

Kwok Yu-seok, the museum's director, Maritime Heritage Research Division, was accompanying us on our tour, and we asked him if the eight million coins salvaged were valuable.

"Not much," he told us. "They had more academic than monetary value."

Another Korean vessel before us had sunk in about AD 900, during the Goryeo Dynasty, and had been salvaged from southwest waters in 1983. This boat measured just nine metres long by about three metres wide, yet had been carrying 30,645 celadon ceramic pieces, as well as quantities of bronze and iron when it went down. Now, I am not much of a seafarer, but even I could deduce that 30,645 of anything, even feathers, was probably excessive weight for a modest-sized craft such as this.

"Do you think maybe it sank because it was overloaded?" I asked Mr. Kwok.

"No, carrying thirty thousand pieces of pottery wasn't unusual for the period," he told us.

The pack-mule vessels of the riverways during the Joseon period are referred to by natives as *hanseon* (Korea boats). Isabella Bird wrote about being conveyed in a sampan from Seoul upstream along the Han River to the interior, but it was actually a hanseon she rode in. The term hanseon was actually a broad reference to a subcategory of boats that typically measured about five metres long, two metres wide, and just under half a metre high.

In shallow rivers, a boatman would propel the vessel along with a long pole. I had seen photos, too, of larger hanseons with massive square sails, the boats stacked to the sky with crates and boxes, looking as if they were ready to topple over at any moment.

Min-jun added, quite adroitly, I thought, "You know how some trucks overturn in Korea because they're overloaded; it was the same with the hanseons. They were overloaded, too."

* * *

Min-jun and I left the museum in late afternoon and went for dinner at a nearby restaurant. In the early evening, we checked in to the Motel Yongbin Bosok Jimjil Sauna, located in a commercial building nearby. Min-jun sought out the showers, of course, while I embarked on a two-hour stroll along the waterfront and south across Yeongsan Dike. The walking path was crammed with parents, kids, and power walkers, and the modern restaurants and cafés along the path were wreathed in bright neon lights. When I returned to the jimjilbang at about ten o'clock, Min-jun was freshly scrubbed.

When I went to fetch a mat to sleep on, to my dismay I couldn't find one. It was not that the jimjilbang had temporarily run out, or that other customers had taken them all, they simply did not have any — we were expected to sleep directly on the hardwood floor! This would never do, of course, so Min-jun and I headed down to the office, where an ajumma sat in a small booth.

"Excuse me, where are mats to sleep on?"

"We don't have mats," the woman stated impassively.

"But how can we sleep without mats?" I added incredulously.

"It's our policy," she said.

"Your policy?"

"Yes."

"But I need to sleep on a mat," I insisted. "I can't stay here if you don't have mats."

The woman refunded us half the fee, and despite it being about eleven o'clock, I decided that our only option was to leave and find other accommodations close by, somewhere that management offered mats. So we packed our stuff, got in the car, and began our search. We found two jimjilbangs in the vicinity, but neither of them had any mats. Mokponians apparently have the strongest backs in the nation! We expanded our search within the city, but couldn't locate another jimjilbang.

I checked the map for the next nearest town. "Let's try Muan," I suggested.

By the time we arrived in Muan, twenty-five kilometres away, it was around one in the morning. Despite assiduously combing the streets, we could not locate a single jimjilbang. I consulted the map again. The next nearest town of any consequence was another twenty-five kilometres away.

"Let's try Naju," I said.

Min-jun was resigned.

At about two o'clock, we stopped in front of the Korea Jimjil Sauna in Naju.

"Do you have mats?" we asked the girl at reception.

"No," she said.

"How can we sleep without mats?"

The young lady shrugged.

We pulled up to a second jimjilbang, and found pay dirt … mats! I paid the entrance fee and Min-jun and I crept into the dark and crowded fourth-floor sleeping area. However, a cacophony of loud snoring immediately forced us to retreat to a quieter second-floor sleeping area, packed with dozens of slumbering parents and kids. We found a small space near a window, which I gladly cracked open, letting the cool night air seep into the stifling enclosure. Satisfied, we lay down on our golden mats.

Unfortunately, in the middle of the large room, a man was lying on a mat with his head propped up on his elbow, watching the big-screen TV, the volume clearly audible. *It was 2:40 a.m.!* Everyone was asleep, or at least was trying to sleep. I had not spent three hours searching three different towns to have my much-needed beauty sleep disturbed by an inconsiderate maverick. I tiptoed over and whispered to him in Korean, *"Sillyehamnida ajeossi, TV soriga keoyo. Kkeojusigesseoyo?"* ("Excuse me, sir, the TV is loud. Can you please turn it off?")

The man shot me a quick, uninterested glance, and replied, *"Aniyo,"* ("No,") turned his back to me, and continued watching his show.

I had expected such a reply; he was, after all, Korean, male, and in his forties. So I pressed on with what I thought was a rational argument: *"Ajeossi, sesiyeoyo saramdeul jumusibnida."* ("Sir, it's three o'clock. People are sleeping.")

He waved me off again. While I was contemplating whether to strangle him or toss him out the window, miraculously, and to my immense relief, an anonymous dozing male patron among the crowd of recumbent bodies came to my rescue.

*"Ne, TV kkeoyo!"* ("Yes, turn off the TV!") came the loud, stern order.

I was saved. Newly emboldened, outnumbering the renegade two-to-one, I brazenly picked up the remote control from the floor next to him, pressed the off button, and watched as the screen went dark. The man said nothing, resigned to the will of this great democracy called South Korea.

I contend that jimjilbangs should enforce a pan-Korea TV curfew; off by midnight, exceptions only made when programs of national importance air, such as Korean World Cup soccer or a presidential election or the final episode of a soap opera.

This night, I slept well, in a hard-mat sort of way.

* * *

Luckily, Naju wasn't that far from the tiny, remote hamlet of Sinchon, which was our intended destination the next day. I had first learned about Sinchon when the *International Herald Tribune* ran a story about a village located in Bukha Township in the heart of the Noryeong Mountains that was home to the nation's most upstanding citizens. The article explained how the good people of the village decided that since there were not enough residents to support a shop, they would establish an unstaffed co-op store, with all payments made on the honour system. A money box sat on the counter, to which cash could be deposited and change made. If someone wanted, for example, ramen noodles, cigarettes, a soda, or a chocolate bar, they would simply deposit the amount owed into the box.

The concept was a resounding success, and nothing ever got stolen. When a local priest mentioned the unusual little place to the local press, however, the story went national. POSCO, Korea's biggest steelmaker, ran full-page newspaper ads with an accompanying photo of about a dozen residents standing and smiling in front of the cottage-like shop. The ad read: "This Store Doesn't Have a Keeper. It Has a Village of Trust."

By mid-morning, Min-jun and I were on our way toward Sinchon, about fifty kilometres north as the crow flies. Unfortunately, the metropolis of Gwangju was smack dab in our way, so we were forced to detour around the south perimeter of the city before proceeding north into the mountains.

The village where the store is located was not easy to find. We drove throughout the backcountry of the area, but really did not have a definitive idea of where exactly it was. Near Danjeon village, we pulled off the road into a small laneway that ran past a few dwellings. There was not a soul around.

"You think this is the place, Min-jun?" I asked, skeptically.

"I'm not sure," he replied.

Just up the lane we spotted a small wooden building, well-worn, with a big front window that resembled a storefront, and pulled over.

"Is that it?" I asked, in disbelief.

"I guess so," said Min-jun, doubtfully.

The door was open, so we stepped inside. There were shelves, but only a few paltry sundry items on them. On the counter sat a coin box.

*"This IS it!"* I exclaimed, though in truth I was disappointed. I had envisioned television cameras whirring, visitors jostling in lineups for the novelty of procuring an item, exiting contently, and proclaiming joyously, "What an experience. I'm so thrilled that I drove the family three hundred kilometres from Seoul through a hurricane in the middle of the night to buy a bag of chips. There's nothing like this back home. Come on, kids, time to drive back to Seoul!"

The POSCO ad photo had shown a shop resembling a cozy little cottage, something you might want to retire in. This place looked more like the tuck shop you would find at Gert and Ernie's Kids' Camp, where your parents dumped you for a week in the summer so they could take a holiday alone.

Min-jun and I stood in the shop, wondering what to do next, and the thought of swiping a candy bar danced in my head. With my luck, though, there would be a hidden security camera in the place and I'd get arrested. At that moment I glanced out the window and froze: across the street, three elderly men were pulling a rope over a stout, low tree branch — on the other end, a big yellow-white dog, the rope secured around its neck as it hung in mid-air. If you have never seen a dog being hung — and I had not — it is a surreal sight.

I instinctively raced out and tried to grab the rope from the men. But they would not let go. I tussled with them for possession. They continued to haul away as I tried to lower the dog to the ground. My adrenalin jacked up, I found myself hurling invectives at them. After perhaps a minute, I managed to lower the dog to the ground, the men backing away, looking stunned.

"Call the police!" I shouted to Min-jun.

A handful of villagers had gathered around and were staring. The dog was still gasping for air. One of the three men approached it.

"Stay away!" I threatened him angrily, a wild look in my eyes.

The man said something to Min-jun, and Min-jun advised me, "Relax, Mark, he just wants to untie the string around the dog's neck."

The man put his hands around the animal's throat and removed an unseen cord, tied so tightly, I had not noticed it. The dog started to breathe more normally. One of the men had retreated to a nearby dwelling, and I could see him hiding what looked like a blow torch attached to a small canister of gas, a device used to burn the fur off dogs after they were dead. Min-jun had called the police. In about ten minutes, a squad car pulled up and two officers got out and conferred with the three men and Min-jun. Min-jun explained to me that if I wanted to, I could press charges against the dog's owner, who would be fined 200,000 won.

"I do," I said.

"We'll have to go to the Buki police station, then."

"Okay."

The dog hopped into the back seat of my car and happily bounded about, wagging its tail. It had escaped death by only a few moments. The dog's owner, seventy-eight-year-old Mr. Jung, who had hauled on the rope, and who was rather unkempt, sat in the back of the police car. We followed the officers to the police station, where an officer informed Mr. Jung that he was being fined 200,000 won for "hanging a dog in a public place."

After a phone call from the police station to a local government official, who explained to us that it was legal to hang a dog in private, but not in public, an officer advised me to return the dog to Mr. Jung. But I knew if I did, the poor old boy would end up on Mr. Jung's dinner plate that night. I offered to buy the dog from him, but Mr. Jung wanted 300,000 won — highway robbery.

I quickly formulated a plan. "I'll return the dog," I countered, "but first I need to take it to the hospital: its vocal cords were injured by the rope."

This was agreed upon. Soon, Min-jun, the dog, and I were in the Scoupe following the police car, moving through town toward the hospital. When we came to a traffic light where the road split in two — left leading out of town into the woods; right into town to the hospital — the squad car turned right, while I darted left onto the country road and sped off.

I was now officially a dog-napper, a wanted fugitive from Korean law enforcement. Min-jun's mouth dropped open. "What are you doing?" he declared, severely distraught.

"I'm taking the dog," I replied calmly, though my heart was racing. This was the first time in my life I had committed a criminal act (excluding, of course, that time when I encouraged my then-twelve-year-old sister to touch an electrified cow fence).

"I can't be part of the plan! I can't get caught. I have convictions for drinking and driving and for violence," Min-jun blurted out.

"For violence?" I asked carefully, seeking enlightenment.

"For fighting," he explained, in Western parlance, probably assault. *Oh my, had I been travelling with a convicted felon?*

The late afternoon sun lay directly behind us, so I knew we were heading east. I glanced at the atlas. The nearest town was Damyang, about twenty-five kilometres away.

Min-jun continued, his voice panicked, "I can't take a chance on getting caught. I'm going to take the bus back to Seoul."

I tried to calm him down. "It's my responsibility, Min-jun. Nothing will happen to you." But he remained tense.

In Damyang, we stopped at a tiny grassy park in the small downtown area. I tried to persuade him to stay, but the conversation somehow turned heated.

"This trip's so much work!" he said vehemently. "I have to read maps, I have to give directions, and I have to make phone calls!"

True. We also had long days. But I hardly considered that occasionally asking a companion to check the map or to make a few phone calls put me into the category of slave-driver. I suppose, though, asking for directions and perusing the atlas could possibly be misconstrued as work, if one had not actually worked before, which I was coming to believe was the case with Min-jun.

He continued, now thoroughly vexed, "And YOU! All YOU do is talk! You talk about this place, you talk about that place!"

True again. During the two weeks we were together, I had tried to engage Min-jun in dialogue, expounding on things we saw and were doing, hoping to get him involved, to elicit some conversation. But he often chose to be a quiet observer rather than a vocal participant.

"It's called conversation. Try it sometime!" I responded hotly. And then I really lost my temper. "Fuck it. Just go back to Seoul. I don't care anymore!"

Min-jun stared at me, mouth agape. "How dare you speak to me like that!" he cried. "You're supposed to be my friend!"

He reached into the back seat, grabbed his little suitcase-on-wheels, and began to stride off. "Don't use my name in the book! If you do, I'll sue you!" he shouted fiercely.

I yelled "You're a mama's boy!" but instantly regretted it. It was a low blow. I shouldn't have said it. He wasn't a bad guy, though he did have an incendiary fuse.

"Shut up!" he called back, as he pulled his luggage along the sidewalk, in search, I guessed, of the Damyang bus station. Min-jun had been with me for exactly fourteen days.

My immediate concern now, though, was for the dog. What was I going to do? I couldn't just drop it off at the police station, which I had just noticed with a jolt of trepidation was directly across the street. Dogs bred to be eaten often spend a lot of time in a cage, so I figured it would enjoy a walk. So, I went to the car, opened the door, and let it wander around the park. It seemed content, skittering about, but it was also very intelligent, because it suddenly cantered to the back corner of the park, turned onto the back road, and disappeared from view. I raced over and peered down the street. Not a trace. It was gone.

This had not been my intention, though now that the dog was free, I must say I was relieved. At least I had deprived its owner, the provincial Mr. Jung, of feasting on dog stew tonight.

I sat down on a park bench to think. I was in a supreme state of angst, from all that had transpired, and not just this afternoon. I was now a fugitive from the law. My days on the road had been long and tiring. I was not sleeping well on mats in the jimjilbangs, which I thought of as emergency disaster centres. And I still had more than half the country to discover. My patience had worn thin. I was out of my groove. My equilibrium was off, my feng shui out of whack. In geomantic terms, I had lost it. I was pissed off. At this moment I hated the trip, and translators, and men who hung dogs, and this country. Koreans were the most hard-headed and inflexible people I had ever met. I believe I fit right in.

There was a truck nearby on the street selling roasted chickens from a back rotisserie, so I paid 6,000 won for a beauty, and went back to the bench to devour it. Then I found an ice cream shop, where I purchased two strawberry milkshakes. Nearby, at a bakery, I procured several pastries (I often eat if I'm depressed). Then, figuring I could do with some exercise, I went in to a nearby Internet room, sat down in front of one of the computers, and gave my fingers a hardy workout.

I got to thinking that with Heju returning from Thailand in eight days, she might want to rejoin me, so I emailed her with the proposal. Her reply was forthcoming a couple of hours later: Yes, she was a masochist and would continue on Mark's Marine Boot Camp — Part Deux. I had lucked out. My feng shui was back!

I also elicited Moonie in Seoul to act as a liaison between myself and the officers at the Buki police station. Moonie told me they requested I deposit 180,000 won into Mr. Jung's bank account the next day to compensate him for the dog. I deposited 100,000 won instead, which I thought fair. But judging from the slew of calls I received over the next several weeks from the police wanting to know where I was, I believe they did not. The next day, I returned to Seoul for a short respite.

(Later, when I was reviewing my plethora of cut-out articles, I came upon the full-page POSCO ad with the photo of the Sinchon villagers in the shop, and there, smiling up at the camera, was Mr. Jung.)

# CHAPTER 16

Back in Seoul, I checked into my neighbourhood jimjilbang, as my flat was occupied by my tenant, Isaiah. The next evening, I took a Saturday drive to meet a friend at a café — the air warm and sultry, as evenings in early June often are — in Jamsil-dong, which translates as "Silkworm Raising Room," a form of sericulture practised in the area during Joseon times. Jamsil is a ten-minute drive from Myeongil-dong, close to Olympic Park.

Rising above Jamsil subway station, at a busy intersection, is the Lotte World Department Store and the luxury high-rise Lotte Hotel. Behind the hotel is the Lotte World Amusement Park, and next to it, a small man-made lake. Underground, inside Jamsil station, four subway lines converge at the subterranean arcade of shops. Above, wide sidewalks brimmed with hordes of mainly young people, shopping or just out about town. The multi-lane road, as usual, was jammed with city buses, cars, and taxis. A kilometre north is the Han River, Jamsil Bridge, and scores of white high-rise apartments. Close by, in Bangi-dong, a backstreet was lined with modern love motels. And in Sincheon, just to the west, the brightly lit backstreets of the entertainment district were packed with young people. An apartment in this part of Seoul will run you a million dollars. But it wasn't always that way. Up until the 1960s and '70s, this area south of the Han River was still predominantly farmland and fields. When it was developed, the roads were for the most part designed in a logical grid pattern; hence why it's easier to find your way around here than in areas north of the river in Old Seoul, where it can be akin to navigating the confusing streets of Old London.

Later, after saying goodbye to my friend, I got back in the Scoupe and puttered slowly around Jamsil in the heavy Saturday evening traffic. I was content to simply people-watch, with no specific destination in mind. Suddenly, I saw a man lying face-down in the middle of four lanes of traffic at an intersection, the motorists slowly and carefully manoeuvring around him. I saw the man's head turn, so I knew he was alive, but no one seemed to be stopping to assist him.

I pulled my car over to the curb and walked back to the intersection where a gaggle of pedestrians was now looking at the prostrate man in the street. I lassoed a couple of university-age fellows from among them and we waded out into traffic, picked the man up by his legs and arms, hauled him over to the sidewalk, and placed him on the ground. No sooner had we done so than he jumped up and darted back into traffic where he proceeded to lie face-down again. Once more, we ventured out into the lanes and lugged him back. This time, however, I sat on him as he lay on the sidewalk on his back, preventing him from getting up.

*"Il-il-gu jeonhwa haesseoyo?"* ("Has anyone phoned 1-1-9?") I called to the onlookers.

*"Aniyo,"* ("No,") someone replied.

*"Jeonhwa haesseoyo!"* ("Phone it!") I insisted.

The man was distraught. "Family! Die!" he yelled in English.

After a while, he relaxed a bit. "Where are you from?" he asked me.

"Canada."

He was slight, maybe 150 pounds soaking wet, and about forty-five. He was trying to say something to me in Korean, but his voice was soft and I couldn't understand him. A young man next to me translated: "He's saying, 'If it wasn't for you, I'd have been killed.'"

He motioned that I bring my face close to his. I did. He smiled and whispered "Friend!" and shook my hand. He had a strong grip. He seemed like a good guy, and I am certain he did not want to die. Koreans can be very emotional, particularly after having downed a bottle or two of soju. I am sure he had lain down on the road on a whim; a plea for help, perhaps. The police arrived after five minutes and put him into a patrol car. I hope they took him to hospital.

* * *

On Monday, I drove the more than two hundred kilometres south to Jeonju to meet the man who would have become the king of Korea were the Joseon monarchy still in place. Jeonju was the cradle of the Joseon Dynasty, when its general, Yi Seong-gye (*Yi* being the former spelling of *Lee*), led the overthrow of the erstwhile Goryeo Kingdom in 1392, and was elevated by Jeonju's aristocratic ruling clan to King Taejo, the first of twenty-seven Yi kings.

The Japanese took steps to end the Joseon Dynasty in 1907, forcing King Gojong to abdicate and sending his crown prince to Japan. In hindsight, it's impossible to say what fate would have awaited the monarchy had Japan not interfered. Perhaps royalty would have eventually unceremoniously been jettisoned by Koreans anyway. During five centuries in power, the Joseon court seemed starkly out of touch with the poor masses. During its declining years, it was also hopelessly corrupt, inept, and in the stranglehold of the omnipresent yangban, who had little if any inclination to create better conditions for the majority of downtrodden citizens. Joseon was virtually powerless to govern effectively at the end.

However, if we imagine for a moment that the dynasty had remained intact (some if its descendants hung on for many decades after in an illusory state, believing they had been ordained as royalty for life), the king presiding over Korea today would be Yi Seok, a grandson of Gojong. Seok's father was Prince Yi Kang — one of Gojong's sons. Yi Kang had fifteen daughters and sixteen sons. Yi Seok was born in 1941. Through the arcane and convoluted Yi royal family tree, the bottom line is that Seok would be His Royal Highness today (trust me on this one).

Just as Ms. Lee Bong-hui, once imprisoned at Seodaemun Prison, had been a window to the Seoul of the 1930s, Yi Seok would be an excellent conduit to life in the royal family, I had decided. I had learned of his existence by reading an IHT feature on his rather topsy-turvy life, and had been trying to contact him for some time, having been given his phone number by Jeonju University, where he taught Yi Dynasty history part-time. A few days earlier, I had finally received a call back from him, and we had made an appointment to meet.

From Seoul, I travelled via expressway toward Jeonju. For a time, the road parallels Gyeryong Mountain, the broad eminence rising more than eight hundred metres up from the plain. South of Gyeryong, the road leads out across Honam Plain and its expansive agricultural delta. Jeonju is located on the eastern edge of the great plain. The city of about seven hundred thousand citizens, like other medium-size urban areas in the country, is busy with cars and people and humming with activity. What sets it apart, though, is that it is the birthplace of the Yi royal family as well as home to several old Joseon buildings that contain the memorial tablets of the kings. It was also the location of the original palace, which was destroyed but was rebuilt.

Jeonju University in located on the western edge of the city. I had phoned ahead and arranged for a student in the English department to act as translator during my visit with Yi Seok.

I pulled up to university's main gate, and the guard asked me through my rolled down window, *"Yeogi museunillo osyesseoyo?"* ("Why are you here?")

*"Yi Seok mannago sipeoyo,"* ("I'd like to meet Yi Seok,") I stated confidently, expecting instant recognition of the famous name.

The guard's expression remained stoic. *"Nugu?"* ("Who?") he asked.

"Yi Seok," I repeated.

*"Naneun Yi Seok mollayo,"* ("I don't know Yi Seok,") he replied.

How strange, I thought. I reached into my file folder on the passenger seat and showed him the *IHT* article, which included Yi's photo.

*"Hangukwang! Geuneun Jeonju dahakgyeoseo yoksa gareuchyeoyo,"* ("The king of Korea. He teaches history here at Jeonju University,") I announced, certain the guard would now recognize Yi.

He studied the photo closely, but not a hint of recognition crossed his face. He was not going to grant me access unless I clarified why I was there, so I phoned the translator and handed my phone to the guard.

After a minute or so, I was waved through. Such is the sorry state of royal affairs in Korea that even the guard employed at the same university that His Majesty teaches at is in the dark about the king.

I met the translator, a personable and intelligent twenty-one-year-old who spoke excellent English. "Call me John," he said. So, I did.

John and I drove east across the flat, rather featureless city to Pungnam-dong, the district where the Yi Dynasty's Gyeonggijeon Palace is located. The area is concentrated but laid out very well, a sort of testament to old Joseon. The street in front of the palace, Taejo Road, is cobblestoned and named after Joseon's first king. There were a couple of handsome cafés and tourist shops, and across the street, kitty-corner to the palace, was the beguiling Jeongdong Cathedral, constructed under the direction of a French priest in the European style between 1908 and 1914. The neighbourhood was also the location of Jeonju Hanok Village, a network of quiet lanes containing about eight hundred traditional hanok. Just west of the palace was the hulking Pungnam Gate, which had been built in the 1700s. There is a lot of history here.

Yi Seok lived in the hanok village, so we drove along the dusty lanes searching for his address, which I had written on a piece of paper. When we rang the doorbell at the front gate, an attractive and regal-looking woman answered.

"Excuse me, is this Yi Seok's home?" we inquired.

"Yes," she said.

We introduced ourselves and told the woman we had an appointment.

She invited us in and graciously led us across the small yard to a handsome hanok. Once inside, we found ourselves in a plain and unencumbered living area with a long, low wooden table in the middle and a wall lined with bookshelves.

John and I sat on the floor at the table and waited. About ten minutes later, His Eminence, Yi Seok, made his grand entrance. He wore traditional Joseon garb. As one might expect, the king possessed a sense of gravity and regality. He was also fit and handsome, with a healthy mane of thick grey-black hair. He appeared considerably younger than his actual age. He was also a bit reserved, down-to-earth, and frank. I liked him.

Yi Seok seemed a bit aloof, though whether this was the result of his blue blood or just his natural temperament, I couldn't say. He understandably chose to communicate in Korean, and conveyed to us that the woman who answered the door was his personal assistant, provided by Jeonju City, though I suspected the two had more than a professional relationship. The king sat cross-legged across from us at the table. He was intelligent, serious, and thoughtful as I began asking about his formative years in Seoul in the 1940s and '50s.

They were privileged times, he admitted, with the extended ex-royal family residing at a palace in Seoul. They were attended by fifty servants, several of whom accompanied Yi to school and delivered his lunch to him. He was not permitted to run during physical education classes, so his principal had to run for him. "We had a Cadillac and a Ford," he added. This was at a time when car ownership was almost unheard of.

Yi Seok's father, Yi Kang, was distant and had little time to spend with the boy. "I had no opportunity to the speak with my father or mother," he said wistfully. "My father was sixty-four when I was born and he had other babies. Of his father's thirty-one children, five were born after Yi Seok came along."

When the Korean War broke out, Yi Seok, just nine years old, and the rest of the ex-royal family, fled from Seoul to Busan for safety, remaining there for eighteen months, until 1952. Back in Seoul, the next decade was extremely trying for the royal family descendants. Syngman Rhee, president from 1948 to 1960, despised the royal family, blaming them for having offered little resistance to the Japanese, allowing them to apparently walk in and colonize the nation. Yi recalled that 1960 was the most dangerous year for the royal family — the government confiscated all the royal property and the extended family was stripped of their assets.

"Syngman Rhee absolutely destroyed the royal family," he added, though the next president, Park Chung-hee, permitted the family to return to the palace.

In the 1960s, as a young man, Yi Seok entered a singing contest at the YMCA, won first prize, and became a college disc jockey, singing at U.S. Army officers' clubs on military bases. His brothers and sisters, aunts, uncles, and cousins thought it undignified — beneath the vaulted airs of the aristocracy — to actually work. But Yi Seok thought differently, and in 1965 he volunteered with the ROK Army and was sent to Vietnam. He spoke about his platoon, and how the men were ferociously relentless.

Back in Seoul, Yi settled into a routine of singing at night clubs. In the 1970s, he hosted a live Friday night variety show on TV. A first marriage lasted one year, a second five. In 1979, when President Park was assassinated and Major General Chun Doo-hwan appointed himself president after a military coup, the royal family palace was given their marching orders at gunpoint. The family dispersed, some moving to America. When Yi's brother died in San Diego in 1980, Yi flew to America on a three-month tourist visa.

"At first I thought the U.S. was wonderful. I visited the Pentagon, San Francisco, San Diego, Los Angeles, and Korean communities. They recognized me as a prince. I even sang in Kodiak, Alaska."

But he was relegated to cleaning pools and gardening in Beverly Hills, and later running Eddy's Liquor Store, located in a rundown area of Los Angeles. He was held up at gunpoint there at least a dozen times. "I pretended to be Mexican, growing a moustache and a beard and speaking Spanish. It was safer that way," he said.

Yi forgot about being a prince. He married an American in a marriage of convenience. In 1992, when a family member died in Seoul, he returned home, his marriage in the United States over. He began singing at nightclubs again, but after a night of drinking, he was hit by a car and spent twelve days in a coma. Yi's life spiralled downward after that, and for several years he had no job, no money, and no home. He visited a Buddhist temple to become a monk, but was rejected for being too old. Contemplating suicide, he inked his will in 2005, which somehow ended up on the desk of a newspaper. When the story went national, Jeonju officials reached out to help. Yi was moved to the city, where he received a fashion makeover and ten new teeth, among other perks.

These days, Yi presides over various civic functions and lectures on royal history at Jeonju University and other places. He laments the paucity of student awareness of Korean history. "Thailand, Spain, and England have monarchies, and Korea once did, too, but the university students I teach don't know anything about the Joseon Dynasty," he stated disapprovingly.

Yi Seok confessed he occasionally pined for his former life in America, but Jeonju seemed to suit him well. Two weeks before our meeting, he had returned from an all-expenses-paid vacation to Hawaii. Not bad for a "might-have-been" king whose goal was now to elucidate the public on Joseon royal history.

After the visit, I took John out for dinner at a restaurant near Pungnam-dong to thank him, drove him back to his university dorm, then returned to the city centre and found a jimjilbang.

* * *

The next day, back In Pungnam-dong, I visited the Gyeonggijeon Palace grounds, which are typically Joseon in style. Underfoot, sandy earth ran between a series of handsome low, modest wood buildings, spaced well apart with plenty of room to move around. Between two of these units in the main courtyard I discovered a series of large paintings along the outside wall that depicted Joseon's twenty-seven kings in full colour. Rather serious, sinister-looking fellows they were, too.

A small group of foreigners was being led through the courtyard by an English-speaking tour guide — a regal-looking Korean woman dressed in a long silk *hanbok* — the formal fashion of Joseon's upper-class. I quietly tagged along while the guide lectured about the palace. Then she led us to one end of the open courtyard, where a set of two mismatched wooden doors stood side by side.

"Exit the door on the right," I heard her say, though I absent-mindedly moved through the one on the left. Immediately, the irate voice of the guide rebuked me: "I told you to go through the right door! It's tradition to go through the right door. It shows respect to the king!"

"But the king's dead," I sputtered abjectly.

"That doesn't matter. You're disrespecting Korea," she continued indignantly. "You're in Korea now. You must obey customs here!"

Oh my. Was she aware that only minutes before, while observing the portraits, an older Korean man near me had passed gas? I thought this would be considered far more sacrilegious than innocently exiting through the wrong door. *Off with his head!* Alas, I was now a pariah — unloved, unwanted, and ignored by the guide — and I slunk away in shame.

I headed across the road to the imposing Jeondong Cathedral, where I was hoping the men of cloth were a bit less judgmental and more forgiving of sinners like me. Construction had begun on the church in 1908, under the stewardship of a French Catholic priest by the name of Father Xavier Baudenet. A plaque in the square in front read: "Many Catholics were executed at this place, including the first martyrs, Yun Ji-chung (Paul) (1791) and Yu Hang-geon (Augustine). Yu Hang-geon's head was hung on this corner stone" — a welcome addition, I am sure, for children playing in the area at the time.

The church was constructed of red-grey brick, now faded, which soars up twenty-three metres (forty-five to the clock and steeple). The building is long and very narrow and incorporates three bell towers. I went in and immediately felt a welcoming coolness — a lovely reprieve from the afternoon's heat and humidity. I sat in one of the pews. I was captivated by the high, narrow interior. Eight stone columns run from floor-to-ceiling on each side of the aisle and the white stone walls are lined with arched stained-glass windows bordered by intricate brickwork. Except for the wooden pews and front doors, everything was made of stone.

Four worshippers sat close to me, praying. I considered praying for salvation for the palace guide, but figured she was beyond redemption. Small groups of visitors poked their heads through the church door and snapped photos. I could have stayed there all day, maybe even for a week; it was blissfully peaceful, and it felt good to be out of the heat. But I had to keep rolling.

My next destination was the small town of Gurye, about one hundred kilometres southeast in the Sobaek Mountains.

* * *

Gurye is one of several distinct mountain areas on the peninsula where more than a few senior citizens live longer than the country's average life span of eighty-four years for women and seventy-nine for men (easy on the soju and cigarettes, fellows). Old-timers in Gurye don't seem to have much problem hitting the century mark. I needed to learn about Gurye's magical fountain of youth. I was not getting any younger myself.

Surprisingly, I conveyed from Jeonju to Gurye along a smooth modern highway that sliced first through the Noryeong Mountains then into the Sobaeks. I had the feeling of being enveloped by the high narrow walls of green that rose up on each side. The scenery here is verdurous and robust. I left the corridor of gloomy lushness and suddenly emerged onto a long, narrow stretch of lowlands by the Seomjin River, along the edge of the Jiri Mountain Massif. It gave me the impression that the entire area was mostly cut off from the outside world. Much of the plain is taken up with agricultural land. I was in Gurye.

I found Gurye City Hall, a modern edifice that seems too large and grand for such a modest-sized town. I was hoping that the officials here could introduce me to a centenarian whom I could speak with, so I poked my head into the large main office. A number of county employees, most wearing white shirts and black pants, sat in front of computers, doing what civil servants in black pants and white shirts did worldwide: playing online poker. I jest.

I explained my quest to them, and, diligence and zealousness being a Korean trait (when I stopped at government offices in other towns, I was without fail accorded attentive and enthusiastic assistance), the employees jumped to life, bustling about and busily checking files and leafing through booklets and notes before producing a list of Gurye's eldest folks. It soon became apparent, however, that the list had not been recently updated, because, as they perused the names, I saw them conferring and crossing out several who they just now were realizing had passed on from this world.

They found the name of a 106-year-old woman, Ms. Go Yeom-nok, and after a few phone calls, it was arranged that I would be transported to Ms. Go's residence by an English-speaking fellow named Mr. Kim Hong-geun. The gregarious and unpretentious Mr. Kim drove me in his SUV, and we were soon running along beside the Seomjin River.

Mr. Kim looked out over the green, wooded hills and the river and remarked candidly, "When I was a boy, there were no trees here. Now everything's tree-covered."

Near the river, at slight elevation at a bend in the road, we stopped on the shoulder and walked up a dirt path that led through the woods. We shortly emerged into a slight clearing where there sat a solitary traditional dwelling. We knocked on the door, and a tiny white-haired woman answered.

Ms. Go looked closer to eighty-five than 106. She wore a loose yellow silk shirt and baggy purple silk pants. She was a delightful breath of fresh air, a gentle, good-hearted woman, the picture of serenity, with a lovely smile. Had I been fifty years older, I would have asked her to the Gurye Kimchi Diner — the tab paid by me, of course.

I sat on the floor opposite Ms. Go and prepared to chat. Alas, she had little to say, and was mainly content to remain silent, absent-mindedly staring into space for spells, probably lost in her private reveries of decades past. After more than a century on this planet, she was entitled to do a little daydreaming. After twenty minutes, Ms. Go had only spoken a few words, so we departed.

Back in the SUV, Mr. Kim opined that Gurye townsfolk tended to reach the century mark because they were not greedy and the air was clean. Back at City Hall, the supervisor generously presented me with a gift of a thick soft-cover book comprising charts and analysis explaining why local citizens lived lengthy lives. It was written in Hangul, so I could not understand it. But fresh mountain air, a healthy diet of local vegetables, and a laid-back environment *sans* stress were among the factors given that could lead to longevity. Having had the pleasure of meeting Ms. Go, however, I suspected it might even be simpler: love everyone and enjoy peace of mind.

I do not mean to aggrandize myself, but I think I meet most requirements enabling me to live to the ripe old age of at least 106, too. I exercise regularly and eat fresh fruit and vegetables. I get too much sleep, do not smoke or drink, and am only occasionally greedy. As a bonus, I have never married, so my life is virtually stress-free. Though, on second thought, I hang around Heju, so chop off several decades due to significant exasperation. I will be lucky if I survive to age seventy.

Sadly, Ms. Go passed away in the next year.

# CHAPTER 17

Prior to my trip, while relaxing in my flat one evening, the phone rang. It was an audibly excited Heju on the line, calling from Daejeon. "Quick … go to your computer," she said breathlessly. "A great white shark was caught off Yeon Island. There's a photo of it hanging from a crane. It's huge!"

My immediate reaction was one of disbelief. "That's impossible. There're no great whites in Korea."

"There are!" she insisted.

I went to my computer, to the website she gave me, and lo and behold, there was the photo of a walloping shark hanging from a harbour crane on Yeon Island, off Yeosu's south coast. It was one of those Megalodon-type sharks — 2.5 tons, fifteen feet long — the kind that like to snack on meaty fellows like me. It had gotten tangled in a fishing trawler's nets and had been hauled aboard.

That's right, the world's most deadly marine predator, which terrorizes swimmers and sometimes draws chunks of legs and arms, or actually the entire bather, was in Korean waters. But here was the thing: except for this obscure website, there was not another venue I was aware of — be it newspaper, TV news, or Internet — that mentioned a single word about the shark. In fact, in all my years in Korea, I had never once read or heard anything in the media about these beasts ever once popping their snouts up off any of Korea's three coasts.

Maybe that was the point: if mainstream media published this little fact, would Koreans and tourists continue to venture into the sea along the beaches during the summer? I smelled cover-up!

Here's the thing, too: prior to this shark being caught, I had spent a year living in Yeosu, which is about thirty-five kilometres north of Yeon Island, and I had also resided for several weeks on An Island, a short distance north of Yeon Island. (I had jettisoned from Seoul to try something new. Having previously taken a ferry through the arresting archipelago of myriad islands off Yeosu's coast, I had decided I'd move to the area to see how I liked it.) That summer, I had swum in the warm, clear, shallow waters off sandy An Island Beach. I now realized I conceivably could have been dinner for Jaws!

After seeing the shark online, I bought a book titled *Great White Shark*, written by shark-diving experts Richard Ellis and John E. McCosker. Inside was a map titled "Known Great White Shark Distribution." On it, the oceans and seas were pale blue, except where great whites were known to hang out, where the areas were dark blue. The temperate waters off the coasts of Australia, North America, and South Africa, South America's west coast, and the Mediterranean were dark blue. I received a bit of a shock when I saw that the Yellow Sea and the Sea of Japan (East Sea), and in fact *all* waters surrounding Korea, were dark blue, too.

Heju had phoned Yeon Island's government office to get the phone number of the fisherman who had hauled in the shark, and had called to ask him if we could meet when we travelled through Yeosu. He had kindly agreed. I was on my way, heading south from Gurye through the coastal mountains. Then it was on to Yeosu, which sits on a peninsula that juts out into the sea, splitting at the port at Gamak Bay into two long arms that continue south to an archipelago of more than three hundred islands. Near Yeosu port, I checked in to the Yeosu Naek Ok Sauna for the night. Before I went to bed, I sent a quick "thank-you" text to Mr. Kim for conveying me to Ms Go's home earlier in the day. His reply came a few minutes later: "My pressure."

I awoke to English-style weather, the sky a thick blanket of ominous grey cloud with a light drizzle, blustery winds, and cool temperatures. My appointment with Mr. Cho Sun-hyen, the fisherman, was on Yeon Island, and we had arranged that I'd take the noon ferry. But as I was about to depart, I thought it prudent to confirm the rendezvous, because, while Koreans can be prone to being a bit lax in affording prior notice to breaking an appointment, they can also be vexed if the opposite occurs. I got Mr. Cho on the line, and was glad I did.

*"Naneun Yeosue itneun eunhange isseoyo,"* ("I'm at the bank in Yeosu port,") he told me.

I was agog. *"Yeondoe myeosiye galgeoyeyo?"* ("What time will you go back to Yeon Island?") I asked.

*"Yeoldusi,"* ("Noon,") he said.

It was eleven o'clock. *"Jigeum mannago sipeoyo?"* ("Can I meet you now?") I asked with some urgency.

*"Ne, ppalli oseyo!"* ("Yes, hurry!") he barked.

I needed to make haste. But I needed a translator, too. I phoned "Kate," a Korean tour guide employed at the small government booth at the foot of Odong Island, just a couple of kilometres east of the port, whom I had met during my time in Yeosu years earlier.

Kate agreed to translate. I motored east, past the old port, to her tourist office. We drove back to the bank, located along one of the narrow congested back lanes behind the port. It was 11:25 when we entered. Mr. Cho was standing at a small table jotting figures into a notebook.

*"Sip o bun yaegihalsu isseoyo."* ("I can only talk fifteen minutes"), he said. He was a buoyant, confident man who appeared older than his forty-nine years. I posed my questions quickly.

He had been born on Dolsan, the long, narrow island of mountains and coves immediately east of the port that was joined to the mainland by a short bridge. On the western edge of Yeosu was the other mountainous peninsula, Hwayang. Between Dolsan and Hwayang lay ten-kilometre-wide Gamak Bay.

Mr. Cho was the captain of a twenty-five-ton fishing boat with a crew of eight. He had been fishing the local waters for thirty years. On the April day he caught the shark, he had lowered a 260-by-45-metre net into the sea just east of Yeon Island, in about 45-metre-deep water.

"We check the nets twice a day," he said. When it was winched up, the great white was in it. "We had to use the crane to haul it onboard. It took thirty minutes to get it in."

"Was it still alive?" I asked, in wonderment.

"Oh yeah," he answered spiritedly. "It was tough and fighting. It had three rows of teeth. It was trying to bite us."

"Were you scared?"

"Oh yeah."

"Was this the first great white you've seen?"

"No," he said.

*Huh?* I sought elucidation. He explained that during the springtime, great whites had been spotted in these waters in the past, but did not get reported because the government did not want to scare the tourists away. This was the first time it had been reported, he said.

But as Bob Dylan sang, times were a-changing, because later I read an article in the English-language edition of the *JoongAng Daily* newspaper, the National Fisheries Research and Development Institute saying that two great whites had been caught — Mr. Cho's, and the other a thirteen-footer hauled in off the eastern coastal city of Yeongdeok, about 160 kilometres north of Busan.

Word of Mr. Cho's shark had spread rapidly through Yeosu's community of *Haenyeo* ("women of the sea") — ajummas who earn their livings free-diving, in wet suits, fins, and masks, down to shallow kelp beds and areas of mollusks, abalone, and sea urchins, bringing their catch to the surface and selling it at local markets. "The divers were scared," said Mr. Cho. "They stopped diving, and it was a month before they got back in the water."

Fifteen minutes after our arrival at the bank, Mr. Cho hurried off to catch his ferry, and Kate dashed off for lunch with her colleagues. I decided that, for old time's sake, I would ride the day's last ferry, at two o'clock, south through Gamak Bay and past An Island to Yeon Island and back. But with a couple of hours to spare, I drove across Dolsan Bridge and continued south to the Yeosu Maritime Science Museum, where I spent an enjoyable hour totally absorbed in the undersea world of fish and other creatures.

A little before two o'clock, I boarded the large roll on-roll off vehicle ferry, rain sprinkling, and stood on the second-level outer deck. We sailed out of the port and under the tall Dolsan Bridge and south into Gamak Bay and past a cluster of low small islands. Motoring past us north into port were fishing trawlers sitting low in the water from their catch. Looking far west across the bay to Hwayang's shoreline, a row of white high-rise apartments was dwarfed by a low mountain ridge that rose steeply behind them. Just south of the bay, we passed another cluster of islands, then, with open seas to the east, we traced the long western shore of Geumo Island, its steep, lush mountains plunging into the shallow greenish waters.

At the far end of Geumo was An Island, only a few kilometres wide and the shape of a fat bird with wings extended. A narrow channel separated the two islands, and when the currents and tides moved at full tilt, the channel acted like a funnel, with the churning water rushing through it, resulting in white-water rapids. On An Island's north shore — one of the few places to land, due to its south and east coasts being lined with rocky bluffs — sat its one tiny village, consisting of a single short, narrow concrete walkway hemmed in by low concrete walls; behind them hunkered a handful of concrete dwellings. There was one post office, a bank, two worn tuck shops, and a small basic restaurant. Adjacent to the village was a long narrow harbour to protect the small fleet of fishing trawlers during typhoon season. Just south of the harbour was a long half-moon-shaped stone beach, and just east of town was An Beach at the head of a long, narrow bay.

During my first stay in Yeosu, I had spent three weeks on An Island. That summer, I visited the beach every day and swam in the sea. I paddled my kayak and tried to sail the used Indonesian outrigger sailboat I had purchased. I quickly learned that being on the beach on a summer afternoon in Korea was much akin to being inside an oven. The life of beach bum was not for me, I decided, and headed back to the mainland and Yeosu, where I signed a one-year contract to teach students English after school at a private hagwon (academy).

The ferry rounded An Island's west shore into the strait separating it from Yeon Island. Even in a vessel as stalwart as this, I felt the broad hull shudder under the stress of the adversarial current. We sailed close to Yeon Island's rocky west shore, then stopped in its sheltered bay for a few moments before heading back to Yeosu.

Back on dry land, in the early evening gloom, I drove north along the city's busy main thoroughfare, past a long line of old shops, automobile repair garages, flat-roof dwellings, apartment blocks, and Mediterranean-style concrete homes. Near a small harbour where Hwayang Peninsula meets Yeosu, in the neighbourhood of Sicheonseo, I enjoyed a light dinner with Kate and her husband in the modern entertainment block.

For old time's sake, after dinner I headed a short distance south along Hwayang's coastal road, past the Soho Yacht Club, and soon arrived at Pattaga Pensions, a series of uninsulated aluminum boxes perched up on the rocks. The owner, Mr. Kim, a grizzled, drinking man, rented out the trailer-like accommodations. I had lived in the one on the top row.

When I moved into it, I insisted I would not be needing gas heating during the winter — in an effort to cut my utility bill — because, as Yeosu locals had blithely explained to me, winters here were "mild." In a story on Yeosu in the *International Herald Tribune*, writer Ingrid K. Williams even referred to the area as having a "temperate climate."

Now, the words *mild* and *temperate* to me invoke moderate spring or balmy fall days, certainly not temperatures cold enough to freeze the gonads off a polar bear. Yeosu, unlike Seoul, would escape the deep freeze, of this I was assured. But I'll tell you that, for many nights during that January and February, it was so bitterly cold in my room that I consider myself lucky to have not suffered from frostbite. And, yes, heating IS a necessity!

On a positive note, the pension offered wonderful vistas of Gamak Bay. Out my large front window, the view was always changing, depending on the weather. I could gaze out and see rolling, sparkling whitecaps on fair days, the inky black water on moonless nights, a light mist or thick white blankets of fog, or the grey, angry swells on stormy days. At dawn, the big, bright orange sun would peak over the mountain ridge on

Dolsan, ten kilometres east across the bay, and bathe the interior of my place with glaring brightness.

In just ten minutes I could be out hiking up the nearby ridge, or paddling my sea kayak, or cycling up and down Hwayang's steep, winding roads through the pristine hilly interior. Heju visited about twice a month on weekends, and we would hike along the coastal plain and shorelines of Hwayang.

One spring afternoon, I was in the pension alone when the rocks below my feet began to rumble and shake. My first earthquake! It only lasted about fifteen seconds, but even experiencing a minor one like that is a sensation that is hard to describe, as if the earth's bowels were shifting, which they surely were.

Earthquakes are rarely felt in Korea, but the volatile Ring of Fire is not that far away. The earthquake-prone zone stretches along Japan's east coast and forms a giant horseshoe along the entire Pacific Ocean coastline from South America to the Philippines. Undersea volcanoes and earthquakes occur along this ring regularly, and South Korea lies just north-west of this active zone.

On another spring weekend, I trudged up the easy path to the grassy, rounded crest along the ridge that rises behind Soho Yacht Club. Looking east, I had a grand view out and over Gamak Bay, where countless small green islands protruded from the sparkling blue-green water, the scene so bold it was as if you could reach out and touch it. Looking west, a wide agricultural plain stretched across to the western shore of Hwayang.

Hawks commonly soar high overhead in the Yeosu skies, and as I lay on my back on the crest under a weak sun, a curious hawk arrived and hovered just five metres above me. Despite a stiff breeze bending the tree branches, the bird remained motionless, fixed to one spot for more than five minutes, only the occasional minute flick of its wingtip keeping it stationary. It was the most extraordinary piece of in-born navigation I had ever witnessed. Finally, deciding I was too big to attack, it tipped a wing and allowed the wind to carry it gracefully and sublimely away, like a dive-bomber, hundreds of metres across to an adjacent ridge.

But despite the many outdoor advantages in Yeosu, I had yearned for the familiarity of my old neighbourhood of Myeongil-dong back in Seoul; Yeosu wasn't "home," and the time had come to depart. So, after finishing my one-year teaching job, I had loaded up my possessions into a large hockey bag and bussed myself back to Seoul.

* * *

It was almost midnight when I left Pattaga Pensions and memory lane and drove the short distance back down the road to the Soho Yacht Club, where, years ago, I had dry-docked my Indonesian outrigger. Amazingly — worn, unused, and damaged — it was still there. Exhausted, I sat in the car in the club parking lot, reclined the driver's seat, and promptly fell asleep.

# CHAPTER 18

I awoke to serenity and quiet. When I checked my watch, I saw it was just a little after seven. I had slept like a log. I got out of the car to stretch my legs and strolled across the concrete square in front of the yacht club. No one was around and there were no cars on the coastal road yet, so it was still and peaceful, the water in Gamak Bay calm and tranquil. I took a few deep breaths of the fresh sea air, then got back behind the wheel and headed out of Yeosu.

As usual, the itinerary I had set for the day was a busy one, and would include exploring the next major island to the east: Namhae.

I drove north to the small city of Suncheon, at the head of the Yeosu peninsula, then conveyed east to Namhae, which is joined to the mainland by the 660-metre-long, 80-metre-high Namhae Bridge, an impressive orange steel suspension bridge that stretches across a narrow strip of dark green sea called the Noryang Strait.

Namhae is the fifth-largest island in South Korea at about three hundred square kilometres. Except for narrow belts of coastline where most of Namhae's villages are situated, much of the island consists of broad, forested mountains. When my parents visited me in 2000, we took the train from Seoul to Busan, and then rented a car and explored Namhae and the next big island east, Geoje. Namhae is laid-back and unassuming, a destination somewhat off the beaten path. That is its charm and allure.

Once over Namhae Bridge, I headed south along a quiet road that rolled along through lovely hills and farmland that reminded me of the English countryside. I soon arrived at Namhae City, which isn't really a city at all, but more of a town, located on the shore of the shallow and muddy Jinju Bay. I thought the town had a somewhat "un-Korean" feel to it — slow, quiet, and unpretentious. I liked it.

After motoring around the island for much of the day, I headed back up-island intent on crossing back over the Namhae Bridge, but on the island side of the bridge, I looked down to the water and saw a most unusual-looking ship moored at a dock. Curious, I drove down a steep side road that led to the water. The ship turned out to be a stunning replica of a *geobukseon*, or "turtle ship," a type of vessel used by Korean Admiral Yi Sun-sin during Japan's brutal invasion of Korea during the Imjin War.

The name "turtle ship" comes from the vessel's squat, enclosed, and almost impenetrable shell comprised of thick bulwark planks. It looked to me like one of those heavy galleons from Roman times. This one had been constructed by the Korean Navy in 1980, with assistance from Korean geobukseon experts.

The 160,000 Japanese troops under the command of warlord Toyotomi Hideyoshi set up base in Busan in 1592, then marched north up through the peninsula to Pyongyang, and spread out east and west of the city, leaving a trail of destruction and death in their wake. But in the sea off Korea's south coast, it was a different story. Admiral Yi and his small but sturdy fleet of panokseon (a slightly smaller, open version of the geobukseon) and a small handful of geobukseon, all loaded with cannon, multiple arrow missiles and archers, and up to 120 rowers, absolutely vanquished the enemy in numerous maritime battles, completely shutting down Japan's proposed and essential sea route up the west coast of the peninsula. Thus, the Japanese ships were unable to convey essential reinforcements, weapons, and food farther north to its many tens of thousands of soldiers. Almost certainly, Admiral Yi's bravery and cunning against huge odds saved Korea from being subjugated by the Japanese.

Korean history books often note that geobukseon was the world's first ironclad ship. But Samuel Hawley, author of the meticulously and exhaustively researched book *The Imjin War*, found little evidence that the ship had been constructed of anything but wood. Still, to build a geobukseon was not easy. It took a lot of manpower and a large supply of timber. Experts believe no more than twenty geobukseon were ever built in Korea. Admiral Yi launched the first turtle ship in March 1592, two months prior to Hideyoshi's assault.

The geobukseon before me was noted as being 34 metres long, 10.5 metres wide, flat-bottomed and keel-less. Short, sharp spears to prevent boarding and two twelve-metre masts extended up from the top deck. On the port and starboard sides were rows of eight portholes for long oars, and up to ten portholes for cannon. There were two more openings on the prow and one at the stern for more cannon. On the bow was a mounted dragon head, and inside it, I learned, four guns armed with gunpowder that sent iron nails flying.

I went aboard. The interior was magnificent, constructed of long planks of light-coloured wood. The lower deck had eight benches on each side that could accommodate eight oarsmen each. Above me was a quasi second deck for cannon, and above that, the "roof." Along with rowers, geobukseon would have had as many as several dozen crewmembers to man the cannon and weapons, meaning about 150 sweaty humans would have been confined to this box during the sweltering Korean summers. Inside must have been a sort of hell. I tried to lift one of the oars, but found it outrageously heavy.

The girth and stalwartness of these vessels was significant. Essentially, Japanese bullets, arrows, and even small cannon fire couldn't penetrate the thick hulls, a seminal reason Yi was able to decimate his enemy. And in two days I would have the opportunity to learn more about the admiral and his battles and turtle ships, when I visited Tongyeong and Hansan Island, which had been his base for part of the Imjin War.

* * *

It was quite late in the afternoon when I finally departed Namhae, and I continued east along the highly indented coastline to Sacheon, a small industrial port city, where I took a room for the night. Sacheon to me felt old, dusty, and dowdy; though, admittedly, the depressing grey clouds weren't helping.

I took a walk through an area on the fringes of the downtown area, and the streets differed little from most of the cities this size that dotted the peninsula. Having spent the past five nights sleeping at saunas on mats, I decided to upgrade this evening, and checked into the modest Songnam Motel. In the lobby I approached the small window, where a shade was pulled halfway down. I lowered my head to see if anyone was there, and received a bit of a fright — inches from my face the weathered visage of an old woman glared back at me — the motel clerk.

*"Sillyehamnida, bang eolmayeyo?"* ("Excuse me, how much is a room?") I asked.

*"Samman won,"* ("Thirty thousand won,") she chirped.

*"Bang, imanocheon won?"* ("Do you have rooms for twenty-five thousand won?") I tried. After all, Koreans were business people, and I guessed she would rather make twenty-five than nothing.

*"Aniyo,"* ("No,") she said firmly. *"Geumyoil, bang samman won."* ("Rooms are thirty thousand won on Fridays.")

I pretended to leave, and, as I suspected, she drew me back. *"Honja?"* ("Are you alone?") she asked.

*"Ne."* ("Yes.")

*"Imanocheon won,"* ("Twenty-five thousand won,") she said. She eyed me suspiciously. *"Honja?"* she repeated. I think she mistakenly believed I was hiding another person who would later join me in the room.

*"Ne,"* ("Yes,") I repeated, and handed her the money.

After I had taken a shower and stomped on the day's worn clothing in the tub, I slipped on a pair of shorts and a T-shirt and walked down to the first floor office to borrow a few hangers. The woman was nowhere to be seen, but as I stood in the lobby, I heard a strange muffled half-dog, half-bear growl emanating from behind the window. I looked over and there was the woman's scrunched-up face again. She was glaring down at my feet. The noise she was emitting was her way of conveying to me that bare feet in the lobby was unacceptable.

* * *

I slept in until noon the next day, wanting to spend every moment I could on a real mattress.

Back in the car, I headed east toward Tongyeong, which is on the Goseong peninsula. I had not been to the small city before. The weather had cleared and it was a smashing mid-June day — not too hot, just how I preferred it: sunny, bright, and balmy minus the humidity. Arriving at top of the peninsula, I proceeded toward Tongyeong, which was at the far southern end. As I drove along the highway, I was never far from the greenish sea.

Tongyeong is a vibrant city of 140,000 residents. It was a Saturday, and every one of Tongyeong's citizens seemed to be out in their cars or walking along the sidewalks. I don't think Times Square on New Year's Eve is even this busy. The city is confined to narrow chutes of land located between clusters of steep mountains and hills, and an amazing number of dwellings, apartments, buildings, and shops have been crammed onto the suitable and available real estate.

I drove through this concrete labyrinth until I reached the port. A kilometre south across the bay I could see the north shore of Mireuk Island, where several freighters were moored. There were also a number of freight cranes. Behind the port rose a steep mountain.

The concrete wharf on the Tongyeong side had fishing trawlers and small merchant vessels docked alongside it. I parked across from the weathered Tongyeong Ferry Terminal and walked over to look at a large map on the wall that showed the multitude of offshore islands — 151 to be exact, forty-one of them inhabited. Hansan Island was seven kilometres southeast of Tongyeong, and a famous tourist draw for Koreans wanting to learn a bit about their famous native son, Admiral Yi Sun-sin. I paid the 8,000 won for a ticket on the four o'clock ferry and boarded with a modest flock of Korean tourists. We motored east out of the bay into the beguiling green sea. This maritime area is picturesque, and both the land and sea were designated as Hallyeohaesang National Park in 1968.

After forty-five minutes, we approached Hansan Island, and docked along a bay on the northwest shore. We debarked and were replaced onboard by another small horde of visitors who were returning to Tongyeong. A walking path, called Hansan Road, led from the dock back around a forested cove. There was not a single shop, dwelling, or building to be seen. I let my fellow passengers go ahead, then strolled on alone. A sign near the dock read:

*Song of Hansan Island:*
*In the bright moonlight at Hansan-do Isle*
*I sit alone upon a lookout pavilion,*
*Wearing a long sword at my side.*
*Full of cares about the fatherland.*

How poignant; I imagined a Korean soldier standing atop the mountain on a moonlit night in 1592, peering out over the surrounding waters, on the lookout for enemy Japanese warships.

The path took me around the small, picturesque cove, then rose gently through the woods to a clearing — a sort of esplanade — where a surprising number of people had congregated. This was the Hansan Great Victory Monument, which marked Admiral Yi's August 14, 1592, Battle of Hansan Island. I joined one of the large tour groups, which was comprised of mainly Korean men and led by an earnest Korean guide. I inconspicuously turned on my mini recorder.

"Do you understand what he's saying?" one of the men in the group asked me in English. It turned out he was one of a large contingency of professors from the prestigious Korea University in Seoul, in Tongyeong for the weekend.

"No, but I'll get it translated later," I told him.

The guide stopped in front of a whiteboard on which someone had drawn two sets of black marks. He explained that one grouping represented the Korean panokseons; the other was the Japanese fleet. The diagram showed that the Korean ships, which were commanded by Admiral Yi, were arranged in a *U*, or "crane-wing," formation. This fleet had the four single-file lines of Japanese ships surrounded. This was an important part of the admiral's strategy — to first contain, and then to fire on the enemy.

Samuel Hawley brought this battle to life in his book *The Imjin War*. A Japanese admiral by the name of Wakizaka led a group of various-sized ships crammed with warriors armed with swords, bows, and arquebuses west from Busan to seek out Yi's fleet. Wakizaka ordered his fleet to anchor north of Hansan Island, between Tongyeong and Geoje Island, in the narrow Gyeonnaeryang Strait.

Yi had fifty-six vessels — a small number of turtle ships and the rest panokseons — which were waiting, hidden from the Japanese ships, off Hansan Island. He sent six of the ships north up the strait to act as decoys to lure the Japanese out into the open. When the impulsive and aggressive Wakizaka spotted the vessels, he had his ships give chase. The Korean ships turned around and retreated to the south with the Japanese in pursuit. Wakizaka's ships sailed right into the centre of Yi's crane-wing formation — the turtle ships in the centre of the semicircle and the panokseons on either side.

The Korean ships fired their cannon, but because it took the men time to reload, oarsmen kept the vessels turning so the guns on the port and starboard sides would be constantly firing. Archers kept the arrows whistling. Yi inexorably tightened the noose, hemming in the Japanese fleet so it couldn't manoeuvre. Japanese arrows and bullets were unable to penetrate the panokseons' thick planks. From mid-morning through late afternoon, Yi's navy kept up a non-stop bombardment.

"Fireballs shot at our ships, which were burned and destroyed," wrote a source aboard one Japanese ship.

Wakizaka himself was hit by several arrows, but survived because he was wearing armour. Forty-seven Japanese ships were sunk, twelve were captured, and fourteen in the rear line escaped. Many Japanese warriors jumped overboard and swam to nearby islands. One Japanese commander committed seppuku, disembowelling himself as his vessel sank. About nine thousand Japanese lost their lives in the battle. Yi lost no ships, and only 123 men.

Our guide stopped us in front of a portrait of Admiral Yi, and said solemnly, "Everyone, bow your heads and honour the admiral," and we did so, remaining silent for about half a minute.

After the tour, one of the professors invited me to ride back to Tongyeong with them on a powerful motor launch that belonged to Chungmu Resort, where the group was staying for the weekend. I gladly accepted. We boarded the vessel at the dock and were soon swooshing noisily across the green water. I was delighted to note that our tour guide on Hansan Island, Park Jeong-uk, was aboard. Corralling a professor to translate, I put several questions to him.

"Why did the Korean ships use the *U* formation?" I shouted, because, despite standing directly next to the guide, it was hard to hear him over the din of the engine.

"Because Lee didn't want his ships to be in a straight line," Mr. Park hollered. "He used that tactic before. He wanted a *U* formation to encircle the enemy, to use his full range of cannon from the sides and front, instead of only firing forward guns."

I next asked about Admiral Yi's propensity for ordering heads chopped off. I had read the English translation of the *War Diary of Admiral Yi Sun-sin* (*Nanjing Ilgi*), written by Yi. The details he kept of his actions, recollections, and politics involving the war were thorough. And I couldn't help noting that he recorded a fair number of executions that he had decreed.

For example, on April 25, 1596, Yi wrote in his diary: "Took a hot bath in the evening. Ordered Minami Uyeon to cut off the head of Sago Youm, surrendered Japanese." Then, on October 30, 1597, Yi penned, "Late in the day I punished two collaborators, Chong Un-bu and Kim Sin-ung's wife, who had led the Japanese to kill our people, and Kim Ae-nam, who had raped a virgin in a literati home, by cutting off their heads and hanging them as a warning."

I realize that the 1500s were a different time. Reading Hawley's gem about the Imjin War, you realize a soldier could be executed for the slightest transgression. Commanders enjoyed absolute power, and on a whim could dictate that someone's head come off. Whether a soldier lived or died might depend on what side of the bed their commander woke up on that morning.

"Why did Yi execute so many people?" I half yelled to Mr. Park.

Mr. Park loudly replied: "He had to. He had to send a message to other soldiers of what awaited [them] if they tried to desert."

All I can say is, I'm terribly grateful that I wasn't born in 1570 in Korea — the perfect age to have been involuntarily assigned to Yi's navy during the war. Personally, I have a close affinity with my neck.

Yi's statue stands tall on Sejong Street, close to Gyeongbok Palace in Seoul, among other cities. A 2014 Korean action film, *Roaring Currents*, about Yi's life and battles, became a blockbuster hit here, drawing a record fifteen million Korean cinema-goers.

The boat dropped our group off at Chungmu Resort, along the west part of Mireuk Island's north shore. Tongyeong lay south across the bay. The word *resort* seemed a stretch; it was more like a small grouping of condominiums with a hotel and small swimming area sandwiched beside the industrial port. I entered Chungmu's formal hotel foyer, crowded with scores of well-heeled, formally-attired Korean guests. I approached the front desk to pick up a business card. The young receptionist seemed indifferent.

A few moments later, I caught a glimpse of myself in the full-length mirror in the lobby. Staring back was, while not quite a homeless person, certainly a scruffy-looking dude in a worn T-shirt, wrinkled shorts, backward-facing baseball hat, sandals, and a five-day crop of facial hair. Being on the road for a couple of months, one tended to forgot about keeping up appearances.

I decided to stroll back to the ferry terminal, a distance of about five kilometres. It was early evening and a lovely balmy night.

It took me a couple of hours to get to the terminal, because I had to seek shelter in a little takeout restaurant when a sudden downpour ensued. Once I arrived, I decided to continue walking along Tongyeong Coastal Road toward a small inner harbour that held a number of docked trawlers and squid-fishing boats. The neon lights from the surrounding shops reflected off the calm black water. I found an Internet room nearby and spent some time catching up on world news and sports. On the road, minus a radio in the car, in a country where English isn't spoken, it's quite easy to get out of the loop.

* * *

I had two days before I needed to be in Busan to meet Heju, who would be taking the high-speed KTX train in from Daejeon, so I decided I would do a bit of sightseeing the next day on Geoje Island, just east of Tongyeong, then check out several coastal cities I'd never visited on my way up to Busan. I spent the night nearby at the very large and formidable Shik Dang 24-hour Sauna on Tongyeong Coastal Road.

The next day was beautiful and I spent the afternoon in Goeje, then made my way along the south coast to Masan, which was a surprisingly hectic little city located along the coast between Masan Bay and a ridge of mountain. I decide to stay the night there.

The following day I leisurely puttered around Masan, then travelled to the adjacent city of Changwon, which also had a bustling and vibrant downtown core, though a more modern road grid system and several public parks. In the early evening I headed east toward Busan, but this route into the city is blocked by a rampart-like mountain ridge. Immediately to the west is the Nakdong River valley and a flat expanse of fertile land measuring about two hundred square kilometres and divided into tens of thousands of agricultural plots. Driving into this vista of open plain and the massive looming block of granite and trees is quite striking.

It was evening when I finally emerged from the tunnels on the east side of the mountain. I was in Busan's northwest sector and I immediately got lost. The streets were an arcane maze, and I realized quickly that my road atlas was useless. I simply tried heading east through the compendium of a million winding tight narrow roads. I stopped every few minutes to check my compass. After an hour, I finally hit a major north–south parkway that whisked me to the port area and the Busan Train Station.

After another hour of fruitlessly searching the entertainment district across from the station for a jimjilbang, I was relegated to the doleful-looking Shinjang Yeogwan Inn — probably the oldest yeogwan in Korea — in a working-class area east of the station. The "lobby" was a tiny, dark area with a little old woman holed up in a closet-like office.

*"Bang, bolsuisseoyo?"* ("May I see a room?") I inquired through the small window.

*"Ne,"* she agreed kindly.

I traipsed upstairs, poked my head into a shadowy cubby hole that apparently would be my room, and turned on the faucet. No hot water. The room was perfect! I went downstairs to pay.

*"Eolmayeyo?"* ("How much is it?") I asked.

*"Iman won,"* ("Twenty thousand won,") she said.

I thought the price was a bit steep for a glorified dungeon, and decided to try a little bargaining. *"Manocheon won, quen chaniyeo?"* ("Is fifteen thousand won okay?") I tried.

*"Ne,"* she agreed with a smile. I don't think the place got many customers, for reasons I could completely understand.

I paid and retired to my executive suite. The dank pillow on the bed smelled as if it had been used by Admiral Yi himself. I extricated a clean T-shirt from my backpack and threw it over the pillow. By this time it was past midnight and I was exhausted. I fell asleep the moment my head hit the pillow. I dreamt that the next day, Heju would shower me with lots of edible goodies she had purchased in Thailand!

# CHAPTER 19

At about noon, Heju burst through the front turnstiles on the second floor of the spacious and modern Busan Train Station along with a rush of other arriving passengers. There was a discernible difference in her. It was now June 19, and I had not seen her since she bailed on the trip on May 6. At that time, she had been dyspeptic and beleaguered. But now she was tanned and healthy, her mood as light and bright as the day was sunny. Four weeks in Krabi — away from me, the imperious slave-driver — had obviously done her a world of good.

After greetings and salutations, Heju filled me in about her trip to Krabi. She had sunbathed and meditated and been the recipient of numerous beachside Thai massages. Then, to my surprise, she declared boldly: "I'm going to move to Krabi!" something she'd repeat a few times over the next few days. "I don't want to live in Korea anymore. I hate it here. I'm going to open a business in Krabi. I'll buy land with palm trees on it and sell palm oil."

Now, it's necessary to understand that half of Heju's brain — the side where the neurons fire up her imagination, dreams, and whims — far out-duels the side reserved for rational thought, logic, and pragmatism.

I had no reason to boast about common sense or reasoning, because the good lord had been asleep when it was my turn to be imbued with those traits. Yet, even I recognized her plan had holes.

"Heju, who'll buy the palm oil?" I wondered.

She thought for a moment. "I'm going to export it," she announced.

"To where?"

She hesitated.

"How much money can you make from exporting it?" I continued.

"I don't know."

"How much will it cost to buy land in Thailand with palm trees?"

She said she didn't know.

"Heju, if you want to start a business," I explained, "you would need to learn the facts about it first. I'm not saying it's not possible to export palm oil from Thailand. All I'm saying is that you're probably not the first person to have the idea. I'm guessing people have been exporting palm oil from Thailand for some time."

Realizing, perhaps, that her notion was not as novel as she had hoped, she confidently announced her Plan B: "Then I'll take a massage course in Thailand and give massages there."

Except, the cost for a massage in Thailand is probably about ten dollars an hour. "You won't be able to give enough massages to save," I cautioned.

So, she announced Plan C: "Then I'll move to Sweden and give massages there." Heju had a Korean aunt who had married a Swedish national and moved to Sweden. She said she could stay with her. Except, EU regulations make it extremely prohibitive for foreigners to land a job on the continent. We let the matter rest.

Heju eagerly presented me with a gift of a one-kilogram block of imported American cheddar cheese that he she had bought the day before at a Daejeon department store. I eyed the lovely dairy product with temptation. Cheese is not a familiar item in the Korean diet, which has long been centred on rice, edibles from the sea, and vegetables. During the next couple of days, we would dine exclusively at breakfast, lunch, and dinner on cheese and baguettes, until the last sumptuous morsel disappeared.

I buoyantly announced, “Here’s my gift to you,” and presented her with a brown paper bag containing four pairs of sports socks I had carefully picked out the day before at a department store in Masan.

She looked at them skeptically and claimed pessimistically, “They were on sale, weren’t they?”

*How could she possibly know? It must be a woman thing.* I feigned hurt. “How can you say that?” I decried passionately. “Just because I occasionally buy a few things on sale, doesn’t mean everything I buy’s on sale!”

She was unmoved. “How much did they cost: a dollar … two dollars each?”

It was hard to fool Heju. Okay … so they were on sale. They cost a dollar each, though I didn’t admit it, of course. Anyway, it was the thought that counted.

Suddenly remembering that ten minutes earlier I had left my road atlas on the public computer near the station’s tourist information desk, I dashed back. It had disappeared! It had only cost thirteen bucks, but it was invaluable to me. Since Day 1 of the trip I had been illuminating, with yellow highlight marker, every road, highway, tunnel, and bridge we passed over or through, and every town, village, city, river, fort, museum, lake, or dam we stopped at. Heju thought I was batty, but I wanted a detailed and accurate recording of our daily wanderings.

“I’ll have to buy another atlas,” I said dejectedly, angry with myself for my carelessness and that the navigated history of the trip was now gone. I was told there was a bookstore in Nampong-dong, just a few kilometres west of there. The Busan Tower was also in that area, so we decided to kill two birds with one stone.

The Busan Tower is hard to miss, being 120 metres tall and located on top of a hill not far from the waterfront. It has a long white concrete stem with an observation deck on top. I had never been up the tower and was looking forward to the ascent. We drove through the busy city streets and parked in a tightly packed area of old residences near the base of Yongdu Mountain Park, the tower above us. We took a treed path along the side of the hill and bought our tickets. We noticed that the tower’s concrete base was badly in need of a fresh coat of paint. It looked as if it hadn’t been refurbished since its construction in 1974.

We rode the elevator up to the enclosed observation platform and proceeded to the outer deck, where we were rewarded with a grand panorama of Busan's vast metropolis. To the east and north, the city sprawls between the sea and the long fingers of the mountains that dominate much of the country's east coast. The ocean of concrete in the densely-packed city was unlike anything I had ever seen before, and I have been to Singapore and Hong Kong. Within the city limits, it seemed there was no green anywhere. I'm sure there were parks here and there, but they were not visible any from our position. Busan Port, the world's fifth-largest, seemed to stretch on forever, an interminable clutter of wharfs, piers, cranes, warehouses, docked freighters, and innumerable rows of brightly coloured shipping containers, stacked high atop one another. Tug boats tootled along in the bluish water, and at the International Ferry Terminal, which lay between us and Busan Station, a large white passenger ship, the *Pan Star*, was casting off on its regularly scheduled voyage across the Korea Strait to Osaka.

Busan, unlike Seoul, was never a capital, nor was it terribly important historically. For most of its history it was just a fishing hamlet and minor trading centre for Japanese merchants. After the Imjin War, Japan and Korea signed a peace treaty that permitted Japanese traders to maintain a permanent post along the coast. They chose Busan.

In 1876, Japan forced a treaty on Korea which mandated that several Korean ports be opened to Japanese trade, and more Japanese merchants arrived in Busan. As late as 1909, Japanese citizens outnumbered Koreans in the village. During colonization, the Japanese conducted major construction projects, establishing wharfs and piers and the East Harbour. In 1914, the village attained city status, but in 1945, its population was still under three hundred thousand. This changed suddenly with the onset of the Korean War, when millions of refugees streamed from Seoul and from areas across the country to Busan, seeking a safe haven from the advancing North Koreans soldiers.

In August 1953, weeks after the armistice was signed, twenty-two-year-old U.S Lieutenant Don Oberdorfer, who later went on to become the *Washington Post*'s Northeast Asia bureau chief, rode the train from Busan north to Seoul, and described the trip in his book *The Two Koreas: A Contemporary History*:

> Our first impressions, at Pusan, were miserable and pathetic. The dirtiest children I have ever seen anywhere evaded MPs (military police) around the train to beg from GIs. One boy crawled around the train on his only leg; what had been the left one was off at the thigh. When our train pulled out, several boys threw rocks at the train.

Once out of Busan, the landscape improved, Oberdorfer wrote, as the train moved through villages by little stretches of valleys between rugged, unadorned crags. "Children line the sides of the railroad and shout 'hello, hello' at the troop train, hoping to be thrown cigarettes or candy or something of value."

Due largely to this sudden influx of refugees to Busan in the 1950s, makeshift shantytowns sprung up here, and some temporary shelters remained in use to the 1970s — the city morphed into a largely unplanned cavalcade of haphazard streets and districts. In 1971, the population reached two million. Today, the city has just over 3.4 million residents and is South Korea's second largest metropolis, after Seoul.

Heju and I came back inside, where a young woman was sitting behind a small wooden desk, stealing long glances of herself in a little hand mirror.

"Are you a guide?" we asked her.

"No, I'm a coin-changer," she said sadly, her job being solely to provide visitors with change for the large swivelling binoculars on the outer deck. I'd say the tower would be a good candidate for an automatic change machine. Back at ground level, we popped inside the old, narrow subterranean aquarium located beside the tower. At the far end was a tank holding small piranha. The university-age student on duty plopped a live goldfish into the water for us. Contrary to how Hollywood portrays piranha, as bloody-thirsty carnivores, I can assure you that Korean piranha, at least, inhale goldfish in one mouthful, like a vacuum cleaner sucking up a piece of dust.

Back in the car, we drove the short distance to Nampong-dong, to a fashionable district packed with university students and a variety of small modern shops and cafés. I found the bookstore and bought another atlas. We then grabbed a snack at a crowded café in the heart of Nampong-dong, then took a long walk through the area. We returned to the Busan station area in the evening and stayed in a room in a yeogwan.

With Heju having been back in Korea for only two days after a month spent on Krabi's long white beach, Busan's concrete jungle must have been a bit of a culture shock for her. But we simply picked up where we left off six weeks earlier. She hadn't even complained yet about me being a task-master. Hallelujah!

* * *

I needed to be in the small city of Gimhae the next afternoon to attend a teachers' meeting at Kaya University, where I would be teaching English at a three-week summer camp. To reach Gimhae entailed breaching Busan's western mountain rampart. We wanted to find an efficient route (an oxymoron) out of the city, so we stopped the car at a local police station near Busan Station that morning to seek advice.

When I showed the officer my road atlas, the page open to a map of Busan, he gave a little laugh and said, "If you use the atlas, you'll never get to where you're going. The streets are far too complicated for that. It's very easy to get lost."

Well, if a Busan cop didn't know his way around the city, how on earth were itinerant visitors like Heju and I to do so? We proceeded to take the officer's advice to get lost, and spent most of the next two hours attempting to manoeuvre our way out. We missed turnoffs, backtracked more than a few times, were constantly checking the atlas, and engaged in numerous small debates centred on the fact that we were indeed lost.

"Heju, if we were supposed to turn left at the intersection we just passed, why didn't you tell me this BEFORE we got to the intersection." I whined impatiently at one point to my unofficial navigator.

"Because how can I read the sign before the intersection if the road sign's the size of a book?" she asked, exasperated. She had an excellent point.

We eventually made our way north and west out of the maze of humanity. I hereby nominate Busan as the world's most confounding megalopolis.

We spent most of a beautiful day enjoying the drive along the fetching shoreline west of the city. We travelled to the coastal town of Jinhae, through Changwon, and finally northeast to Gimbae later in the afternoon.

* * *

After my meeting at the university, which didn't wrap up until nine o'clock, we stayed the night in Gimhae, then returned the next day in the pouring rain to Busan and took a room at a yeogwan by the train station to wait out the downpour.

The following day, with the sky still overcast and light rain falling, we made our way east into Nam-gu, the heart of a congested residential area of the city, and into the grounds of the United Nations Memorial Cemetery. We paid a small fee at the front gate and walked into a vast sea of green grass, surrounded by a wall and a continuous row of tall evergreens. Everything was meticulously landscaped and manicured. Neat rows of shrubbery and bushes were interspersed with precise rows of small granite headstones or white crosses.

During the Korean War, a total of 40,896 foreign soldiers from seventeen different nations were killed, 36,516 of them American. Between 1951 and 1954, about eleven thousand soldiers were buried here, thousands more the following year. But America, Belgium, Columbia, Ethiopia, Greece, Luxembourg, the Philippines, and Thailand eventually transported their war dead back home for burial, though the remains of 2,300 foreign soldiers, including thirty-six Americans, still remain.

We strolled through a block of gravestones belonging to fallen Turkish soldiers, and stopped in front of some to read the inscriptions. I was taken aback by how consistently and collectively young these soldiers were. Many were only in their early twenties when they died. I jotted a few inscriptions into my notebook. About twenty-six thousand Canadians also volunteered for the Korean War: 516 lost their lives, 1,212 were injured.

Had these young men lived, many would now be in their eighties. It seems we as a human race are incapable of living peacefully. When we left the grounds, I was feeling depressed and introspective.

From the cemetery, we drove east across the densely packed metropolis to Busan's southeast sector, to Haeundae Beach, the country's most famed piece of sand. While not the biggest at 1.5 kilometres long and a hundred metres wide, it is without a doubt the most popular, the choice of not only the young and hip and those who want to be seen, but of families, too. Every July and August, newspapers and TV news splash images of up to a hundred thousand bodies crammed shoulder-to-shoulder the entire length of the beach under a sea of many thousands of oversized colourful umbrellas. If you enjoy your neighbour resting his beer can on your stomach, his elbows gouging your shoulder, I suppose this beach is the place for you to be during summer vacation.

As we approached Haeundae, it was like entering a mini-Manhattan. We drove along Marine City Road, where clusters of sleek steel and glass luxury high-rise condo towers have been built. We've the Zenith Tower A has eighty floors and is 301 metres (988 feet) high. It is the tallest residential structure in South Korea and the tallest building in Busan. Think about that. It's the height of many of the mountains on the peninsula. My question is, What if there was a fire? Did suites come equipped with wing suits and parachutes? If the power goes out, do residents have to traipse down eighty flights of stairs to take Fido for a walk? I would not want to reside in We've the Zenith, though there's no danger of this ever occurring, because a single condo unit can cost as much as three million dollars, according to a newspaper article I read.

We found the modest Busan Yacht Club along Marine City Road, where a sailboat named *Forerunner-2* was on dry-dock. I learned about *Forerunner-2* after I had arrived in Seoul in 1995, and followed with interest a series of dispatches in the *Korea Times* written by a twenty-four-year-old Korean, Kang Dong-seok, who was sailing solo around the world in the boat. Kang's honest, descriptive, and colourful chronicles from exotic islands and ports, and the people and places he encountered, made me feel like I was sailing along with him.

*Forerunner-2* was larger than I expected — 9.2 metres long and weighing in at ten tons. A plaque informed us that Kang was the first Korean to sail around the world. He had stopped at many ports, and his voyage of seventy thousand kilometres had taken three years and five months to complete. In one report, Kang confessed resolutely that if he had to choose between his sailboat and a woman, he'd pick *Forerunner-2*.

We drove along Haeundae Beach Road, which paralleled the famous beach. It was lined with high-end motels and condos, the area around it completely geared to tourism. About 15 million visitors come to Busan's beaches each year.

We parked the car along the beach road. Because the late afternoon was chilly and blustery, there was only a smattering of people, in long pants and sweaters, out on the sand. The throngs hadn't arrived yet. We strolled down onto the sand and joined the other rogue beachgoers.

I floated my thermometer in the surf and discovered the water was a chilly twenty degrees Celsius. In Busan and along the east coast during summer, the sea is typically three to four degrees cooler than off the west and south shores, which are under the influence of the warm, north-moving Kuroshio Current, which originates in the South China Sea. But the Tsushima Current, so named for the large Japanese island sitting fifty kilometres south of Busan, draws its source from the colder Sea of Japan (East Sea). Busan waters are under the influence of both the colder Tsushima Current and warmer Kuroshio.

These two currents meet between Busan and Tsushima Island, and tumultuous sea conditions can result where they collide. Once, I was taking the high-speed ferry, which slides along the water surface on what look like skis, from Tsushima Island to Busan and the vessel was encountering the jostling of the two currents in the form of very tall and rolling waves. Moments after balancing precariously atop one monster that would have capsized the *Poseidon*, I squeaked fearfully to the purser: "Can this ferry tip over?"

He gave me a smile reserved for kids, and replied (as a loose suitcase slid back and forth along the aisle of the rolling ferry) that it was scientifically and physically impossible for this particular vessel to tip. But hadn't a similar statement been made about *Titanic*?

Heju and I crossed the beach road and went in to a McDonald's for dinner. Surprisingly, Heju seemed content, probably because we were sitting indoors on real chairs at real tables, using forks and knives (albeit plastic ones), rather than munching on baguettes and cheese in the car on the fly or in a yeogwan.

After the meal, now dusk, we began our journey up the east coast, aiming to make the border with North Korea, about 450 kilometres away, in a couple of weeks. We were finally heading in the general direction of home, and I could sense the finish line. It was June 22.

# CHAPTER 20

The east coast of the Korean peninsula is profoundly different from the south and west coasts. For one, the Sea of Japan (East Sea) has an average depth of more than five thousand feet and descends steeply offshore. The Taebaek mountain range runs close to the shoreline.

The Taebaeks average about 1,500 metres, reaching their greatest heights in the north. Because they run so close to the coast, water run-off tends to be minimal, with just short streams and occasional coastal lagoons and sandbars. There are, however, scores of beaches. The tidal range along most of the coast is just over one foot — barely noticeable — and the coastline, except for Yongil Bay in Pohang, is relatively straight. There are only two notable islands, Ulleung and Dok, the first a volcanic outcrop 150 kilometres offshore. The sea here often appears a vivid blue.

Speaking of the sea, Koreans are adamant that prior to Japanese colonization of the peninsula, the body of water located off the east coast was known as either the East Sea or the Sea of Corea. Japan unilaterally renamed it the Sea of Japan, they argue. I can recall seeing the name Sea of Japan in my geography textbook when I was in elementary school. A 1782 map drawn by geographer J. Bayly, *A New Map of China*, indicated the body of water as the Sea of Corea. The Korean government has lobbied hard to have the sea renamed the East Sea, however, and today it is commonly referred to as both the Sea of Japan and the East Sea.

Because of the natural barrier formed by the Sobaeks (through the centre of the peninsula), and the Taebaeks to the east, it has been historically difficult to access the east coast, and the region has been largely isolated from the more populated west. In fact, moving north from Daegu to the border along the east coast, there are no major cities or highways. If one looks at a night-time satellite image of the peninsula north of Daegu, the entire eastern half is in almost complete darkness.

During the summer, the cold Tsushima Current originating in the East Sea is the most dominant. Affected by both cold and warm ocean currents, the east coast has a great variety of fish, and is one of the few areas in the world where both tropical and coldwater species can be caught within an area of a few kilometres.

I was glad that, except for a short stretch, we would not be travelling on expressways as we made our way along the east coast. Instead, a series of lonely, quiet coastal roads thread their way north past myriad fishing villages to the border, the rugged sea often in sight. Along the road one passes scatterings of typical coastal dwellings, most of them single-storey concrete structures with blue, green, or orange roofs.

Not far from Busan, we came upon a desolate stretch of beach, and spotted a couple of empty concrete bunkers that looked like German Second World War pillboxes. The bunkers, once used by the ROK army as lookout posts from which to spot North Korean spies, were overgrown with weeds. In Simon Winchester's *Korea: A Walk Through the Land of Miracles*, he mentions wandering on foot along these eastern beaches during his trek north up through the peninsula, and encountering military arc lights, barbed wire, and pillboxes.

A few kilometres north, we stopped on the side of the road near the tiny village of Taebyondung. There were two more pillboxes here, as well as a small lighthouse. From a rocky, windswept bluff overlooking the water, we had a wonderful view of the coastline, which was littered with boulders; the water was clean and clear, with a greenish hue. A strong tang of salt permeated the fresh sea air as we watched the surf crashing against the rocks below. You wouldn't want to swim in this stretch of water, let me tell you.

We got back in the car and continued on to the next village, Wolnae, in the larger village of Gori — home to the Kori Nuclear Power Plant. Built in 1976, the plant was Korea's first such facility. Today, there are four different nuclear sites in South Korea, and a total of twenty-three nuclear reactors that supply the country with about a third of its energy needs. A large road sign on the coast road read, IF YOU REPORT A SPY SHIP IT'S WORTH $150,000. IF YOU REPORT A SPY IT'S WORTH $100,000.

"Heju, if you pretend to be a North Korean spy, I can turn you in and make a hundred thousand dollars," I teased.

She was unimpressed. "It is a common joke in Korea," she replied.

Despite not having covered much ground since leaving Busan, we had stopped at several places along the way and before we knew it, it was already early evening. In the little seaside village of Jinha, fronted by alluring Jinha Beach, we paid just 30,000 won for a large room in L Motel that looked to me like a $150-a-night condo at a swanky resort.

In the morning, we drove toward Ulju County and the tiny seaside village of Sinri. I had read an unusual story in the *JoongAng Daily* newspaper about some of the town's residents who dove for a living, gathering abalone, sea urchins, and other creatures in the local waters. Because warm water being discharged by the nearby nuclear plant was negatively affecting sea life in the area, the local government decided to reimburse the Sinri divers for potential lost wages. The Ulju government — obviously of a benevolent nature — offered a maximum of about 150 million won (US$125,000) to each diver.

Up to this point, Sinri had about fifty registered female divers and one lone male. Yet, when applications for financial reimbursement came in to the Ulju government, they were from Sinri college students, office workers, eight villagers over the age of seventy-five, one disabled person, and two children. The number of Sinri divers had suddenly ballooned to at least 232 from the town's 267 households. Suddenly, sixty-six of them were men, too.

In the article, an Ulju County official admitted there was no official test or certificate needed to become a diver. "Practically anyone can register," he explained.

Sinri's waters were obviously bobbing with 232 happy people of the sea, so Heju and I decided to drop in for a visit. When we turned onto the deserted laneway leading down to the water and Sinri's tiny town square, the late-morning sun was bright and baking hot. There were a couple of old, concrete dwellings on the laneway, bleached from many decades of the sun's glare, but not a soul around. We stopped and waited to see if someone would appear and about ten minutes later an elderly man came ambling along the lane.

Heju called out the open window when he drew near: *"Sillyehamnida ajeossi, diva iseyo?"* ("Excuse me, sir, are you a diver?")

*"Aniyo,"* ("No,") he replied.

We entered one of the bunker-like dwellings that seemed to double as a restaurant, and asked the ajumma there if she was a diver.

*"Aniyo,"* she answered.

Next door, we tried the Sinri Pharmacy. We asked the pharmacist — a handsome woman in her seventies with intelligent eyes — if she was a diver.

*"Aniyo. Naneun yakgukeseo siponyeon il haesseoyo,"* ("No, I've been working at this drug store for fifty years,") she replied.

We parked the car and walked along a dusty lane toward the water. Around the corner was an old mom-and-pop shop. We poked our heads in and found three retirement-age citizens sitting around shooting the breeze. We went in to say hello.

*"Anjeuseyo,"* ("Have a seat,") invited the good-natured shop owner, Mr. Lee.

The floor in the store was concrete and the shelves appeared to have not been dusted or restocked in ages, holding only a haphazard and meagre smattering of sundry items, including cans of food whose expiry dates probably lapsed in the 1800s. We chatted with Mr. Lee and the two others, Ms. Ji and Mr. An, for a while. Ms. Ji had been a diver and Mr. An a diving team manager. Being veterans of the sea, I inquired, half in jest, if they had ever encountered a great white shark in the local waters.

To my absolute astonishment, Mr. An said yes.

"In 1995, I was the manager of a small crew of women diving off the west coast near Anmyeon Island [near Seosan]," he recounted. "We were in about seven metres of water, and one of the divers was under the boat. Suddenly, a shark surfaced with her in its jaws. When it went under we never saw the woman again."

I gulped, and asked if he was sure it was a great white.

Mr. An nodded solemnly. "Oh, yeah. They're the only ones that eat people."

Well, actually, tiger sharks, bull sharks, and lemon sharks have also been known to take chunks out of us, too, though I assumed he knew the difference between one of those and a great white. What he said next made me gasp. "Great whites have babies along the west coast, too." This was the first I had heard of that. I had swum in those waters.

Heju and I got up to leave after chatting with the trio for about an hour, buying them a couple of bottles of soju before departing. I suspected Mr. Lee was already into the nip a bit, because he reached into his breast pocket and proudly displayed his little pacemaker. Then things got stranger: in front of the shop, a tiny woman, who I guessed was about eighty and had been walking past, stopped directly in front of me, looked me in the eye, and with a grim resolution asked if I could give her a piggyback ride. I'm not joking.

I contemplated doing so, but thought it a bit undignified to be galloping about town with a granny hooting and hollering like a cowgirl on my back. I politely declined. But then the shopkeeper, Mr. Lee, and his pacemaker wanted in on the action, and ordered me to jump on his back for a piggyback ride. He, too, was serious. But he looked to weigh all of about 150 pounds.

"I think I'd be a little heavy for you," I said.

This did not discourage him in the slightest, and he flexed his biceps and insisted brightly, "No problem, I can lift you!"

He would have, too, but I didn't want to be responsible for him succumbing to a heart attack after hauling me around town. Sinriites were in the wrong business: standup comedy was their forte.

Heju and I strolled down to the deserted waterfront, where a small harbour with a concrete break wall protected a few moored fishing trawlers. The water inside the break wall was glassy smooth and dark green.

"No divers here," I mentioned to Heju.

"None," she agreed.

We walked over to a row of low concrete dwellings, where a quartet of townspeople was squatting outside by a tap, gutting and cleaning freshly-caught fish. One of the women, Ms. Jang, told us she had been diving there for thirty-five years. Then she motioned to the small woman crouching on her haunches next to her. "That's my mother," she added. "She dove too. She's eighty-six."

The younger Ms. Jang was very proud. "I'm famous here. I can dive to fourteen metres ... and hold my breath for three minutes."

These *haenyeo* belong to a group of female divers commonly found in coastal areas in East Asia. It is thought women's bodies are more resistant to spending long hours in the cold water and many continue to work into their seventies. These divers are most renowned on Jeju Island.

Along Jeju's east coast is a little village called Hado, home to roughly five hundred haenyeo and the Jeju Haenyeo Museum. I had read in the newspaper about how ten kilometres off Jeju's southwest coast, on the flat, treeless, and windy Mara Island — a rocky outcrop about a mile long and just several hundred metres wide, with a population of less than two hundred — female divers traditionally brought home the bacon. That is, until a regular ferry connected Mara to Jeju in 1992. The men folk had essentially stayed home, unable to fish because of rough seas, or farm because big waves smacked against bluffs and dispersed saltwater into the soil. The men looked after the kids and tended to drink and gamble. The women earned the money diving. Gender roles had been reversed. The women were the tough breadwinners; fellows less forceful and more gentlemanly, with an emphasis on "gentle."

Ms. Byun, an elderly diver on Mara, said of her husband: "He was so nice and tender. He was very feminine. I couldn't tell whether he was male or female. So I never begrudged having to feed him."

The advent of a ferry service brought with it tourists, and part-time tourism-related jobs, which the men claimed.

Ms. Jang, the proud and confident diver in Sinri, told Heju and me that there were about thirty full-time and seventy part-time divers active in the town.

"How many are men?" I asked.

"About six," she said.

When we mentioned the financial compensation, Ms. Jung said it didn't bother her that townsfolk who weren't divers had submitted applications. "Everyone knows each other. We're all neighbours."

We left the town's soon-to-be-wealthy residents, and headed toward Ulsan, about twenty kilometres farther up the coast.

* * *

We entered at Ulsan's eastern edge, and crossed a low bridge over the Taehwa River. The river flows down from the Taebaeks and empties into the sea about a dozen kilometres southeast of the bridge. With the weather having suddenly turned overcast, and threatening dark clouds amassing, the river was a steely grey.

When the country's manufacturing industry began in the mid 1950s, the areas in and around Seoul and cities in the southeast — particularly Busan, Daegu, Pohang, and Ulsan—were chosen as industrial bases. Up until 1962, Ulsan had been a small fishing village, but when President Park designated it an open industrial port, that changed. Beginning in the 1970s, the number of factories in Ulsan skyrocketed, and the population has now quadrupled from 250,000 to more than one million. Today, Ulsan is America's Pittsburgh, an industrial juggernaut, home to some of the world's largest manufacturing plants, including Hyundai Motors, Hyundai shipyards, and an SK Energy oil refinery. Just seventy kilometres north of here, in the city of Pohang, is POSCO, one of the world's top-producing steel mills. Not bad for little Korea.

Over the years, pollution took its toll on the Taehwa River, as it became choked with factory waste water and residential sewage. Upriver, wastewater was discharged from farms. Eventually, the water turned a dirty brown, foul-smelling and unsafe for drinking or swimming. When, in 2000, a mass of 10,000 mullet fish floated to the surface, dead from the pollution, this environmental debacle became a catalyst for change and local government, businesses, and residents finally said "Enough!"

Waste water from residential homes was instead sent through a new pipeline to a sewage disposal plant. Farmers upstream built tanks to collect sewage and runoff water. Industry followed new regulations governing safe water disposal. A sandy spit along the river, a convenient spot where people had habitually disposed of their garbage, was transformed into a park.

Between 2003 and 2005, half a million tons of sludge was dredged from the river bottom. Thousands of company employees and civic groups volunteered to pick up and remove garbage from the shoreline and to plant flowers. Thirty thousand tons of well water was flown in daily and dumped into the river to revitalize it. In the end, the Ulsan government spent $250 million on the clean-up efforts.

By 2004, the water was clean again, minnows and smelts had returned, and egrets flocked to feed on them. The following summer, a national swimming race was held on the river, drawing 1,200 competitors.

We drove east to the mouth of the Taehwa River, where Ulsan's blue-collar city streets rolled up and down near the sea. After spending some time on a concrete jetty looking out at the grey sea and the industrial port, and chatting with local shipbuilders, we headed north through the city past the Hyundai shipyards. In the 1980s, Simon Winchester visited these same shipyards. In his book he lamented the demise of the British shipbuilding industry, supplanted by the ruthless efficiency of Ulsan's massive yards, which could churn out huge vessels in much less time and for far less money. Yet, more than three decades later, Ulsan's yards are ironically experiencing somewhat similar circumstances as Chinese shipyards are now producing ships cheaper than what the Koreans can build them for.

* * *

We were on our way from Ulsan to Gyeongju and the Silla Dynasty, just forty kilometres north. We drove up the quiet coastal road, the surf grey and agitated on this overcast morning, producing sizable choppy waves. We passed a series of little roadside fishing villages typical along the east shore, simple houses with colourful blue, green, or orange shale tile roofs. There was a sense of isolation but also of the rugged and raw beauty of the sea.

We stopped at Bonggil Beach in Yangbuk Township to check out King Munmu's underwater tomb. When the Silla king died in 681, he requested that he be buried just offshore. We parked at the popular tourist site and wandered out onto the sand. But we left disappointed, as there was no boat available to convey visitors the two hundred metres to the exposed reef of rocks where the king's tomb was submerged.

The Silla Dynasty had comprised a series of walled town-states from 50 BC to AD 660, in the eastern half of the Korean peninsula. It had then conquered both Baekje to the west and Goguryeo to the north, and ruled the entire peninsula until 935. Silla had been a grand dynasty. Its capital, Gyeongju, was cosmopolitan and progressive.

"In the ninth century, it was certainly one of the great cities in the world," Patricia Bartz wrote of Gyeongju, whose population at the time was estimated to be between six hundred thousand and one million. Paper, silk, hemp, cloth, lacquer-ware, pottery, and bronze, silver and gold trinkets were produced. Trade and cultural ties were established with China and Japan. Sciences and math were studied. Buddhism flourished, temples becoming wealthy under the state, monks powerful.

But due to corruption and power-hungry kings who failed to assuage angry lords and aristocrats, rebellion became a constant concern, and the Silla dynasty easily fell to a new dynasty in the north, Goryeo.

We headed west through the sea of rolling green ridges in Gyeongju National Park toward Toham Mountain, which is the site of a renowned granite carving of Buddha called Seokguram (meaning "stone cave hermitage"). Guide and history books refer to the carving and the grotto in which it now sits in glowing terms. I had not yet seen it, and was eagerly anticipating doing so.

We parked in a lot on the broad wooded mountain where there were a few small tourist shops, and bought our tickets. The path was lined with trees, and we followed it until, nestled against the forested slope, we came to a simple traditional wood structure with a double black-tiled roof. Inside, we found ourselves in a narrow shadowy hallway with a glass partition separating us from Seokguram Grotto. In the centre of the grotto, which had been built over the carving around 776, was the granite likeness of Buddha himself.

The sculpture was grand, carved from white granite and 3.5 metres tall, sitting atop a carved lotus. Buddha wears one of those calm, wry expressions of his, as if he is contemplating the meaning of life. A soft yellow glow bathes the domed inner chamber, and the smooth granite is exquisite, arching up gracefully about nine metres.

We asked the guide in the hallway how much the Buddha weighed.

"Between forty and one hundred tons," she said. I was surprised — I would have guessed just a few tons.

"How was it moved here from where it was carved?"

"No one knows," she said. "It's like the pyramids."

The guide speculated that perhaps Europeans had a hand in constructing the grotto, alluding to the fact that they could have moved along the Silk Road to Korea. And in the seventh century, the reverse may have occurred, with Koreans perhaps trekking to Rome along that ancient road, she said.

At an RAS lecture on Buddhist history I had attended, the speaker said that in the seventh century, thirteen Korean monks had separately embarked from Korea for the epicentre of Buddhism at the time: India. They had travelled along the Maritime Silk Road, southwest by sea from Korea to today's Thailand or Malaysia, where the monks would have likely spent some time at the local monasteries. They would have then trekked west across today's Myanmar, likely accompanying a group of merchants for protection, then by ship across the Bay of Bengal to India. There awaited them five hundred or more overland kilometres until they reached the holiest of Buddhist sites, Bodhgaya, and its elaborate Mahabodhi Temple, carved in about 260 BC and located in the Bihar State in northeast India.

It's unknown what happened to the monks after they arrived in India. There's no record of them making it back to Korea. Likely, they stayed in India.

It was early evening by the time we returned to the car and began to descend Mount Toham, located on the eastern edge of Gyeongju. From our vantage point near the top of the mountain, we looked out over the spacious basin in which the city of Gyeongju is built, and the hills and ridges surrounding it. The small fields were of various shades of brown and green in the grey light of dusk, and not a single high-rise apartment building blighted the landscape. It was a tranquil scene, so different from what we were used to seeing in the towns and cities.

* * *

The following morning was overcast as Heju and I left a motel on the outskirts of town and drove in to Gyeongju. We were on the lookout for large earthen burial mounds called tumuli. And as we headed along the Taejong Road, in the southwest part of city, we couldn't miss what we were searching for as we came to a long park, lush and green, that seemed to stretch back forever. In it, there were a number of large, round grassy humps, and the one in the foreground was of such mass that I suspected aliens had sent it to Earth as a sort of pre-welcome gift.

This monster tomb, known as Hwangnam Daechong (Hwangnam is the area where we were and *daechong* means "big tomb"), is as tall as a seven-storey building and well over a hundred metres wide. Also referred to as a *tumulus*, it is just one of twenty-three such burial mounds scattered throughout in the park, which is aptly called Daereungwon (meaning "Big Tomb Park").

When one of Silla's long line of fifty-six kings and queens died, he or she was usually allotted a grand tomb. Some tombs, though, were also made for the aristocracy, as well as generals and government officials. More than 670 of these tombs — some no larger than a few metres in diameter — dot the city and the surrounding farmland. Hwangnam Daechong is the tallest tumulus in Gyeongju.

Heju and I walked through the wrought-iron front gate into Big Tomb Park, which was lined with tall trees. The grass was pristine and beckoning me, and I had the urge to kick off my shoes and run through it barefoot. Lawns and grassy parks are a rare commodity in Korea. Instead, we followed the path a short ways to a forty-foot-high tumulus near Hwangnam Daechong. There was a tourist office beside it, and several groups of Chinese and Japanese visitors standing around outside. We went in and found a guide who spoke English and was willing to give us a short tour of the tumulus.

"Who was buried inside?" we asked.

"We don't know," she told us. "It didn't contain written records. But we call it 'Cheonmachong.'"

The reason for the name, which translates as "Heavenly Horse Tomb," is that when the tomb (the body estimated to have been interred in the fifth century) was excavated between 1973 and 1975, the image of a galloping horse was discovered inside painted on a saddle. Horsemanship had been an important skill of the Silla military. There were 12,000 artifacts, including a gold crown and various pieces of jewellery, unearthed from the tomb. Today, Cheonmachong is the only tumulus that is open to visitors, and it has been reconstructed as a museum, allowing people to view a cross-section of the tomb and inner chamber.

Over the centuries, despite the fact that the Mongols in the 1200s and Hideyoshi's Japanese troops in the 1590s destroyed many of the wooden structures and carried off myriad treasures, these tombs have been left untouched by grave robbers. This is likely because of the labour that would be involved in removing the tons of earth and stone that sit atop them. In 1921, though, during an excavation to repair a nearby home, a gold crown was unearthed. The Japanese excavated several tombs in the area at the time, and the artifacts discovered are on display at the National Museum of Korea in Seoul. The excavation of one tomb in 1926 was assisted by future Swedish king Gustav VI Adolf, himself an archaeologist. But it wasn't until 1973 that Kim Jeong-ki, an expert in Korean traditional architecture, was appointed by President Park Chung-hee to conduct more digs. Mr. Kim and his team discovered many thousands of valuable Silla artifacts and gold crowns in both the Heavenly Horse Tomb and Hwangnam Daechong, and many of these are on display at the Gyeongju National Museum.

Digs continue at a slow pace to this day, though the vast majority of tumuli remain untouched. Thus far, only five royal tombs have been positively identified, and these belong to kings Hyeondeok, Heungdeok, Muryeol, and Wonseong, and to Queen Seongdeok.

Heju and I entered Cheongmachong with the guide. The interior was cavernous, the walls arched, forming a rounded ceiling. Around the perimeter were glass cases holding artifacts. There were replicas of a gold crown, a sword, a saddle, a whip, stirrups, medicine bottles, tweezers, and a behemoth of a gold belt — the originals all held in Gyeongju National Museum.

"Silla's ancestors came from Mongolia, where horses were common," our guide told us.

The king's belt measured 125 centimetres in length. She informed us that he would have been two metres tall and very fat. When his coffin was opened, however, there were no bones or ashes inside. They probably disintegrated, she guessed.

After the tour, Heju and I headed outside and strolled back through the park, which we amazingly had to ourselves. It was tranquil and quiet. "This is where my Kim family is buried!" Heju declared proudly. When Heju is feeling despotic or sovereign-like, she takes the opportunity to remind me that she is of royal blood and the descendent of Silla's King Gyeongsun.

Actually, Silla royalty was engendered from three leading family clans: Bak (Park), Seok, and Kim. We passed a tumulus that experts believe may belong to King Michu, who was the first Kim to sit on the throne (AD 262–284). Maybe Heju did have blue blood. Perhaps all this time I had been mistakenly referring to her as Heju, when her real title was "Your Highness Heju." She would have appreciated that.

We walked on and soon found ourselves in another greenspace, Wolseong Park, the path winding through another grassy area containing more tumuli and ancient Silla stone relics, including a large pond and a 1,400-year-old weathered but exquisite brick astronomical observatory. There was not a whiff of concrete or a vehicle in sight. How lovely! I commend Gyeongju officials for having done an absolutely superb job of preserving the area's natural beauty. It was quite satisfying to be transported back 1,500 years. And it is nice at night, as well, I hear, with the pond, observatory, and tumuli all lit up.

It was dark by the time we returned to the car, and headed across Taejong Road to Noseo-dong, a bustling district of narrow lanes, bright lights, and modern amenities, which included a KFC, a McDonald's, and a Pizza Hut. The juxtaposition from second-century pastoral beauty to a world of twenty-first-century fast-food did not elude us. We took a room at the aptly named King Motel. We freshened up before strolling back to the KFC: on the way in, Heju had eagerly declared that she wanted to have chicken for dinner.

Sadly, when we entered the restaurant just before ten o'clock, we were informed that they were clean out of chicken and closing in a few minutes. The duchess was understandably disappointed.

# CHAPTER 21

The Hahoe Folk Village (pronounced *Ha-Hway*) is a traditional Joseon settlement that dates back to the 1500s. It is located west of the small city of Andong and is one of only seven villages of its type that is still operational. It appears today pretty much unchanged since its inception by an extended aristocratic clan of Ryus (or Yus) back in the sixteenth century.

Today, 235 residents — 85 percent of these being Ryu ancestors — still live in the village. I had read that about 1.7 million people visit here annually. Even Queen Elizabeth II toured it in 1999, and former U.S. president George H.W. Bush and his wife Barbara were here in 2003.

In the sixteenth century, with Andong a hotbed of political conservatism, the local Ryu clan was prominent. Prime Minister Ryu Seong-ryong, who led the efforts during the Imjin War, was born here in 1542. Admiral Yi Sun-sin stopped by Hahoe to discuss the war.

Heju and I were here for slightly less critical issues: I was to appear in a documentary film being shot about traditional Korean hanok. We had met the filmmaker, Whang Sung-yean, while taking a Peter Bartholomew–led tour around the palaces in Seoul earlier in the year. I suppose that because I put forth a series of queries to Peter, Mr. Whang believed I'd make an inquisitive host for his latest film. He coordinated his schedule to meet us and film the first part of the documentary in Hahoe. (Later, after my trip was over, I would take a dozen sorties across the country with Mr. Whang and his crew to continue filming.)

The day after our stop in Gyeongju, Heju and I travelled north along lonely winding roads into the heart of the looming, omnipresent Taebaek mountain range and on to the city of Andong. From there we heading west toward Hahoe on a road that ran alongside the Nakdong River, a pastoral area bordered by low, gently-sloping mountains, an area of orderly farming plots with the odd small farm dwelling scattered here and there. What was most appealing to me about the village was that, as we approached, we could see there was not a single apartment building, nor, in fact, any sign of modern development or commercial property. Heju and I parked and followed a path that passed through agricultural plots and finally into the village itself, a concentrated hub of 126 hanoks that had been constructed of red clay and wood, some with thatched roofs, others tiled. A low, crumbling wall of faded red clay ran along the path.

If the town's aim was to retain the atmosphere that existed here five hundred years ago, they have succeeded. Winslow Homer himself would have been honoured to paint this bucolic setting. Hahoe is nestled on the sandy east bank of the languorous Nakdong River. On the opposite shore, a steep red cliff rises up.

In Joseon days, there was a rigid and hierarchal social order here: ruling yangban families resided in the most desirable properties in the centre, while the next section out was reserved for independent landowners, followed by tenants. The least-desirable area was designated for the lower-class citizenry — merchants and artisans.

We rendezvoused with the two-person camera crew (Mr. Whang had business to attend to in Seoul) and a Hahoe resident, Mr. Ryu Pil-seok, a fortyish, fifteenth-generation Ryu descendant who Mr. Whang had hired to be our guide for the next twenty-four hours.

Mr. Ryu was very proud of his family heritage. "During Joseon, about seventy percent of Hahoe villagers were Ryus. The other thirty percent were servants," he said. "In the old days, we only wanted Ryus. Ryus were yangban, very intelligent."

Today, Joseon-era yangban get a bad rap, and probably deservedly so. By most accounts, they were collectively abhorred by the poverty-stricken masses, not only for their haughty airs, but because they often didn't work. Yangban were part of the traditional ruling class or gentry. This highest echelon of society — including the royal family and the ruling class, and current and past yangban officials and their family members — enjoyed much privilege. They were the educated — well-versed in Confucian classics, awarded government posts — and they owned landed estates and serfs. Only yangban were permitted to live in large houses and to wear luxurious garments. But many were idle and sponged off their relatives and the rest of society. They established legal and social barriers between themselves and the middle class by marrying among themselves and having yangban children by concubines.

Professor Suh Ji-moon of Korea University wrote that "yangban were the Korean equivalent of the British 'gentleman.'" Both lineages date back more than two thousand years, she said, and both expected to maintain high moral and refined personal standards, to uphold the structure of society, to guard their culture by suppressing the "ignorant and ignoble masses." Yangban were modelled after the *junzi*, the figure of moral perfection defined by Confucius. They were "deadly" oppressors of the masses, added the professor, and in no small part responsible for the demise of the Joseon Dynasty.

George Foulk was positively disdainful of them: "Get rid of these 'grand loafers,'" he wrote. One afternoon in early winter in 1895, Isabella Bird looked out from afar over Jongno Street in Seoul and saw a long line of white that she initially thought was snow against the drab monotones colours of the city, but then realized it was throngs of yangban dressed in white, aimlessly drifting en masse like the ebb and flow of an ocean tide. The men simply shuffled, pretending to be busy and to look important.

Mr. Ryu led us to a corner of the village, to a hanok called Yangin House, which is more than five hundred years old. The camera rolling, our coterie of five knocked on the door, which was answered by a small and rather bewildered occupant, Ms. Kim Myeong-gyo, who told us she was ninety-three years old. Ms. Kim grinned, exposing gums with few teeth, and informed us happily that she had married a man from the Ryu clan when she was just fifteen. "I rode in a palanquin on my wedding day!" she said brightly, adding that she had also attended school with President Park Chung-hee.

"How was he as a student?" I asked.

"He was tough. He liked to fight. He always had to win," she said.

Off we traipsed through various areas of the grounds, the cameraman stopping to shoot footage, often with me in the scene as a silent thespian. The day had turned out to be a muggy one, and the afternoon dragged on slowly.

In the evening, shooting continued as I took tea-drinking and calligraphy lessons from crusty yangban men who were not terribly hospitable. Then, filming mercifully over for the night, we returned to have dinner outside in the garden at Mr. Ryu's hanok before retiring, along with the two members of the crew, in an independent hanok room located on his property.

As I soon discovered, the hanok's thick walls of mud and clay were excellent sound absorbers — a bazooka could have been fired outside and we wouldn't have heard it. I imagine it is like sleeping in an underground bomb shelter. The silence allowed me to enjoy an outstandingly sound and uninterrupted sleep. Yet the very design that ensured the silence was also a flaw: there was only one small window in the room, and my impression was that we were enclosed in something that resembled a tomb. That is, until we were awakened at eight o'clock the next morning (far too early for my liking). The cameraman wanted to shoot me looking out the hanok window from about ten different angles. Thus far, though, I had barely spoken a word on camera. It slowly dawned on Heju and I that I had not, in fact, been hired for my chiseled jaw (or weak chin), deep intellect (or pontificating soliloquies), and mesmerizing baritone voice (or youthful tenor); rather, it seemed I was to be a silent extra, a minion, a failed B-level thespian. When the documentary, entitled simply *Hanok: Korean Traditional House*, was finally completed, more than a year later and after having traversed thousands of kilometres across the peninsula and spent endless hours being filmed, I discovered that while it was quick-paced and professionally done, most of my scenes had been left on the editing room floor. I was on screen for a total of about five minutes.

After more traipsing through Hahoe in the late morning heat, we rode in Mr. Ryu's van to a picturesque area of forest and hills along the Nakdong River, where the Dosan Seowon Confucian Study Hall had been erected in 1572.

In their heyday, seowons were a mainstay of young yangban students (who, after their years of study were done, would become adult yangban loafers). There were more than seven hundred seowons across Korea. But in 1871, the Daewongun, the regent of Joseon — young King Gojong's father — promulgated the Seowon Abolishment Act to curtail their power, and ordered many of the institutions destroyed. Seowon numbers were reduced to just forty-seven.

In recent years, there has been a seowon renaissance of sorts, with about 150 being refurbished and offering weekend seowon retreats for youngsters. In one newspaper article, an accompanying photo showed a group of Korean children at such a retreat, wearing traditional yangban garb and sitting on the floor at low tables learning about proper tea-drinking protocol. From the glum and weary expressions on their young faces, it seemed the kids enjoyed the experience as much as getting a measles shot.

Dosan Seowon sits snugly on the lower slope of a hill. It is constructed of heavy wood planks and is C-shaped, the building open at one end with a courtyard in the middle and a long porch running along the front. Nearby stands a grand wooden gazebo with thick floor planks and support beams that looked as dry as a bone. Heju and I sat on the floor, a slight but refreshing breeze taking the edge off the humidity. Birds darted in and out of the nearby woods. It was immensely peaceful there.

A seowon guide, Ms. Oh, a formal and good-natured woman, sat with us, and she and Heju were soon engaged in a spirited tit-for-tat debate about the merits, or lack thereof, of Confucianism during the Joseon period. Heju had no time for it; Ms. Oh thought it divine.

Each person in society had a defined role. An individual knew his or her place. Confucianism dictated whom one could marry, if one could receive an education, one's occupation (or lack of), and where one could reside, what clothes to wear, how to behave and speak in public, among many other things.

In the Analects of Joseon, Confucius wrote: "Let the ruler be a ruler, the subject a subject, a father a father and a son a son."

The Joseon period, to me, didn't sound like as much fun.

"Confucianism was responsible for having brought peace and harmony to Korea," Ms. Oh insisted politely.

Heju contested that, in fact, rather than peace, for much of Joseon, the Yi family royal court had been plagued by strife, infighting, civil unrest, and murder, and that the proletariat had been repressed and squeezed by the rulers. Ms. Oh countered that the fighting mainly involved other countries attacking Korea, which seemed to be a commonly held view. But, if one examines the five centuries of Joseon rule, there were only two major foreign attacks: by Japan during the Imjin War and by the Manchus in the 1600s. The French, U.S., and Japanese incursions on Ganghwa Island between 1866 and 1875 aren't classified as full-fledged battles.

The Imjin War and the Manchu invasion were devastating, but two major wars did not constitute a besiegement by numerous nations. Professor Andrei Lankov compared Korea during Joseon to European nations at the time, and noted that far more battles and warfare were fought by the latter. Korea, he said, had been comparatively more peaceful when it came to warfare with other nations, and that Korea's past centuries were actually relatively stable in comparison with Europe's. No fan of Confucianism myself, I unilaterally scored the debate a victory for Heju, and for democracy the world over.

Back at Hahoe Village, near the parking lot, stood a modest outdoor coliseum-like stage, where I was given a lesson on the ancient art of mask dancing, and was filmed doing it. Each year, in the early fall, the city of Andong holds a ten-day Mask Dance Festival. My dance teacher was Lee Sang-ho, the country's pre-eminent master in the discipline. He was short and slight and now in his seventies, but he had performed on this stage in front of both Queen Elizabeth II and President and Mrs. Bush. Mr. Lee gave me a wooden mask to put on, and demonstrated to me a few "simple" dance steps. I could barely see out of the tiny eye slits in the mask, and with camera rolling, I shuffled about on the stage ungainly trying to mimic my teacher. Heju, sitting in the cheap seats, could not contain her laughter.

I could tell that Mr. Lee was silently contemplating how a reasonably coordinated person could make such a disaster of such easy instructions. I couldn't disagree. Afterward, he explained patiently that my lack of dancing prowess was due to culture differences. "When Westerners dance, they tap their feet and use the bottom half of their body," he said. "When Koreans dance, they use their top half and shoulders and hands. Korean energy flows top to bottom. Western energy flows bottom to top."

So there you have it. No wonder I can't groove.

In mid afternoon, after having spent an intense and tiring twenty-eight hours at Hahoe, my movie agent, Heju, and I were mercifully relieved of our duties. We said our goodbyes to the crew and our host before heading to Andong City for the night.

The next afternoon was spent strolling along the Nakdong River's silty banks. We opted to stay another night in town.

* * *

Late the following morning, Heju and I left Andong and hopped on a country road that meandered out of the city and through a beguiling area of rolling hills, forests, lush green farmland, and verdant orchards of apples and pears. The fragrance of chestnut trees in bloom was overpowering as we drove along, car windows down.

We stopped at a little roadside hamlet in Waryong Township for lunch. Inside the restaurant we were greeted by the ajumma, whose smile was so wide, her teeth so white, I thought her dentist had installed new dentures that very morning. As we sat on the floor at the low table waiting for our bibimbap (rice with assorted vegetables), a steady stream of older men began wandering in and slipping off into a separate room. I counted about twenty fellows.

"They're here for a town meeting," the ajumma explained. "Once a month they have a party, so that's why there are no women." I guess in these parts women don't have much of a say in local politics.

After lunch we continued northeast into the wilderness of the Taebaek Mountains, so looming and rugged, the scene reminded me of film footage I'd seen of the Alaskan landscape. We headed east toward the coast.

Heju was planning to catch a bus to Daejeon the next day, Sunday, as she needed to be back at her teaching job on Monday.

When we reached the top of a very broad mountain crest and saw a restaurant perched there, we had to pull over. We sat at a low table by the large windows and ordered tea, taking in the panorama. The view out over the valley far below was incredible, the dense forest stretching to the horizon. I kept thinking that one would not want to get lost alone out here.

After our break, we continued east for a short distance until, in a small sliver of a wooded valley walled by 3,300-foot Mount Baegam, we pulled in to the little town of Sotai, which I wanted to see. I had read about the area being a tourist destination due to its abundant underground natural hot springs and above-ground spas.

But what was immediately obvious as we descended into the village was that its glory days seemed to be over. Nothing seemed to move. There were no cars on the roads and we could see no people on the street. The few buildings in town were worn and old. The town seemed moribund. We decide to stop at the Baegam Koryo Hot Springs Hotel, and in a small lobby we spoke to the manager. A glass dome had been constructed over the pool, and there were currently two customers in the water. Yes, he conceded, Baegam had been the place to visit … up until the eighties. But when Koreans' average personal incomes began to rise, they were able to travel further afield, and they abandoned the town in droves as they headed to more exotic destinations.

We hopped back in the car and drove a little ways before pulling in to the Baegam Hot Springs Hotel Phoenix. Inside, two clerks proceeded to ignore us as they happily continued playing their board game in the empty lobby.

We left the former hotspot and got back on the road that would take us to the sea and toward our next destination — the port town of Hupo.

When we reached the water, near Pyeonghae, we merged onto a road that ran along the coast and headed south. As we drove, we could hear the breakers crashing loudly onto sections of rugged windswept beach and rocky outcroppings. The water near the shore was turquoise green, but farther out it appeared a deep dark blue. There was not a soul out on the sand. Along the roadside we passed a smattering of dwellings with orange and blue tile roofs.

Hupo is a small town, utilitarian but pretty, and the location is idyllic, situated as it is on a hint of a natural harbour, with the Taebaeks sloping gently down to the water. At the port, several breakwalls have been built, one forming a large square harbour where a fleet of fishing and squid trawlers were docked. A few warehouses and fish-processing facilities also line the shore.

A squid-fishing boat that was tied to the wharf had its engine running, and the captain was testing the high-powered lights that ran the length of the vessel. Even during the day, the lights blazed bright and hot.

At night, when the vessels were out at sea, these lights attract plankton, shrimp, and small fish to the surface; in turn, this drew the squid, commonly found at depths of between seventy-five and six hundred metres, up to the surface and into the waiting nets.

Despite the fact that Heju and I were standing ten metres away from the boat, we could still feel the intense heat generated by the bulbs. We shouted to the captain over the din of the engine, asking what the temperature was under the lights.

He hollered back, "I don't know? But they're hot enough that they'll sunburn your face."

"How much does one bulb cost?"

"Forty dollars!"

"How long does one last?"

"About six months."

I had read that a single squid vessel could produce up to 300 kilowatts of light power. And, since one kilowatt equals about ten 100-watt light bulbs, the three hundred kilowatts of luminance from this boat would ostensibly equal three thousand 100-watt bulbs. Little wonder why, on satellite photos taken of this region at night, the lights from these boats are visible out at sea.

We returned to the car and drove along the coastal road through town. While we were stopped at a traffic light, a large orange-red tour bus pulled up behind us. Hearing and feeling the thudding and pulsating vibrations of techno music emanating from within, we looked back and discovered that the aisle of the bus was crammed with stout ajummas with permed hair who were rocking to the beat. These must be Korea's notorious dancing ajummas, who commandeer tour buses and order helpless drivers to turn up the tunes.

* * *

It was July first, Heju's departure day, and the late-morning sky was steely grey, a steady drizzle falling as we drove along the coastal road to the Hupo Bus Station, just outside of town. We pulled up in front of a small old building with a few plastic chairs out front, and Heju bought a ticket for the next bus bound for Daegu, where she would transfer to another that would take her on to Daejeon.

We sat in the car for forty minutes before the bus finally pulled in. Heju had been along on "The Endeavour: Part Deux" for exactly thirteen days. I thanked her, wished her a safe trip, and we said our goodbyes. Then she was gone. I sat alone, rain splattering the windshield. In two days I had to be 150 kilometres north in the coastal city of Gangneung to meet a Korean man from Seoul who had answered my online ad for a translator. He had agreed to accompany me for the final week of the trip.

# CHAPTER 22

I arrived at the Gangneung Train Station at about seven thirty the next evening. I had spent the day before exploring the area inland west of Hupo, and that day I had slowly motored up the coast to Gangneung, where I was scheduled to meet Park Tang-won, my new translator. He was already waiting for me when I pulled up. We said hello and went into an austere little snack shop across from the station to chat.

"Call me T.W.," he said.

T.W. had greyish-brown hair and a rather boyish face. He was a bit below medium height and seemed calm and circumspect, emitting a rather quiet and defeated air. He said he had been teaching English to kids in Seoul for the past thirteen years. "My dream's to move to Mokpo and open a fishing business with my brother," he confided.

Later, as we stood next to my Scoupe, T.W. said, "Why don't we take my car?" He had an almost brand new Renault Samsung SMF-5.

I had assumed T.W. knew we'd be using my car. "It's better if we take mine," I explained, "I've been using it the entire trip. I have to stop and start constantly on the road to take notes, and I wouldn't be able to do that if you were driving."

T.W. smiled and answered assuredly: "Mark, if we take my car, you're the boss. I'll stop wherever you want. You order, I'll do it."

I didn't entirely believe him, but against my better judgment, I transferred a few of my things into a gym bag, parked my derriere onto the admittedly well-padded and comfortable passenger seat, and settled back. I had given up my admiral status for that of a mere navigator. I had an ominous feeling this would not end well. I left the Scoupe in the train station lot.

In the city core, we checked into a twenty-four-hour jimjilbang in Okcheon-dong, and I took a jog through the neighbourhood of labyrinthine back lanes lined with shops, bars, and market stalls.

I had been to Gangneung a handful of times, and had not been able to warm to it. To me, it was well-worn and depressing. With 230,000 residents, it's the largest city north of Pohang along the east coast. When I returned to the jimjilbang, I showered and placed my mat near T.W.'s and went to sleep.

In the morning, I discovered immediately that T.W., like Min-jun, had risen with the birds. I tried to sleep a bit longer, but found it hard, sensing my colleague wide awake and waiting for me. We were on the road in T.W.'s car at the ungodly hour of eight a.m.

Steep, densely wooded hills encroached on the coastal road as we puttered along the exposed rocky shoals on the seaside. Our first destination was the Unification Security Pavilion, part of the Gangneung Unification Park, located south of the city in an area called Aninjin. I wasn't sure what to expect from the ambiguous sounding title. The word *unification* was to me a warm, fuzzy reference to the potential reunification of the two countries, while *security* denoted force and weapons.

Later, as T.W. and I walked through the small museum-like hall, it was obvious that the curator had no interest in the North and South ever unifying. Prominent information displayed included the fact that North spies had triggered a remote-controlled bomb they had placed aboard a Korean Air Flight bound from Baghdad to Seoul on November 29, 1987. The plane had exploded in midair, killing all 104 passengers and eleven crew. There was also information about how in Rangoon, Burma (now Yangon, Myanmar), on October 9, 1989, North agents planted a bomb targeting South Korean president Jeon Du-hwan. The bomb exploded and killed fourteen South Korean officials and four Burmese nationals.

Behind a glass case were items found inside a North Korean spy submarine that had run aground just down the coast in 1996. In the case, among other weapons, was a made-in-Canada Browning 9 mm handgun and hand grenades. When T.W. and I departed after an hour, I concluded that "Separation Museum" would have been a more apt title for the attraction.

Just a few minutes away was Unification Park where the North Korean submarine had come aground. We pulled up to a narrow concrete wharf where a large destroyer was docked. Nearby, in dry-dock, sat the dull rust-coloured sub.

On September 16, 1996, a local taxi driver heading home in the pre-dawn darkness spotted the marooned North sub just offshore. He alerted the local police and soon the area was buzzing with thousands of ROK troops searching for the sub's crew. With the cover of the heavily-wooded Taebaek hillsright there, the crew of the submarine and the commandos had fled into the wilderness, planning to make the arduous trek back to North Korea. In response, the South launched its largest manhunt in history — far bigger than the one that was still trying to track me down and haul me to jail for dog-napping.

When the sub had run aground, I had been living in Korea for about a year, and over the next forty-nine days, I recall that the airwaves and newspapers provided constant reports on the hunt to track down the infiltrators.

The Unification Park manager, Kim Yeong-bok, was a rather humourless man to whom I put a slew of questions about the incident. To most, Mr. Kim's reply was "I don't know." He finally pointed to a small sign by the sub. "That's all we know — what the sign says."

The sign gave us all the sub's specs, but not much else. I'm sure Mr. Kim knew more than he was letting on, but for security reasons was being evasive. He did concede that the infiltrators had likely first headed west, inland toward Goebeong Mountain to get into more remote territory.

I hadn't heard of Goebeong Mountain, so I inquired about its location.

"I don't know," replied Mr. Kim, though he obviously did.

My atlas indicated it was twenty-seven kilometres northwest, and I decided that we'd head there after we left the wharf. Perhaps some of the residents living around Goebeong Mountain had seen the North Koreans all those years ago? I asked Mr. Kim if he could provide us with the name of a village there.

No he couldn't. He said he would have to phone the Korean Central Intelligence Agency to get permission to tell us. I told him not to bother. But I noticed a small, glossy pamphlet at the information booth, and on the cover was a diagram of the route the North Koreans trekked.

"May I take this?" I asked.

"I'll have to check with NIS," said Mr. Kim as he picked up his desk phone and dialed (I assumed) the local NIS office. He then handed the receiver to T.W., who conversed with someone on the other end for a few moments.

"We can't take the pamphlet," said T.W., after finishing the call. "If we want more information, we have to call the military."

Oh my, this was getting ridiculous!

Next, Mr. Kim took us into the claustrophobic 32.5-metre sub. The interior was markedly narrow, and it didn't seem as if there was anywhere for the eleven crew and fifteen commandos to sit, rest, or sleep. There were no seats, cots, or bunks. Some may have slept in the empty missile tubes, Mr. Kim suggested. These were hardy North Koreans.

Two years later, in 1998, another North sub ran aground, again off Gangneung. Obviously, the North either built lousy subs or its captains were inept at reading maps. When the South's military opened the mini sub's hatch, they found the five crew members inside dead from self-inflicted gunshot wounds.

As we made our way to the car, T.W. confided that while inside, he had done a bit of covert sleuthing and ascertained that one of the villages the North soldiers had passed through was called Doma. I checked the atlas and was pleased to see that the town was only about twenty kilometres away. *Good job, T.W.!* I thought. We were on our way.

When we got to Wangsan County, we took a side road that followed a creek through a narrow valley with nine-hundred-metre ridges rising up on either side. There was a narrow band of agricultural plots and a few small farm dwellings along the far side of the creek. This was Doma. It was foggy, and ribbons of mist hung in the upper section of the ridges as we walked across a bridge that spanned the creek and knocked on the front door of one of the houses. The door was answered by a friendly farmer by the name of Cho Bang-suk, who immediately asked us in. Mr. Cho told us that Doma had been the military staging ground for operations to hunt down the enemy after a water canteen belonging to one of the North commandos was found along the creek. The ROK military camped out here in tents, he said, and during the night they shone bright searchlights into the mountains, their helicopters roaring overhead.

"It was like a battle zone," said Mr. Cho, speaking of the many thousands of soldiers and Special Forces that pitched tents around the village and hunted down the enemy. "Our houses shook from the usually five or six helicopters hovering near the summit at night. It was scary. We couldn't sleep well. We usually drank in the evenings."

Several days after the troops arrived, Mr. Cho told us, he was walking in the village when he heard a dog barking fiercely at a cornstalk. This was soon followed by many shots fired from an automatic rifle. Dead in the hail of gunfire was a young North Korean.

As the fugitives moved north, people ended up dead. Three elderly villagers picking mushrooms in the mountains north of here were found shot. In the small city of Inje, seventy-five kilometres north and just thirty-five kilometres south of the border, a commando threw a hand grenade into an ROK military post, killing five soldiers. A total of four civilians and eight ROK soldiers were killed by the enemy.

The bodies of the eleven crew members from the sub were found in the local mountains, apparently killed by their own compatriots, likely for being unfit to trek through the harsh backwoods at a quick enough pace. Of the fifteen commandos, thirteen were hunted down and killed by ROK soldiers. One surrendered and is now living in South Korea. And one remains unaccounted for. The manhunt lasted from September 18 to November 5.

We spent several hours talking to a few of the villagers in Doma, and departed at dusk for Taebaek City — about seventy kilometres south. Taebaek City is the highest elevation city in the country, at seven hundred metres above sea level. It boasts the springs of the Nakdong and Han Rivers, as well as the only casino in the country where Koreans can legally gamble. There is also a coal museum and Taebaek Mountain National Park. It didn't get much better than that in my mind, and I planned to see them all.

As we drove south, I attempted to engage T.W. in conversation, but a couple of sentences seemed to be his arbitrary limit. He wasn't one for extended conversation.

After ninety-minutes, as we emerged from the evening's darkness, the bright lights of downtown Taebaek City suddenly appeared. And what a pleasant surprise the city was. The long main street we drove along was bustling and prosperous, with shops, restaurants, and lots of pedestrians out and about. I imagined this was how Aspen, Colorado, might look. Later, though, I learned that the reality was much different here: the town and local region were economically depressed, and unemployment had remained high after many of the region's coal mines were shuttered in the late 1980s and early 1990s.

We continued on, hemmed in by towering mountains, and just southwest of the city, among the trees at the base of Mount Taebaek, we found Family Boseok Sauna. We would stay the night. The next day would be a busy one — I had planned to visit a number of different places.

* * *

T.W. and I left our accommodations about nine o'clock the next morning. Although the day was grey and foggy, the alpine grandeur was still evident; I inhaled the thin, cool air.

Not for from the jimjilbang, along a base slope of the stalwart Taebaek Mountain, we parked the Scoupe and walked a short ways up a path to the modern and rather formidable-looking Taebaek Coal Museum. We had arranged to meet the museum's researcher, Chong Yun-sun, and he was there already, waiting for us. Mr. Chong wore a spiffy suit, and his hair was thick, black, and well-coiffed. Mr. Chong was a Taebaek native, and in 1968, at the age of seventeen, he had begun drilling part-time in a local mine. He earned about 13,000 won (about US$50) a month, which was considered a good wage at the time. In comparison, the average pay for a factory worker in South Korea then was just 8,400 won (about $32) per month. After attending university, he began drilling full-time. After working underground for a time, Mr. Chong was promoted to a job in a mining company office.

Coal mining in Korea, he said, began with the Japanese in 1937. They dug twenty-two mines in what is today North Korea and thirteen in South Korea. The Japanese shipped the mined coal by rail to Donghae, a blue-collar city northeast along the coast, then by sea to Japan. Japanese coal was of low quality and they required a better grade to fuel their warships.

Mining flourished between the mid-1950s into the 1980s in Taebaek. At its peak, more than 60,000 miners were excavating 24 million tons annually. In the 1960s in Korea, there were eight government-owned mines, five that were privately-owned consolidated ones, and many small, private ones. Much of the coal was earmarked for making *yontan*, small pressed-coal briquettes introduced in the 1920s to fuel stoves and to heat homes. In the sixties, there were about four hundred yontan factories across the country; today only fifty remain, yet about a quarter of a million households still rely on yontan for cooking and heating. Each winter, newspapers publish photos and stories about volunteers going door-to-door delivering free yontan to those in need, usually the elderly.

Two factors combined to cripple eastern Gangwon Province's mining industry: a flood into the country of cheaper Chinese coal and the switch to oil and gas. From the late 1980s to the early 1990s, 340 coal mines — many small and privately-owned — were permanently shuttered. As a result, during those years Taebaek City's population dwindled from 125,000 to 50,000. Twelve thousand miners lost their jobs. By 2003, only three million tons of coal was being excavated by just six thousand miners. And today, nationwide, only five mines remain open, and just two of those are in the Taebaek area. The region was forced to reinvent itself, and turned to tourism: four golf courses, three ski resorts, a high-elevation sports training centre, and a casino have been built. As well, ecotourism is promoted, the region becoming well-known for its wealth of hiking and climbing opportunities.

But before it could become a legitimate outdoors destination for weekend warriors and outdoor enthusiasts, Taebaek City and the surrounding area had to be cleaned up. The ground used to be caked in coal dust, the streams were polluted, the fish were dying, and the roads remained unpaved. "It used to be black," Mr. Chong recalled. "School kids would draw pictures in the coal dust. They couldn't wear white because their clothes turned black. Even on sunny days we had to wear boots because of the dust. There weren't many trees either; farmers had burned them to make farmland or chopped them for firewood."

The transformation has been remarkable, and as far as we could see, little evidence remains of the town's former unhealthy environmental state.

When T.W. and I left the museum at midday, the sun was finally peaking out through the clouds after a full week of depressing greyness. We took a scenic route that wound through the stalwart mountains to the Daihan coal mine, the country's largest and oldest mine, established in 1936 by the Japanese. On the way in, we drove by the tall grey form of a vertical mining shaft at the side of the road; at the mine site, a broad, sweeping forested slope loomed over the small office building below.

The manager of the Daihan mine, Mr. Kim Young-jin, conceded that the prospect for long-term continuity of the mine was bleak. The mine's seventy-five-year production limit would soon come to an end. Engineers were digging deeper and deeper, making new shafts every day in an effort to get to the coal. "It's getting scarcer to find," he said. Apparently a vein had been discovered near the Taebaek Coal Museum, one that would offer a thirty-year supply of coal, but government approval was still needed before mining could begin.

Mr. Kim led us behind the offices to the mine shaft entrance, where two rail tracks descended into the darkness to a vertical depth of nine hundred metres into an unseen network of 450 kilometres of narrow horizontal tunnels. Soon, faint beams of light began to appear from deep within the shaft, and a few minutes later, a clutch of solemn, silent miners — flashlights mounted on their yellow helmets, faces darkened from coal dust — emerged into the sunlight. They proceeded to rinse the grime and soot off their boots and faces.

Mr. Kim enthusiastically expounded on the merits and advantages of living in Taebaek, and among them he mentioned the cool summers at the higher elevation. "If it's 29 degrees in Seoul, it'll be just 21 or 22 here. And there aren't any mosquitoes!" he boasted.

* * *

Back in Taebaek City, T.W. and I had lunch, then strolled along the main street to Hwangji Park, a pretty little green space located behind a little gate in the heart of downtown. The warm rays of the late afternoon sun filtered through the trees and the mountain air was refreshing. To test Mr. Kim's theory that it was hotter at sea level, I used my mobile phone to call my pal, Moonie, in Seoul. Moonie sounded like he was one step away from death, and said Seoul was under debilitating humidity and plus thirty-degree heat. My thermometer showed just twenty-three degrees. Mr. Kim was right!

Little Hwangji Pond was in the centre of the park, its water a bright bluish-green and crystal-clear. As I watched, a brook trout and a solitary catfish slowly glided through it. In the centre, a little stream of water found the surface from the underground spring. A sign stated: "This is the starting point of the Nakdong River. The temperature of the pond is always fifteen degrees. Every day, 5,000 tons of water flow out from the spring. The pond has a diameter of one hundred metres. The altitude is 700 metres (2,300 ft)."

To think that a tiny trickle of water escaping from the pond and flowing south morphed into the nation's longest river, which meanders 525 kilometres before emptying into the sea near Busan, was hard to believe.

Back in the car, T.W. and I drove southwest, back to Taebaek Mountain area, to the spring of Korea's second-longest river, the 514-kilometre South Han. Off the main road, in a forested area near the base of Daedeok Mountain, we got out and hiked along a trail that rose gradually through the woods and a small meadow. It culminated at a small, shallow limestone pool called Geomryongso Pond. It was barely the size of a bathtub. A trickle of water slid over the edge and flowed downhill, where it converged with a trickle of water from another nearby spring.

"This is the Han River, producing 2,000 tons of water a day at a constant nine degrees Celsius," the sign informed us.

Despite both springs being just twenty miles from the east coast, the Taebaeks block their flow in that direction. And despite their proximity to one another, the Han flows west unimpeded, while the Nakdong is forced south.

The sun was starting its early evening descent as we drove back in the direction of the city, and just north of it found Chujeon Station, the highest-elevation train station in the country at 855 metres. In fact, due to the elevation, snow had fallen there as late as April. We strolled along the platform by the tracks and the rail line disappeared in each direction behind the thickly wooded slopes.

A sign on the wall read WELCOME TO THE STATION CLOSEST TO THE SKY.

Two young station employees were playing catch on the platform. T.W. and I entered the red-brick building that served as the large one-room station house. The manager, Lee Su-hyeong, was a stoic man to whom words did not come easily. The station wasn't busy, conceded Mr. Lee. Only one passenger train stopped here each morning at nine o'clock.

"Do passengers get off the train?" I asked.

"Rarely," Mr. Lee said.

"Do any get on?"

"No one."

"Is it lonely here?"

"Yes."

The Taebaek Line runs east from Jecheon, ninety kilometres west, to Baeksam Station, near Taebaek City.

Up until the mid-1980s, Chujeon Station was an important rail cog in the region, and about 100,000 tons of coal was loaded monthly here onto the freight cars. Fifteen full-time employees worked at the station. Times were so propitious, in fact, that there was a local saying: "Even dogs in this town wander around with a ten thousand won bill in their mouths."

"Now we have only three employees and load ten thousand tons of coal a month," lamented Mr. Lee.

Chujeon Station's other role is rather ignominious: if a passenger or freight train rolling by needs to wait on the single line for another train to pass, it can do so here.

From the station, it was a short drive to the Gangwon Land Casino, a gaudy hotel and casino complex. We ventured inside, but it was so jam-packed that we stayed just an hour.

It was about ten o'clock when we checked into a jimjilbang at the base of Hambaek Mountain, just a short drive west of Taebaek City.

The jimjilbang stood alone, a rustic, handsome place adorned in neon lights. After showering and having a soak in the hot tub, T.W. and I had a late meal in the snack bar before throwing down our mats. T.W. lay supine and began watching TV. It was near midnight, and I knew he was exhausted, having been up since about five in the morning.

"You had a long day; you should try to sleep," I suggested.

"Not yet," he said. "I have to wait at least an hour after dinner to digest my meal before I sleep."

"Why an hour?" I asked.

"Because my stomach feels funny if I sleep right after eating. And scientists say you should wait at least forty minutes after a meal before you sleep."

I wondered if a stomach knew the person was sleeping or lying awake watching TV.

T.W. said it did. "When I watch TV, I lie down with my head on my elbow like this," he said, indicating his body was on an angle. "Food gets digested faster this way. But when I sleep flat, my food digests slower."

*T.W. has earned his paycheque today*, I thought. Not that I paid him, *per se*, but you know what I mean. I was dog-tired, too, and was soon out like a light, lying flat on my mat. My dinner had my permission to digest as slowly as it desired.

# CHAPTER 23

Our next destination was the village of Haean, which lies about 150 kilometres north of Taebaek City, right near the border. Haean is commonly referred to as the "Punchbowl" — not a reference to a post-season U.S. college football game, but rather to the bowl-shaped area where ROK and UN troops engaged in bloody, close fighting against the Chinese and North Koreans soldiers during the Korean War. Both sides were essentially dug in along the 38th parallel from the summer of 1951 through the summer of '53, dying over a few kilometres of contested real estate. Other U.S.-named battle spots, such as "Heartbreak Ridge" and "Bloody Ridge," are also located around the Haean basin.

When T.W. and I left the sauna that morning, the sky was a bright hazy white, the air was fresh. Our first destination was to be the town of Yeongwol, about sixty kilometres west, where T.W. had a preacher friend he wanted to visit. We took Route 38, which wound through a narrow cleft between low, steep granite eminences, a shallow river accompanying us part of the way. The Taebaek Rail Line ran alongside, the tracks moving in and out of the tunnels burrowed through the rock. Between some narrow gaps, it ran across old rail bridges buttressed by stone girders. We motored along slowly, enjoying the scenery. We had the road virtually to ourselves.

On the way, just west of Taebaek, we passed through the town of Sabuk, which gave us a grim reminder that the halcyon days of mining here are gone. Rows of abandoned low-rise apartments and rusted-out buildings, their walls grimy, their windows shattered, stared out at us. An elevator mine shaft rose high into the sky. A shantytown of decrepit concrete homes was juxtaposed with a handful of new apartments. When the mines were shuttered, the mining communities were largely abandoned.

About an hour later we entered Yeongwol, a pretty, slow-paced little town located on the banks of the Han River and surrounded by mountains. After a two-hour stop at the preacher's house, we took No. 31 toward Haean. We had the twisty up-and-down blacktop to ourselves, the mountains here rising up to 1,200 metres. We passed through the sparsely populated alpine county of Pyeongchang, where, in February 2018, the Pyeongchang Olympic and Paralympic Winter Games will be held. The Games' venues will be spread out across the county and east to Gangneung City.

Much of the snowfall in South Korea occurs here in the north Taebaeks, and the area averages more than two metres of the white stuff annually, most accumulating between late November and late February. Fifty kilometres northeast of Pyeongchang City, the little mountain town of Hoenggye will be the site of the Olympic Medals Plaza and Olympic Plaza and a temporary 40,000-seat stadium at which the opening and closing ceremonies will be held.

T.W. and I threaded our way through vast tracts of forest so remote that there weren't even any of the requisite tiny villages that normally dot the roadside every few kilometres. I was becoming nauseated as we slowly ascended and descended the hills and drove around the many curves, so we took advantage of a rest stop by the side of the road where there were several tented stalls and a few women selling snacks.

"In the old days, guys in the military used to hate being assigned to the mountains in Gangwon," said T.W., who was a former platoon leader during his two-year compulsory military service. "Roads weren't paved then and it took all day to hike down from your post to pick up supplies."

As we moved towards Inje, the road paralleled the lovely Naerin River, the only river that flows north in the country, with clear water and banks of granite. At Inje, it meets up with the south-moving Hangyeryeon River to form the singular Soyang River, which veers westward.

Instead of taking the tall bridge over the Soyang into Inje City, we continued along No. 453 toward Haean, the Hangyeryeon River now running alongside us. We were just thirty kilometres from the border. "Somewhere past Inje, the Civilian Control Zone begins," said T.W., referring to the restricted area south of the DMZ operated by the military.

When we finally entered the township of Haean, I realized I had completely misjudged the scope of the basin. I had imagined the Punchbowl to be about the size of a large football stadium, but it actually covers more than sixty square kilometres, an expansive green area surrounded by an almost continuous wall of mountains. About sixty million years ago, this had been an active volcano.

The town itself was in the centre, dominated by agricultural plots; not an apartment or commercial centre to be seen, only a smattering of farmhouses. If you blinked, you would miss the tiny, dusty town of Haean and its short main street with only a couple of restaurants, two hardware stores, and a couple of mom-and-pop shops.

We doubled back, and on the edge of the Punchbowl checked into a little homestead called "Punch Bowl Minbak." I checked the odometer on T.W.'s car, and found we had added three hundred kilometres since leaving Taebaek.

After showering, I took a late-night jog into Haean. The mountain ridge to the north was backlit by bright ROK floodlights that shone down into the DMZ. It reminded me of a scene from the movie *War of the Worlds*, when Tom Cruise and his son are by a hill on the other side of which are the alien tripods, the night sky is ablaze with explosions and fires.

* * *

We were to begin the morning with a tour of the nearby Fourth Tunnel, secretly hollowed out under a mountain by the North in 1976 and discovered by the South in 1978, followed by a tour of the Eulji Observatory Post. It was already hot and hazy, and an ominous band of thick fog that hung over the north ridgeline seemed to be drifting slowly toward us. I worried that the fog would severely hinder our view out across the DMZ into the North.

At a guard post along the road, a soldier explained to us that the official order of the tour was tunnel first, observatory second.

"T.W., can you ask him if it's possible to visit the post first, the tunnel second? I'm worried the fog will be over the ridge soon."

*"Aniyo,"* ("No,") replied the guard. Tunnel first, post second.

I asked T.W. to ask again, but he bristled, silent and stone-faced, and refused. I waited a few moments before asking him again, "T.W., I'm only asking you to try one more time."

He reluctantly mumbled a few words to the guard, who responded with the same answer. We were waved through. At this point, T.W. was seething. He enunciated slowly, "In the Korean military, there are strict rules that we must follow." And that was that. I had crossed a line. From that moment on, I was a pariah and permanently in T.W.'s doghouse.

After a stop at a nearby hall to sign up for the tour, we boarded a shuttle bus that took our small group first to the tunnel, then up a steep, twisty road to the Eulji Observatory. At the crest of the hill was an ROK sentry post manned by guards with machine guns. Three layers of wire fence ran along the ridge. A large information centre faced the four-kilometre-wide DMZ. Despite some fog having rolled in, partially obscuring the horizon, the view was extraordinary. Laid out before us was a vast green valley and, farther away, rolling ridge after rolling ridge.

I removed my binoculars from my backpack. "No photos!" an ROK soldier ordered.

"It's not a camera — they're binoculars," I told him. Thankfully, I was permitted to use them.

After the tours, T.W. said he wanted to visit a war monument and fort located about twenty kilometres away. We headed southwest on the Punchbowl's only road, No. 453, quickly ascending into the rugged hills that ripple north to the horizon. The terrain here is rough and the ground looked bone-dry, able to support only shrub-like vegetation. We passed a remote military barracks where several dozen young ROK soldiers were training on a dirt field.

After driving for nearly an hour without finding what T.W. was seeking, we returned to Haean, T.W. giving me the silent treatment. We stopped at a small war museum near the minbak that I wanted to see, but I left after only a few minutes. I was mad. With T.W. refusing to converse, there wasn't much point in continuing with him.

I spoke frankly when I got back to the parking lot, conceding that I knew why he was angry with me. T.W. responded tersely, telling me he was quitting the trip. And that was that. I grabbed my bag out of the backseat. He backed up the car, threw it into drive, and hauled out of the lot, leaving me stranded in the Punchbowl without wheels. He had been with me for three days and four nights.

*Good riddance, T.W., and don't accidentally drive off a high Taebaek mountain cliff on your way back!* I thought.

I sat on a bench in the lot, the mid-afternoon sun bearing down on me like a hot laser, and soundly cursed T.W. I figured I could either hop on a bus and head to Gangneung to retrieve my car, or remain in the Punchbowl permanently, silently swearing at my ex-translator. I preferred the latter but chose the former, and trudged along the road toward town. I waited at a bus stop and, twenty minutes later, an old public county bus squeaked to a halt in front of me.

"*Eodie gaseyo?*" ("Where are you going?") I called to the driver.

"*Inje,*" he said.

Good enough. I hopped aboard. About a half-dozen country folk made up my fellow passengers. An hour later, at the Inje bus station, I approached the ticket window to inquire when the next bus for Gangneung departed and was told an hour and a half. I bought a ticket and strolled outside to look around downtown Inje. What a surprise! The tiny city — sandwiched between the Soyang River and the lower slope of a low, steep rock face — was bustling with throngs of pedestrians. Three- and four-storey buildings contained restaurants, shops, and PC rooms — it could have passed for fashionable Gangnam. I had wrongly expected Inje to be sleepy and slow.

I stopped in at an Internet room to check my emails, but it was packed with young ROK soldiers in uniform playing military video games. I hastened to another one, but it, too, was crammed with servicemen. Finally, at a third, although also brimming with military men, I managed to secure the lone empty computer. It was Saturday, a day off for the troops. *Was anyone left to protect the border?* I wondered. If the North's generals ever decided to launch an attack against the South, Saturday would apparently be a good day. Don't tell them I said so, though.

Back at the station, I boarded the country bus destined for Gangneung. My six fellow passengers this time were young women in their late teens or early twenties, all dolled up, I assumed, after having met up with their soldier beaus in Inje over the weekend. We headed east along Route 44, toward the coastal town of Yangyang, where we would stop briefly before continuing south to Gangneung. On the way out of Inje we entered Seorak Mountain National Park, a 373-square-kilometre swath of steeple-like peaks and ridges, some rising more than 1,500 metres. There is a singular mountain named Seorak, but also a broad area — the Inner Seoraks west of Inje and the Outer Seoraks to the east, nearer the coast.

Route 44 through the park was impossibly twisty and narrow, as it threaded through Hangye Valley, a V-shaped wedge of land squeezed between steep granite walls. Along the road flowed a narrow little stream that tumbled over the rock. The occasional roadside kiosk, where ajummas sold snacks to visitors hiking along the river, popped up along the way. Some had a little table and chairs set up, but with no road shoulder, the bus passed dangerously close to the brave customers sitting in the chairs.

The trip progressed slowly, the bus unable to travel at more than thirty kilometres per hour due to the many tight turns. The driver was constantly shifting and grinding the gears, braking then accelerating, and I was soon nauseated. The sky was bright and a marvellous shade of blue, but all of a sudden we were encompassed by a solid blanket of dense white fog that reduced visibility to near zero. Ten minutes later, just as quickly, we were out of the soup and back into the bright sunshine.

My original plan had been to head back to Gangneung with T.W., then swing slowly west with him along the remote border to Seoul. But I decided that I'd skip the border part. Gangneung would now be my final destination. I was relieved. After about four months, the end was here.

After arriving at the Gangneung bus station, I took a taxi to the train station to pick up my Scoupe. I then drove to a yeogwan nearby, showered, and took a long evening stroll through the old downtown area. To celebrate the journey's conclusion, I treated myself to dinner in a restaurant.

Afterward, I decided to catch a movie, so I wandered on foot through a curiously enervated area of downtown in search of a movie theatre. Finally in luck, I rode an old elevator up to the fourth floor of a building and stepped off into a small lobby. I was the only person there, and the ticket girl seemed surprised to see a customer.

On the wall were two movie posters for films I had never heard of. One was called *Taxi Ride* — not to be confused with *Taxi Driver*, the 1976 Academy Award–nominated film starring Robert De Niro and Jodie Foster.

*"Taxi Ride joeun yeonghwa eyo?"* ("Is *Taxi Ride* a good movie?") I asked the girl.

*"Ne,"* ("Yes,") she said.

But, unwilling to gamble ninety minutes and 8,000 won, I departed.

I did eventually locate a second theatre, this one also a small independent: worn, virtually empty, and very hot. I saw *Ocean's Eleven*, years after its release date. There were twelve people in the theatre for the 11:20 p.m. showing. As for the film, all I can say is that if you've just finished a long, tiring journey through a country, it's a vapidly pleasurable way to eradicate ninety minutes of your life.

The following day a steady rain was falling, so I was limited to visiting the interesting but formal-sounding Chamsori Gramophone Museum and Edison Science Museum, which essentially was a showroom for about every gramophone ever produced.

There were also other archaic-looking electrical items on display: a stock ticker from 1871, an electric iron, a toaster, a hair curling iron, and a waffle cooker — all visually interesting. There were bits of information about Thomas Edison and his inventions, too. But I think it would have been a good idea to have some hands-on displays. For example, maybe a bowl of batter to discover what it was like to toast waffles in 1880.

The highlight was when the owner of the museum ushered me in through a side door in the lobby wall leading to a secret private theatre with rows of seats, a movie screen, and large speakers. He went to the front and pushed a few knobs. Appearing on the screen was a video of the opera quartet Il Divo performing at a sold-out concert in, I believe,

Greece. The voluminous music and angelic voices filled the space. I was as close to heaven as I might get. After twenty minutes, though, the man ushered me back out of the hall and I found myself returned to the world of mere mortals, standing in a smattering of raindrops.

The next day, the sun was shining brightly in a blue sky so I decided that the day would be for me, and I'd spend it by the sea doing nothing but relaxing. So I slipped on a T-shirt and shorts and headed over to Gyeongpo Beach, one of the country's most popular, and one often patronized by university students. The long stretch of soft yellow sand seemed to go on in both directions forever. The sea was sparkling, a lovely, expansive deep blue. A row of restaurants and motels lined the road behind the beach. Despite it being the middle of the summer, and a perfect day, there was barely a soul on the sand. I was in heaven.

I plunked down my beach towel in a narrow sliver of shade under an empty lifeguard post and immediately stretched out. I fell into a most welcome and luxurious sleep.

I awoke with a start and checked my watch: nearly four o'clock. I'd been out cold for a couple of hours. And I was also no longer in shade, the sun having turned parts of me a bright red. I decided to cool off by taking a dip, so I fit my swim goggles over my head and walked into the surf. As far as I could tell, I was not only one of the few people out on the sand, but I was the only person in the water. Not bothered, I dove in. The sea was invigorating.

I swam out a bit and made a series of shallow dives to the sandy bottom. The water was crystal clear, and I could see that the bottom quickly descended to unspeakable depths where lurking marine monsters would surely end my life. I began to swim along parallel to the shore about ten metres out. Life didn't get better than this! A few minutes later, though, I became cognizant of the repeated sounding of a shrill whistle. Treading water and looking toward shore, I spotted a young male lifeguard, maybe eighteen years old, standing on the sand by a small group of friends. He was waving frantically at me. I couldn't understand what he was all riled up about.

Apparently, I had done something that was against the rules, but I couldn't think what it could be. I wasn't drowning, so that couldn't be it. I wasn't ogling female bathers, because there were no bathers to ogle. There was no exposed fin of a nearby prowling great white shark that I could see. Then it suddenly occurred to me: I was swimming too far from shore. You see, ten metres from the shoreline to Koreans might as well be interminable. In the country's long history, I don't believe any Korean has actually ever swum in its seas or lakes. Instead they float on rubber devices and inner tubes near to shore so their feet will always be in contact with the ground. It's not that Koreans can't swim. I have watched them zip past me like Michael Phelps during lane swims at my local indoor pool. It's because they're curiously and illogically afraid of deep water.

The lifeguard wouldn't be pacified until I got out of the water, and, not feeling like arguing, I complied and returned to my towel to sleep some more. I woke up ninety minutes later, the afternoon fading, and gathered my stuff and returned to the car. Thoroughly relaxed and groggy, I opted to extend my indulgent mini-vacation for another night, so I got a room at a large and airy but empty jimjilbang near the beach.

Early the next afternoon, I departed for Seoul, and about three hours later, I was home in Myeongil-dong. My trip was unceremoniously over. My odometer informed me that the Scoupe had accumulated over eight thousand kilometres, equivalent to driving twice across the United States. Heju and I had begun the pan-Korea part of the trip on April tenth; it was now July tenth. It seemed very anticlimactic. One thing I knew with certainty: I wouldn't be driving tomorrow.

# CHAPTER 24

Unofficially, the trip wasn't really finished because I continued to attend Royal Asiatic Society meetings and to query strangers old enough to have experienced Japanese colonization and the Korean War. If I went somewhere on the peninsula, I'd jot notes on the geography and geology. I continued to read the newspapers daily.

In early fall, I attended an RAS meeting in Seoul at which the guest speaker was a New Zealander by the name of Roger Shepherd, who had recently accomplished quite a feat: he had hiked northeast about 735 kilometres from Jiri Mountain in South Jeolla Province, through the Sobaek and Taebaek Mountains, with his trek culminating on the east coast at Goseong, in Gangwon Province, at the border with the North. Roger had tackled what's known as Baekdu-Daegan Trail.

*Daegan* means "trail ridge," and *Baekdu* refers to Mount Baekdu, the tallest eminence in northeast Asia — an extinct volcanic cone rising 2,744 metres on the North Korea-China border. For much of Korean history, citizens have considered Mount Baekdu to be sacred and spiritual.

While the total distance from Jiri Mountain to Mount Baekdu is about 1,400 kilometres, Roger had stopped at the border, unable to continue all the way to Mount Baekdu. The Baekdu-Daegan Trail in the South moves mostly along ridges ranging from a low of two hundred metres above sea level to as high as 1,915 metres. Roger said there was a path to follow, though it was unlike the renowned Appalachian Trail in the eastern United States, not always well-marked.

The tall, lanky, and bearded New Zealander stood before the packed RAS crowd, presenting slides that he'd snapped along the trail, many from atop ridges and peaks, seemingly in the clouds, many of them wide, panoramic views. Roger completed his adventure with his pal, Andrew Douch, and for the ten weeks the pair slept in tents, casual alpine huts, minbaks, and even outdoors in a traditional public gazebo.

After the meeting, Roger said he'd be returning to the trail for a couple of weeks to do follow-up research for a book he was writing about the long trek. He said he would be driving a motorcycle into the Sobaek and Taebaek Mountains. I offered him the use of my Scoupe for the two weeks, since I wasn't using it, and he accepted, which was why, a couple of weeks later, I found myself driving southeast from Seoul to the northern edge of the Sobaek Mountains, to the juncture where they begin their southward bend after moving west from the Taebaeks. It is between Goesan on the north edge of the range, and Mungyeong, thirty kilometres away on its south perimeter, that the narrow and winding Mungyeong Pass has permitted foot travel over the centuries between the top and bottom halves of the peninsula.

It was early evening when I arrived in the rather foreboding area of Mungyeong, where the looming Sobaeks blocked out the descending sun. At the base of this stalwart eminence I met Roger and we rented a room at a yeogwan, spending the evening in conversation. He had been a policeman in New Zealand, but while doing a short stint in Korea as an English teacher, he had fallen in love with the alpine terrain and now lived here. He established a business, Hike Korea, which leads foreigners on alpine treks.

The next morning, I followed Roger as he trod along the old Mungyeong Pass road and trail. He was deep in thought and diligently jotting down notes, focused and engrossed in his task. He didn't say much. After a while, I thought it best to let him continue alone, and he drove me to the local station so I could take the bus back to Seoul. Roger went on to author *Baekdu Daegan Trail: Hiking Korea's Mountain Spine*. On subsequent adventures, he spent a total of six months in North Korea trekking an additional two thousand kilometres, including all the way to Mount Baekdu on the Chinese border. He also led a group of New Zealand motorcyclists south from Siberia, down through North Korea, then all the way to the south coast.

That summer, before I had met up with Roger, I had driven to Jiri Massif in South Jeolla, the start of the Baekdu Daegan Trail, for a hike with a friend from the RAS.

Jiri Mountain National Park's 472 square kilometres straddle three provinces and include the country's second highest peak at 1,915 metres. After the hike, I perused the atlas to decide how best to navigate my way back to Seoul, and noticed a road, No. 19, that I wasn't familiar with. It began at the southern foot of Namhae Island and continued up through roughly the centre of the peninsula, through the Sobaeks, and seemed to disappear somewhere in Gangwon Province. *What a route!* I thought, anticipating taking the route that wound its way for more than four hundred lonely kilometres through the mountainous interior.

I got on No. 19 just west of the national park, and it quickly ascended into a series of S-turns that snaked up the side of a broad mountain. Then, my goodness, what a treat: a fabulous vista unfolded to the north, an uninterrupted view out over the vast Sobaek range. The sheer scope of the panorama was amazing: green and broad, ridge after ridge after ridge of long slopes reached to the horizon. Roger refers to the Sobaeks as still largely "unexplored." He isn't kidding.

When I reached the pinnacle of the first broad hill, I noted that a long, twisty road led down the other side. I decided to let gravity do its job and save a little fuel by disengaging the automatic gearshift from Drive, and slipping it into neutral to coast. *Wheeeeeee! How fun*, I thought as the car quickly accelerated downhill. In hindsight, I don't recommend doing this, particularly when there's a long, steep drop to the valley floor directly to one's left. I applied the brakes as I neared a sharp curve, but brakes don't seem to have much effect when you're in neutral, or at least they didn't in my Scoupe. My heart rate immediately doubled as the car's speed did, too. I pumped the brakes hard, but they were largely ineffective. My pulse rapid, I shifted back to Drive and the brakes re-engaged. Fortunately, I lived to tell the tale.

For the entire length of Route 19, I kept the Scoupe puttering along at between forty and sixty kilometres an hour, which was absolutely fine with me. I moved contently through the lovely, secluded green valleys, past small hamlets, up and down and over and around the lush hills and alongside more prominent eminences. It took me the entire afternoon and into the early evening to get from Jiri Mountain National Park to around Wonju — about one hundred kilometres southeast of Seoul — where I reluctantly left independent-spirited and hearty No. 19. If someone were to ask me how best to experience the peninsula's unspoiled ruggedness in a car, I'd highly recommend the drive.

* * *

Now that the trip was really over, I could begin to sum it up. Compared to the hardships that George Foulk, Isabella Bird, Mark Napier Trollope, Simon Winchester, and Roger Shepherd, among others, encountered on their treks and wanderings through Korea, mine had been a cakewalk. Yet I believe Heju and I, too, had suffered for our art. Heju had sacrificed by taking off four months off work. And I swore I had become shorter. That's right, because I noticed with some alarm that when I was sitting behind the wheel for up to ten hours a day over three months, slouching in the bucket seat, my chest and stomach seemed to morph into one. It became difficult for me to ascertain where one began and the other ended. I suspected I had shrunk at least an inch. In the four months, though, I feel we barely scratched the surface. It would take years to really explore all that the peninsula has to offer.

It was strange how distances were relative. The distance, say, from Busan to the Punchbowl — approximately four hundred kilometres — is about the same as from New York City to Washington or from Toronto to Ottawa, yet on a map of those countries, the distance barely registers. From a Korean perspective, however, those four hundred clicks are formidable. Also, consider how instantaneously the world would open up to South Korea were that baneful border not there. Instead of having to board an airplane to leave the peninsula, one could hop in a car, head north, then turn left and drive ten thousand kilometres to Paris, or journey south through China, then Nepal, or even continue on to India. The possibilities would be endless.

I hope that one day that border will fall. It seemed as if the Berlin Wall was there one day and gone the next. Anyway, it's likely Koreans will face another, more pressing problem before that happens. Due to a low birth rate that seems to be holding steady in the South at approximately 1.21 children per woman, the government forecasts there will only be about 44 million South Koreans living in the country by 2050. I realize I'm in the minority here, but I don't think fewer Koreans in an already overcrowded peninsula would necessarily be a bad thing. There would be fewer cars on the road, more available seats on the subway, less competition for students to get into the top universities. And more jobs.

I don't think Koreans at heart have changed much since the days when British captain Basil Hall encountered them along the west coast of the country in 1816. They were aggressive forces of nature then, and they still are. Back then, they wore white hemp and cotton garments and straw shoes, they farmed and fished and lived simply in villages grouped by bloodlines. Today, they might don suits and ties and designer clothes, but underneath the polish, I think they're the same audacious salt-of-the-earth folk of centuries past. I'm not sure this modern, urban, fast-paced lifestyle spent in high-rise apartments and frequenting high-end shopping malls suits their souls.

I have a soft spot in my heart for Korea and Koreans. When I'm in Canada or another country, and I hear the distinctive staccato hard sounds of the language, I often want to stop and say hello and try to use a bit of my Korean. I have an affinity for them. They are like no other people I have met. No matter how quiet, deferential, or unassuming they might seem, they won't be dismissed, forgotten, or ignored. Failure is not an option for them. At times they try too hard; their energy, drive, and will are unstoppable. Forgive them this, for they are Korean.

Having spent some of my thirties, all of my forties, and part of my fifties — half my adult life — in Korea, I have mixed feelings about the country. I'm not sure exactly when, but maybe after five or six years there, the special feeling I experienced as a rookie in 1995 slowly began to wane. But I wouldn't have stayed there for so many years had I not felt a kinship with the peninsula and its people. When I'm back in Canada, though, and someone asks me how I enjoy living in Korea, I pause and say cautiously, "It's high-energy and hectic, and the kids are great, and there's lots of teaching work there … but …"

There's always that "but." After nearly sixteen years on the peninsula, I believe I'm no further ahead in my understanding of Koreans than when I first arrived. They are still an enigma to me, and I'm sure they always will be.

Were I in a foxhole on a battlefield, the enemy perilously close, I'd choose a Korean as my partner. Preferably an ajumma; they take no prisoners. Hopefully not a monk; they'd surely negatively comment on my stomach.

# ACKNOWLEDGEMENTS

First of all, I owe a big debt of gratitude to Kim Heju in Korea, who took four months off from her job to accompany me on the trip. When the manuscript was finished, Heju also spent months and innumerable hours on the phone and online, contacting professors, officials, and guides — experts on Korean history, palaces, architecture, geology, military, and railways, among other subjects — to confirm countless bits of information.

Thanks to my aunt, Irene Cameron, for gifting Bill Bryson's *In a Sunburned Country* to me on my birthday. Without having read his book, the seed to pen mine wouldn't have been planted.

I must thank Mr. Bryson, too, for producing such enjoyable material.

I'm grateful to my aunt Shirley Ferwerda — who owns perhaps the largest personal collection of novels written by British authors in the world — with whom I shared long, enjoyable conversations about writers and books. Thank you for taking the time to read my manuscript and for offering valuable insights.

I fondly remember my uncle Maarten Dake, who passed away in 2013, and with whom I had many pleasurable discussions about Korea and about the book.

I'd like to thank Dundurn for taking a chance on a first-time author, in particular editorial director Carrie Gleason. I'm also grateful to senior editor Allison Hirst, who spent countless hours on the manuscript to help forge a more descriptive and focused end-product. And to Sylvia McConnell, a freelance editor who introduced the manuscript to Dundurn, thank you.

Many people we met on the trip gave their time and shared information: on Sorok Island, Park (Elizabeth) Seong-hui, Kim Gwang-mun, and Choi Yong-gap; Gu Yun-ja on Ganghwa Island; Yi Seok in Jeonju; former Seodaemun prisoner Lee Bong-hui; Jeong Dong-hwan at Château Mani; Cho Bang-suk in Doma; Ryu Pil-seok in Hahoe; in Taebaek, Chong Yun-sun; Kim Hong-geun in Gurye; at No Gun Ri, Nam Jeong-hyeon and Yang Hyae-chan; the venerable Jae-An at Jogye Temple, and Ryo Myoung and park ranger Park No-san at Gyeryong; Cho Sun-hyen, fisherman on Yeon Island; Ban Ki Moon's second cousins in Haengchi; "Kate" in Yeosu; Cedric at Jakwansa Temple. And much gratitude to Park (T.W.) Tang-won and "Min-Jun" for accompanying me.

Roger Shepherd, Victor Teplyakov, Lee Yong-jo, Samuel J. Hawley, Peter Bartholomew, and war historian Sin Jong-tae took time to confirm parts of the manuscript. Andrei Lankov and David A. Mason shared their knowledge on Korea. Jungnam Chi and Kyunghee (Boyeon) Lim were supporters and shared ideas. Thanks to my long-time Korean friend, Moon (Moonie) Seok-mo. I'd like to thank Daryl Bergman and his wife, Jenny (Yunkyung) Lee, who provided me with a space in their Toronto home where I could write. And finally, sorry to those I have forgotten to include here; thank you all for your assistance.

# BIBLIOGRAPHY


Adams, Edward B. *Through Gates of Seoul: Trails and Tales of Yi Dynasty*, Vol. 1. Seoul: Sahm-bo Publishing, 1970.

Allen, Horace N. *Things Korean: A Collection of Sketches and Anecdotes, Missionary and Diplomatic*. New York: Fleming H. Revell Company, 1908.

Barris, Ted. *Deadlock in Korea: Canadians at War, 1950–1953*. Toronto: Macmillan, 1999.

Bartz, Patricia M. *South Korea*. Oxford: London Clarendon Press, 1972.

Bird, Isabella L. *Korea and Her Neighbours*. New York: Fleming H. Revell Company, 1898.

Bryson, Bill. *A Walk in the Woods: Rediscovering America on the Appalachian Trail*. New York: Broadway Books, 1998.

Carlson, Lewis. H. *Remembered Prisoners of a Forgotten War: An Oral History of Korean War POWs*. New York: St. Martin's Press, 2002.

Clark, Donald N. *Living Dangerously in Korea: The Western Experience, 1900–1950*. Norwalk, CT: EastBridge, 2003.

Cook, Harold F. *Pioneer American Businessman in Korea: The Life and Times of Walter Davis Townsend*. Royal Asiatic Society, Korea Branch: 1981.

Diamond Sutra Recitation Group. *King Sejong the Great: The Everlasting Light of Korea*. Vol. 2, Korean Spirit and Culture Series. Pohang, Korea: Yong Hwa Publications, 2007.

Eckert, Carter J., Ki-baik Lee, Young Ick Lew, Michael Robinson, and Edward W. Wagner. *Korea Old and New: A History*. Seoul: Harvard Korea Institute, 1990.

Ellis, Richard, and John E. McCosker. *Great White Shark*. Stanford, CA: Stanford University Press, 1991.

Ha, Tae hung. *A Trip Through Historic Korea*. Vol. 2, Korean Cultural Series. Seoul: Yonesei University Press, 1960.

Ha, Tae hung. *Behind the Scenes of Royal Palaces in Korea (Yi Dynasty)*. Seoul: Yonsei University Press, 1983.

Hall, Basil. *Voyage of Discovery to the West Coast of Corea and the Great Loo-Choo Island*. London: J. Murray, 1818.

Hamel, Hendrik. *Hamel's Journal and a Description of the Kingdom of Korea, 1653–1666*. Translated by Br. Jean-Paul Buys. Seoul: Royal Asiatic Society, Korea Branch, 1994.

Hanley, Charles J., Choe Sang-Hun, and Martha Mendoza. *The Bridge at No Gun Ri: A Hidden Nightmare from The Korean War*. New York: Henry Holt and Company, 2001.

Hawley, Samuel. *The Imjin War: Japan's Sixteenth-Century Invasion of Korea and Attempt to Conquer China*. Seoul: Royal Asiatic Society, Korea Branch. Berkley, CA: Institute of East Asian Studies, University of California, 2005.

Ilta, Zen Master. *Everyday Korean Buddhist Practices*. Translated by Brian Berry. Seoul: Hyorim Publishing, 2009.

Kang, Chol-hwan, and Pierre Rigoulot. *The Aquariums of Pyongyang: Ten Years in the North Korean Gulag*. Translated by Yair Reiner. New York: Basic Books, 2001.

Kim, Agnes Davis. *Unrealized Challenge*. Seoul: Yonsei University Press, 1982.

Kim, Myong-taek, ed. *Korea Tour-Road Atlas* (Chinese-English Edition). Seoul: Chung-ang Atlas Co., 2007.

Kirk, Donald, and Choe Sang-Hun. *Korea Witness: 135 Years of War, Crisis and News in the Land of the Morning Calm*. Seoul: EunHaeng Namu, 2006.

Kirkbride, Wayne A. *Panmunjom: Facts about the Korean DMZ*. Seoul: Hollym International Corp., 1986.

———. *DMZ: A Story of the Panmunjom Axe Murder*. Seoul: Hollym International Corp., 1984.

Nahm, Andrew C. *Korea: Tradition and Transformation: A History of the Korean People*. Seoul: Hollym International Corp., 1988.

Nahm, Andrew C, ed. "Korea Under Japanese Colonial Rule: Studies of the Policy and Techniques of Japanese Colonialism [Proceedings of the Conference on Korea, November 12–14, 1970.]" Center for Korean Studies, Western Michigan University, 1973.

Nilsen, Robert. *Moon Handbooks: South Korea*. Emeryville, CA: Avalon Travel, 2004.

Oberdorfer, Don. *The Two Koreas: A Contemporary History*. New York: Basic Books, 1997.

Palais, James B. *Views on Korean Social History*. Seoul: Yonsei University, 1998.

Russ, Martin. *Breakout: The Chosin Reservoir Campaign, Korea 1950*. New York: Penguin, 2000.

Sands, William Franklin. *Undiplomatic Memories: The Far East 1896–1904*. London: John Hamilton, 1904.

Shepherd, Roger, and Andrew Douch. *Baekdu-Daegan Trail: Hiking Korea's Mountain Spine*. Seoul: Seoul Selection, 2011.

Sonjae, Br. Anthony An. *Discovering Korea at the Start of the Twentieth Century*. Seoul: The Academy of Korean Studies Press, 2011.

Spencer, F. Robert. *Yogong: Factory Girl*. Seoul: Cheng and Tsui, 1988.

Steers, Richard M. *Made in Korea: Chung Ju Yung and the Rise of Hyundai*. New York: Routledge, 1999.

Tucker, Spencer C., ed. *Encyclopedia of the Korean War: A Political, Social, and Military History*, Vol. 1. Santa Barbara, CA: ABC-CLIO, 2000.

Underwood, Horace G. *Korea in War, Revolution and Peace: The Recollections of Horace G. Underwood*. Seoul: Yonsei University Press, 2001.

Underwood, Lillias H. *Underwood of Korea*. New York: Fleming H. Revell Company, 1918.

Vol. XLI of *Transactions*. Seoul: Royal Asiatic Society, Korea Branch, 1964.

Vol. 68 of *Transactions*. Seoul: Royal Asiatic Society, Korea Branch, 1993.

Vol. 80 of *Transactions*. Seoul: Royal Asiatic Society, Korea Branch, 2005.

Vol. 85 of *Transactions*. Seoul: Royal Asiatic Society, Korea Branch, 2010.

Winchester, Simon. *Korea: A Walk Through the Land of Miracles*. London: Grafton Books, 1988.

Yi, Sun-sin. *Nanjung Ilgi: War Diary of Admiral Yi Sun-sin*. Translated by Tae-Hung Ha. Seoul: Yonsei University Press, 1977.

# ABOUT THE AUTHOR

Mark Dake has worked as a sports reporter, a tennis coach, and a copyeditor. From 1995 to 2012, he worked as an ESL teacher in Seoul, Korea, and has travelled through thirty-five countries in North and South America, East Asia, and Europe. Mark currently splits his time between Toronto and Seoul.

You can visit him at markdake.com.